The Silver Women

POLITICS AND CULTURE
IN MODERN AMERICA

Series Editors
Keisha N. Blain, Margot Canaday, Matthew Lassiter,
Stephen Pitti, Thomas J. Sugrue

Volumes in the series narrate and analyze political
and social change in the broadest dimensions from
1865 to the present, including ideas about the ways
people have sought and wielded power in the public
sphere and the language and institutions of politics at
all levels—local, national, and transnational. The
series is motivated by a desire to reverse the
fragmentation of modern U.S. history and to
encourage synthetic perspectives on social movements and the state, on gender, race, and labor, and
on intellectual history and popular culture.

THE SILVER WOMEN

How Black Women's Labor Made the Panama Canal

Joan Flores-Villalobos

PENN

UNIVERSITY OF PENNSYLVANIA PRESS

PHILADELPHIA

Published by
University of Pennsylvania Press
Philadelphia, Pennsylvania 19104-4112
www.upenn.edu/pennpress

Printed in the United States of America on acid-free paper
10 9 8 7 6 5 4 3 2 1

Hardcover ISBN: 978-1-5128-2363-9
eBook ISBN: 978-1-5128-2364-6
Library of Congress Cataloging-in-Publication Data
Names: Flores-Villalobos, Joan, author.
Title: The silver women : how Black women's labor made the
Panama Canal / Joan Flores-Villalobos.
Other titles: Politics and culture in modern America.
Description: 1st edition. | Philadelphia : University of Pennsylvania Press,
[2023] | Series: Politics and culture in modern America |
Includes bibliographical references and index.
Identifiers: LCCN 2022017511 | ISBN 9781512823639 (hardcover) |
ISBN 9781512823646 (ebook)
Subjects: LCSH: Foreign workers, West Indian—Panama—History. |
Women foreign workers—Panama—History. | Women, Black—Panama—
History. | West Indians—Panama—History. | Panama Canal (Panama)—
History. | Canal Zone—History.
Classification: LCC F1577.B55 F56 2023 | DDC 972.87/500496—dc23/eng/20220525
LC record available at https://lccn.loc.gov/2022017511

To Feliks Garcia and Arthur Keller

CONTENTS

Women of Silver and Gold

April 24, 1907, must have been a hot, muggy day in Empire, a busy industrial town near the train tracks of the Panama Railroad. Empire was the head-quarters of the central division of the Isthmian Canal Commission (ICC), the administrative body that oversaw the construction of the Panama Canal. Empire was always a hotbed of activity, home to engineers, steam shovels, and foreign workers digging the deepest point on the Canal, the Culebra Cut. That day, Jane Hall, a Jamaican woman who owned a boardinghouse, walked out of the U.S. District Court of the Canal Zone after winning a civil case against one of her tenants.[1] Hall alleged that her tenant had vacated his rooms without proper notice and had not paid three months' rent at the agreed price of twelve dollars Panama silver a month. After a lengthy case and appeal, the court ruled in her favor and awarded her the equivalent amount, nine dollars along with court fees, in United States gold.

Hall's payout was notable because, within the U.S. territory of the Canal Zone, West Indians rarely received pay in gold coin. The payroll system un-equally divided the wages and benefits of the official Canal workforce. Skilled workers, almost entirely white Americans, were placed on the "Gold Roll" and were paid higher salaries than for equivalent jobs in the United States. They received their wages in gold American dollars. Meanwhile, the more than 150,000 migrant West Indian men who made up the majority of the "unskilled" workforce were placed on the "Silver Roll," only eligible for much lower pay rates in local coin, usually Colombian silver pesos. Officials, employees, and residents alike came to understand these categories as racialized—Gold as white, Silver as Black—even beyond the payroll. As all ICC services and facilities were designated for either Gold or Silver Roll personnel, the unique pay structure effectively extended racial segregation throughout the Canal Zone.

Into this arrangement came West Indian women like Jane Hall, who were for the most part not official employees of the Canal Commission. As Black women, they inevitably had to deal with the racialized labor scheme and spatial segregation that defined the Canal Zone, but as uncontracted workers, they did not have to function strictly within the roll system. Jane Hall owned her own independent businesses—three boardinghouses in Culebra that sheltered Silver workers who could not acquire decent housing from the ICC. She charged rent in silver because it was what workers had, but sometimes paid in gold for services and, as in her civil case, sued to receive back rent in gold. Other West Indian women similarly evaded the binaries of the roll system, moving across white American "Gold" spaces in their work as domestic servants, higglers (market women), and laundresses, and demanding gold as payment from their clients. West Indian women like Jane Hall played a crucial, double-edged role in the Canal construction. On the one hand, they built a provisioning economy that fed, housed, and cared for workers, in effect subsidizing the construction effort and its racial calculus. But, working outside the umbrella of the ICC, they also found ways to skirt, and at times challenge, the legal, moral, and economic parameters imperial authorities sought to impose on this migrant workforce—to function beyond the boundaries of silver and gold.

As historians since the 1980s have firmly established, the Panama Canal was realized as much through the exploitation of a racialized class of workers as it was by American ingenuity.[2] What is less visible, and less understood, is the project's dependence on the domestic and care labor of West Indian "Silver women."[3] West Indian women sustained Silver Roll workers, providing food for those underfed by segregated Canal Zone cafeterias, laundering clothes daily for those who worked in dusty construction sites, and fostering links with legal and commercial institutions in their newfound homes on Panamanian territory.[4] They were equally central to the survival of white Americans, who in the early construction years depended on the provisions of West Indian market women, as they had scant access to fresh foods from the commissary and lacked knowledge of local products. West Indian women took care of white American children and cleaned white American homes, physically maintaining the image of an orderly domestic sphere. In short, West Indian women's labor made the United States' imperial project possible.

The Canal's construction was realized by a multiethnic and multinational migrant workforce, but the bulk of unskilled laborers came as contracted labor from the Caribbean. Nearly half of the Canal's contracted labor force hailed from Barbados alone.[5] When they arrived in the Canal Zone, these migrant workers found the beginnings of a company town—they were expected to reside, eat, and labor under the purview of the ICC. As a way to divide and control the labor force, the ICC organized all company services under the racially segregated roll system. Beyond differentiating pay, the ICC also provided white Gold workers with higher-quality housing, food, and recreation than it did Silver workers. Black West Indian or Silver workers received substandard food in outdoor mess halls, whereas white workers could sit at indoor tables with a decent meal. Silver workers could not stay in Gold hotels or enter the local YMCA open to white Americans. They received no paid vacation or sick leave. They lived in overcrowded, shared bachelor barracks and had limited access to married housing, whereas Gold Roll workers received private rooms or spacious, screened-in, family homes. Silver workers were assigned to the most dangerous jobs on the line.

This gap in services for Silver workers meant that everyday life and work in the Canal Zone depended on support systems outside of formal labor arrangements.[6] It was instead Black women who fed, cared for, and sustained Silver laborers. In the earliest years of construction, authorities worried about worker retention and considered the benefit of having West Indian women in the Zone, surmising that West Indian men "won't work anyplace without their women."[7] Women cooked and sold foods that West Indian men preferred, using local produce that the mess halls could not procure. They found and kept homes outside of ICC housing, where West Indian families could reside together. They supplemented, and sometimes surpassed, their partner's incomes by performing paid domestic service for white Americans, contributing to family savings. The ICC encouraged this uncompensated labor in order to relieve their own burden in maintaining the Silver workforce.

West Indian women's work extended beyond the Canal Zone. They also sustained the larger circuits of regional labor migration that staffed the construction. They kept homes on the islands, saved and distributed remittances, and took care of children left by their departing kin, supporting family members' migration as part of household strategies. Women's care work thus undergirded the racialized migratory labor system that enabled American imperial expansion in the early twentieth century. They did not merely provide support for projects of imperial infrastructure—rather, these undertakings could not have happened without them. The history of the Panama Canal cannot be fully understood without accounting for West Indian women's labor of social reproduction, in Panama, the Canal Zone, the islands, and beyond.

Though equally subject to racial discrimination and segregation, Black women workers were not deeply integrated into the formal regulatory mechanisms of labor relations in the Canal Zone—they did not hold contracts, were not paid exclusively in silver coin, and had little access to official ICC housing.[8] Though a few held contracts as teachers or nurses, most West Indian women worked outside the official realms of ICC authority as servants in Gold Roll homes or higglers who sold their wares across the Zone. Still, Canal Zone authorities sought and found different ways to manage this informal workforce. Through their legal and regulatory institutions, including police, courts, private investigators, and the sanitation department, Canal Zone authorities produced moral categories and legal frameworks that defined Black women as immoral, criminal, and pathological, even as they relied on their labor. These institutions and rules gave the ICC broad power to surveil, arrest, and deport West Indian migrant women.

In addition to illuminating how indispensable their labor was to the construction of the Panama Canal, this book also chronicles how West Indian women became a persistent source of anxiety for the U.S. Canal administration. West Indian women were particularly disquieting imperial subjects for the Canal administration since they migrated beyond the purview of the ICC, settling in the borderlands of the Canal Zone, where they could tend their own homes, care for their own families, and establish a degree of autonomy. Black women's work, paradoxically undergirding the entire construction process while simultaneously seen as outside the realm of economic or productive labor, presented a problem of labor management for Canal authorities.[9] These women's provisioning of Silver workers exposed the incompleteness of integrating the Canal labor force into the lofty Progressive ideals of administrators as Silver workers mostly opted out of the company system of housing, food, and recreation in favor of West Indian women's services. Women's labor of social reproduction threatened the fantasy of successful imperial control of the Canal Zone enclave—even as the project depended on it.

West Indian women's presence and labor in the Canal Zone thus fundamentally shaped a gendered and racialized mode of imperial governance during the construction era. As women's labor lay outside their sphere of influence, Canal management upheld an imperial "military-sexual complex" that associated immorality, prostitution, lack of productivity, and disease with West Indian women.[10] Administrators criminalized nonnormative intimacies among West Indians, making cohabitation without marriage and interracial relations illegal. They surveilled moral behavior in the Zone and Panama through local police and private investigators, used deportation and internment to punish West Indian women, and abandoned their responsibility to provide for West Indian workers, eventually expelling West Indians from Zone residences altogether at the end of construction.

Yet U.S. imperial authority in the Canal Zone, particularly in the early years of construction, was not a monolith. The ICC held a diffuse and contested sovereignty over the area, tested by its critics stateside and by its failures in retaining a labor force, regulating morality across its borders, and negotiating with Panamanian political power.[11] Imperial power also manifested in heterogeneous ways across different departments and administrators, who held competing ideas on how to govern the Canal Zone. While the upper echelons of the ICC spoke of morality, its white employees on the ground in search of company or entertainment often found themselves at odds with these expectations. West Indian women, who traveled to Panama without labor contracts, without paid passage, and without access to official company services, functioned mostly outside the main arteries of U.S. imperial authority. They settled among other West Indian migrants in Silver enclaves within the Canal Zone such as Jamaica Town, or in Panamanian neighborhoods like Guachapali, could skirt the roll system, and traversed spaces where U.S. power faltered—the river laundries of Taboga, the bars and restaurants of Bottle Alley, the boarding houses of El Marañon.

West Indian women thus developed a double-edged relationship to the U.S. imperial project and its violent exclusions—subsidizing its economic developments but subverting its moral logics.[12] West Indian women had a drive to secure material wealth promised by the Canal venture but migrated against the express wishes of American authorities and worked outside of their purview. They maneuvered within a legal system that criminalized their social and sexual lives. They disputed the devaluing of Black lives in the face of the tragic deaths that disproportionately affected Silver workers. And while they created infrastructural support for the contracted Black labor that undergirded U.S. empire, they also nourished West Indian immigrant communities by recreating the institutions and patterns of Afro-Caribbean life in Panama. U.S. imperial authority in Panama held an almost inescapable monopoly of power, but this power had its limits, and women capitalized on their narrow opportunities to carve out niches of material benefit and physical safety for themselves and their kin.[13] They did so through specific gendered and diasporic strategies of social reproduction, mobilizing their flexible labor, legal and financial claims-making, and kinship networks to secure income and survival.

The Canal Zone was a moral universe jointly created by the contradictions of U.S. imperial governance and the paradoxical strategies of West Indian women. Women affirmed the extractive labor economy of the Zone while simultaneously remaking and redeploying its moral categories in a multisided engagement with imperial authority. West Indian women's assertions of their own modes of living, working, and loving often stood in opposition to imperial expectations, such as in their continued commitment to cohabitation without marriage, made illegal in the Canal Zone in 1905. At other times, West Indian women repurposed the same racialized and gendered norms of morality used against them, such as when directing the language of deviancy toward fellow West Indian women. Their practices thus did not function within a tidy binary of accommodation versus resistance.[14] Rather, West Indian women made their lives under conditions of dispossession and exclusion that forced them to navigate between the social reproduction of imperial racial capitalism and the social reproduction of West Indian lives.[15] For example, when women leveraged a discourse of victimhood in front of Canal authorities to secure spousal support, they deployed hegemonic ideas about dysfunctional West Indian families *in order to* uphold the validity of their criminalized unions, thus forcing U.S. administrators to follow through on the financial and legal obligations that came along with the common-law partnerships that the same system criminalized. This edgewise negotiation of empire secured West Indian women's survival, their economic futures, and the social reproduction of their kin at the same time as it affirmed the moral economy of the Canal.

As currency in exchange for their labor, silver linked Black migrants to imperial investments in infrastructure and global finance. West Indian women were excluded from formal employment and rarely registered on the official payroll, but the promise of money nevertheless drew most of them to the Canal Zone. For West Indian women, silver and gold were not just a form of potential wealth or a monetary transaction.[16] They also served as symbols of racial discrimination, objects of contention with white bosses and customers, tokens of loyalty from a partner, links to their migrant family members sending remittances, or as the owed wages of a deceased loved one. Silver and gold run as threads throughout each of these women's practices, tied as deeply to intimacy and kinship as they were to labor.[17] While distinctly marked by the racial segregation of the Canal Zone, women yet managed to function outside of the strict margins of the roll system—they demanded to get paid in gold coin from their American customers and traversed across segregated spaces in the Zone in their everyday domestic work. Centering on "Silver women" locates them as pivotal, if unrecognized, economic actors within a history dominated by overarching narratives of imperial finance and contracted labor. West Indian women in Panama challenged the racialized economic parameters imposed by imperial authorities and mobilized understandings of wealth and value that accounted for their own economic and emotional priorities.

West Indian male laborers continue to dominate narratives of early twentieth-century Caribbean migrations as the essential symbol of diasporic connection and the Caribbean entry into modernity.[18] The highly mobile, literate, modern, and politically active Black West Indian man recurs throughout histories of the period in figures like Claude McKay and Marcus Garvey, structuring what scholar Michelle Stephens has criticized as the "masculine global imaginary" of diaspora.[19] This continued assumption of Black men's predominance in early twentieth-century migrations—demographically, politically, and culturally—has diminished Black women's powerful interventions within migrant Caribbean communities.[20] It has distorted, as well, our understanding of large-scale imperial projects, which historians have solidified as struggles between a fully formed imperial administration and male contract laborers while ignoring the essential everyday labor of social reproduction that operated in the shadow of infrastructural behemoths.[21] Looking at West Indian women during this period turns our focus away from the desires of empire, the boundaries of the nation-state, and the narrowness of patriarchal Caribbean mythologies. It relocates the Canal construction period as a time of conflict, negotiation, and contingency between an imperial authority not yet solidified in its power and a growing migrant community that far exceeded the official workforce.[22] This book prioritizes Silver women's social, political, and economic creativity in the long wake of emancipation as they "endowed free status with meaning," in the words of Jessica Johnson, through their migration and survival.[23]

Black women's survival in Panama was pragmatic and rooted in everyday, personal struggles. Women at times reaffirmed the moral categories of empire, mobilized these discourses against other Black women, and privileged individual profit over community safety. Nevertheless, their individual actions collectively maintained the migrant West Indian community by providing care, food, and domestic labor where U.S. authorities did not, and defending the moral status and financial futures of migrants. The fruits of their labor spanned the Caribbean, establishing business and legal relationships outside the confines of U.S. empire. They also collectively disturbed U.S. power and its norms of gendered inclusion, questioning the extent of the ICC's incursions into West Indian enclaves and exposing the project's dependence on women's entrepreneurial labor. These strategies of social reproduction, embedded in long-standing Afro-Caribbean circuits of kinship and obligation, nurtured West Indian migrations throughout the early twentieth century, linking places like Harlem, Cuba, and Costa Rica. West Indian women's strategies of social reproduction did not merely sustain them on an individual level; they also sustained the physical, economic, and political perpetuation of a global Caribbean diaspora.

Borderlands of Imperial Labor

Panama declared its independence from Spain in 1821 and entered into a voluntary union with Colombia as an autonomous federal state. Though the isthmus had long served as a crossing for people, goods, and ideas, it was generally considered a backwater of Colombia for most of the early nineteenth century. This would all change with the beginning of the Gold Rush, which precipitated a race to find a faster route between the Atlantic and Pacific Oceans. Between 1848 and 1856, Panama became the main point of transit for labor migration, the site of the world's first transcontinental railroad built by the Panama Railroad Company (PCC), and a key node in America's military and financial empire.[24] The construction of the railroad thrust Panama into two main developments of the nineteenth century—the expansion of informal U.S. empire, and the voluntary labor migration of nonwhite people toward the productive sites of imperial investment, primarily from the postemancipation West Indies. As with the Canal, these earlier projects of U.S. "manifest destiny" in the Caribbean basin, starting with the railroad, relied on the exploited labor of contracted Black male workers and uncontracted Black female workers who subsidized the social reproduction of this workforce through their domestic and care labor.[25]

These patterns of labor migration would intensify with France's attempt at building a canal three decades after the railroad's completion. From 1881 to 1889, more than 84,000 West Indian workers arrived in Panama to work for the Compagnie Universelle du Canal Interocéanique de Panama under Head Engineer Ferdinand Marie de Lesseps in an attempt to replicate the success of the Suez Canal.[26] These migrants came not only as Canal workers but also as merchants, domestics, clerks, photographers, doctors, pastors, and newspapermen.[27] They traveled by the regular fortnightly service provided by the Royal Mail steamship line as well as by the common small boats that regularly left Kingston's harbor. Passage on a steamer cost twenty-five shillings.[28] By 1884 the *Star and Herald* had begun to call Colón "the new Jamaica," and indeed the island and the isthmus grew closer during this period as the transit in people, merchandise, and news between them thickened.[29] In 1885, of 12,875 workers, 9,005 or 70 percent were Jamaicans.[30] During the decade of the French venture, Panama grew a reputation for lavish excess and corruption—an enclave of champagne, guns, gambling, prostitution, and rampant speculation. An American resident described the period as a "carnival of depravity."[31]

At the time, most West Indians treated Panama as a brief sojourn. The number of returnees remained high throughout the French construction, outweighing emigrants by 1884. It was during this period that the mythology of the "Colón Man"—the West Indian male returnee from Panama who flaunted his newly acquired wealth with gold watches and rings—developed.[32] This was not the experience of most migrants, though the ideal of the Colón Man retained a powerful hold on Caribbean consciousness throughout the following decades. Many Jamaican migrants received horrific injuries or perished from disease; the ICC's chief sanitary officer William Gorgas calculated that, at the height of work under the French company, about a quarter of employees died per year.[33] Some never returned at all.

In 1889 the years of delay and grift finally led to the crash of the publicly owned Compagnie in a spectacular scandal. Some seven thousand West Indians repatriated, but many stayed and formed communities around Colón. The experience of the French Compagnie would shape the path of the United States fifteen years later in multiple ways. Its early efforts at excavation and infrastructure set the foundation for further American construction (the Americans would repurpose many leftover French structures and machinery). Its well-publicized failures provided a cautionary tale of immorality and mismanagement gone awry. Finally, its allure for West Indian workers seeking their fortunes meant that by the time of the United States' arrival, Jamaicans had well-established routes of migration and exchange with Panama. Many were already there, embedded in the early communities they had formed in Colón.

In 1903 the Republic of Panama, aided by U.S. military intervention, declared its independence from Colombia.[34] A few weeks later, without the participation of any Panamanians, the Hay-Bunau-Varilla Treaty granted sovereignty to the United States over the ten-mile-wide strip of land that was to become the Canal. The year 1903 thus marks the legal birth of the Panamanian nation and the start of American colonization of the Canal Zone, which extended ten miles on both sides of the planned 51-mile-long structure.[35] The two terminal cities, Colón and Panama City, remained under Panamanian sovereignty, but they were separated from the Zone by a porous and unregulated border. By crossing the street, visitors might pass into the sister towns of Cristobal and Ancon under U.S. sovereignty. Within the 436-square-mile territory of the Canal Zone, residents and visitors could experience the austere and highly standardized architecture of the American company town, be subject to U.S. law and police surveillance, and face strict racial segregation.[36] Though the Canal Zone and Panama technically functioned under separate jurisdictions, in practice these spaces were tightly linked; residents traversed across them continuously throughout the construction era for work and entertainment, while U.S. diplomats, administrators, and sanitation officials repeatedly intruded into Panama's sovereign territory. West Indian women, less beholden to the patterns of construction, transited across these borderlands of empire as part of their daily work.

The ICC, which reported directly to Secretary of War William Howard Taft and worked under the leadership of the chief engineer, presided over the Canal Zone. On May 6, 1904, Theodore Roosevelt appointed John Findlay Wallace as the first chief engineer. He would only last a year. Roosevelt then appointed John F. Stevens, counting on the civil engineer's previous success in building the Great Northern Railway. Stevens soon buckled under the challenges of the Canal and resigned in 1907. He was replaced by Colonel George Washington Goethals, whose militaristic leadership proved more durable, and who would oversee the construction of the lock-system canal to its successful completion in 1914. As the quick turnover of chief engineers in the early years indicates, the decade of construction was a moment of precarious transition during which the U.S. administration strained to govern the Canal Zone and bring its promises to fruition. Amid this tumult, as power and borders shifted, West Indians traveled to the isthmus.[37]

The ICC sent labor recruiters across the Caribbean Sea to Barbados, Jamaica, St. Lucia, Grenada, and Guadeloupe. Each island government reacted differently. In 1893 Jamaica passed the Emigrant Labourer's Protection Law, stating that anyone who wished to emigrate to certain "proclaimed places"

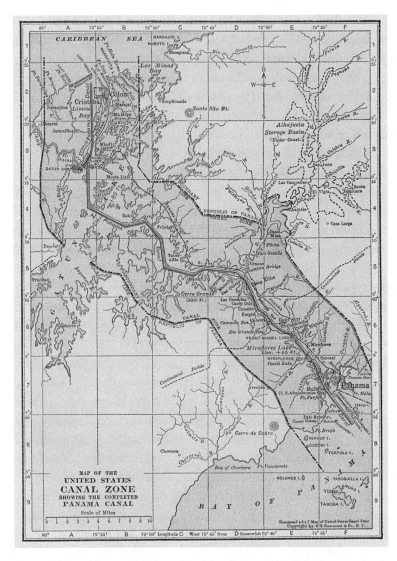

Figure 1. Map of the completed canal and Canal Zone, 1930. C. S. Hammond and Company, [1930..1935], accessed August 3, 2021, https://texashistory.unt.edu/ark: /67531/metapth288682/m1/1/, The Portal to Texas History, University of Texas at Arlington Library.

as decided by the governor, had to obtain a permit and fulfill certain conditions. The law was revised in 1905 to directly address Panama recruitment efforts.[38] Jamaican laborers needed either a contract and a recruiting agent prepared to pay £1 to the Distressed Emigrant's Fund or the backing of two people with property worth £10. The contract had to clearly state the terms of the job engagement and had to be approved by a police inspector. The British government stipulated these conditions as a safeguard against spending public money to assist Jamaicans abroad. It feared repeating the earlier financial disaster of repatriating Jamaicans who had left to work on the French canal. The law had the effect of limiting unskilled worker emigration from Jamaica since only workers who already enjoyed financial security could meet its conditions. This was borne out by the eventual predominance of Jamaicans in higher-paying skilled jobs in the Zone, such as artisans, managers, policemen, and teachers. Women who wished to travel to Panama ran into difficulty if coming from Jamaica since most of them could not obtain a contract in advance and were generally regarded as less financially secure. They would have to travel with some existing financial support, if they followed official routes. However, Jamaica's proximity to Panama and previous history of informal migration meant that migrants could and did travel by their own means.

This was not the case for the islands of the Lesser Antilles, which lay further from the isthmus and lacked established sea routes to Panama. The ICC focused much of its efforts on Barbados, placing its main recruitment station, headed by agent William Karner, at Trafalgar Square in Bridgetown (now National Heroes Square). Barbados placed no financial restrictions on emigration until 1911, when the number of emigrants had already begun to decline. The government did, however, seek limited controls through the Emigration Act of March 18, 1904, which required a magistrate to oversee contracts. Almost half of the contracted labor force (19,900 workers) came from Barbados.[39] Yet more than 20,000 men and women arrived without contracts (historian Velma Newton estimates it could have been as many as 40,000).[40] During the recruitment period, Barbados is estimated to have lost a third of its population to Panama.[41] Barbadian women could travel more easily to Panama than their Jamaican counterparts, as long as they could pay their passage. Migration from Barbados was thus markedly working-class in comparison to Jamaica, as they did not have to pay an emigrant's fee. Barbados also served as a central terminal for migrants from other islands. For example, ICC agents recruited in Grenada, but most Grenadians traveled first to Barbados before taking the twelve-day steamer to Panama.[42] The ICC also sent agents to Guadeloupe and Martinique in 1906, but the French government rescinded their permission to recruit in 1907. Some French West Indians nevertheless traveled on their own through Castries or Bridgetown.

Panama and the Zone presented new racial landscapes for migrants from majority Black islands, and an introduction to "American-style" segregation. However, many West Indians had experience migrating to different intra-Caribbean locations for temporary work and were likely accustomed to the uncertainties of labor migration in an imperial enclave. Migrants also traveled with their own prejudices toward West Indians from other islands—enmities exacerbated by differences in language, class, and skill level. Though West Indian migrants could not consistently rely on the British for support, they did at times request intercession on their behalf from the British consul in Panama, Claude Mallet. Their identification as British subjects often created tension with the governing bodies of the Canal Zone, who derided West Indians' attachment to Britain's colonial authority. However, the British consul and the islands' colonial governments held little sway over the Canal Zone or their British subjects living under U.S. sovereignty. Though aware of the issues West Indians faced abroad, Colonial Office administrators more often than not left Panama migrants to fend for themselves and did not substantially challenge the ICC's attempts to expand its legal authority over British subjects.

Despite their class and national differences, all West Indian employees of the Canal Commission had to contend with the roll system, which differentiated pay rates for skilled workers on the Gold Roll and unskilled West Indian and other foreign laborers placed on the Silver Roll. Gold Roll rates were 25 to 50 percent higher than for equivalent jobs in the United States. Silver Roll rates were far lower and had no relation to wages of equivalent workers in the United States. These rates were based on the "wages prevailing for tropical labor in the Caribbean area," though they were higher than what these men could make in their islands of origin as plantation workers.[43] In practice, in the early years, this meant Gold employees were paid in actual gold American coin, while Silver employees were paid in local currency, silver Colombian pesos or Panamanian balboas. Workers on the line had to walk up to the "pay car," which would make regular stops along the railroad tracks, and show their metal ID tag to receive their wages. By the end of construction, all workers came to be paid in American dollars, but pay rates remained sharply divided. The system was never exclusively a racial hierarchy and inconsistently categorized workers based on skill, nationality, and race.[44] In 1908 President Theodore Roosevelt issued an executive order that privileged citizenship as the main category for the Gold Roll and limited it to American and Panamanian workers. However, throughout construction, Goethals and other officials interpreted the laws in ways that made the system increasingly rigid and racialized. Though some foreign white employees from places like Spain or Greece were placed on the Silver Roll, they could also be paid under Gold Roll rates.[45] African Americans were placed primarily on the Silver Roll—their race trumped their citizenship. Skilled Black West Indian workers remained on the Silver Roll under the category of "artisans"—their race trumped their skill.[46] While the payment scheme did not affect women as directly, the roll system nevertheless structured their lives. West Indian women did not have access to ICC services, for the most part, but still had to navigate the racial segregation of the Canal Zone. If they lived within the Zone, it was in segregated "native" or Silver towns with little access to services and poor sanitation.[47] If they wished to use facilities like the commissary, they had to use the Silver one. But, for Black women, the roll system presented a more porous barrier.

Throughout the construction years, the fantasy of a perfectly organized American labor colony remained mostly that—a fantasy. The spread of disease and the heavy rains, combined with the task of recruiting and maintaining a transnational labor force, made governing the Canal Zone a challenge for its series of early chief engineers. Denied company married housing, West Indians settled in privately owned tenements across the Canal Zone and Panama, distancing themselves from dependence on U.S. institutions. White American employees and migrant laborers from the West Indies, India, China, and Spain traversed across the Zone border to Panama and gathered in its saloons and gambling houses, with little regard for segregation. The strategies of social and labor control used to manage the Canal

Zone and its border, in the early years of construction, failed to contain the diverse populations who sustained the project.

Along with the American roll system, West Indians had to contend with Panama's distinct but overlapping ideas of race. As in many other Latin American countries, the myth of mestizaje prevailed as one of the foundations of Panamanian national identity.[48] This discourse maintained that, during the colonial period, white, indigenous, and African-descended people intermixed so freely as to dilute their individual differences into a single, mixed racial identity. This trope's predominance has led to continued structural discrimination for both Afro-descendants and indigenous groups throughout Panama.[49] The racial and social geography of Panama would change significantly with the advent of the Gold Rush, the Panama Railroad, and the interventions of the French throughout the nineteenth century. By the turn of the twentieth century, the arrival of the ICC and its strict architecture of segregation, along with the rapid influx of West Indian immigrants, set the stage for a hardening of racial lines and the growth of xenophobia in Panama.[50] West Indian immigrants' reception in Panama as unassimilable interlopers, tainted by their Blackness and their association with American empire, contradicted popular notions of the country's racial harmony. Panama's racial politics and its limited national sovereignty shaped the experience of West Indian women who were often the subject of moral suspicion by Panamanian state actors.

Some West Indians chose to live in Panamanian territory during construction to avoid the policing, overt racial segregation, and lack of housing within the U.S. Canal Zone, despite the higher rents. After 1912 many West Indians were forced to leave the Zone altogether following an official depopulation order that expelled all but white American employees.[51] As they settled in adjacent areas of Panamanian territory, West Indian women found local iterations of the criminalization and discrimination they faced in the Zone. The combination of U.S. imperial pressures and nascent Panamanian anti-Black xenophobia placed West Indian women in a particularly vulnerable situation, casting them as dishonorable women and vectors of disease. Panamanian elites enforced the desires of the ICC to police Black women and impelled West Indians to live in the only housing available to them—cheap tenement buildings alongside red-light districts, owned by elite Panamanian families.[52] Yet, in Panama as in the Canal Zone, West Indian women sought to meaningfully lay claim to their new communities and challenged Panamanian notions of honor and respectability through their encounters with local courts.

The construction of the American canal intensified the workings of racial capitalism in Panama and across the Caribbean. Increasing flows of money brought more and more migrants to the region, where they faced hardening regimes of labor discipline and racialized notions of American and Panamanian sovereignty. These ideas came together in these borderlands of empire in ways that exacerbated Black women's vulnerability as they dealt with segregation and exclusion in the Zone while marked as racial "others" in Panama. Yet these spaces of contested governance and clashing visions also served as the openings where Black women could shake off, at least in part, the surveillance they faced from American and Panamanian authorities, and enact their practices of intimacy and economic flexibility. In the multiracial saloons of Panama City, the tenement buildings of Empire or El Marañon, the newly formed Canal Zone courts, and the public streets where they could market their wares, Black women fought for their autonomy and survival.

Silver Archives

Record Group 185, held in the National Archives and Records Administration of the United States at College Park, Maryland, holds the biggest collection of original documents regarding the construction of the Panama Canal. Within this archive, only nine subcategories make direct, extended reference to West Indian women, despite their crucial role in providing domestic and care labor throughout the decade of construction. These documents fall into only two categories—miscellany or criminalized sexuality. West Indian women do not even appear in categories where one would expect them to, such as "Laundry Service." The danger of this archive is that it suggests West Indian women in the Canal Zone either did not matter or served the sole function of sexual objects.

The imperialist projects of the United States in the early twentieth century maintained a "fantasy of empire" through their administrative documentation,

eliding the tensions of colonial expansion by creating a comprehensive tex-
tual corpus of knowledge that silenced or contained subjects that fit uneasily
within its project.[53] The Isthmian Canal Commission valued above all the
efficient management of labor with an eye toward fast completion of the Canal. The great majority of the general files maintained by the commission
thus concern administrative and technical issues under categories such as
"Force" and "Buildings—Construction, Maintenance, and Disposal." Anything not covered under these subjects fell under miscellany, including
"Holidays" and "Amusement." The logic is clear. Work and administration
(defined through subcategories of efficiency, scheduling, and infrastructure)
prevailed, while amusement and intimacy were relegated to crime or miscellany.

   This book probes the margins where U.S. imperial power faltered and
West Indian women made do. It confronts the silences and hierarchies of
knowledge enshrined by American sources, using conceptual roadmaps laid
out by Black feminist scholars and scholars of gender and U.S. empire to approach this archive critically while accounting for Black migrant women's
own practices and logics.[54] While imperial documents often denigrate Black
West Indian women, at their edges lie women's own strategies of what Saidiya Hartman calls "trying to live when you were never meant to survive."[55] I
use criminal investigations, memoirs authored by white women, administrative correspondence, and other sources meant to flatten Black women to instead reveal their everyday strategies of survival and negotiation. The West
Indian women in this book evaded capture by Canal Zone police, talked back
to their bosses, quit their jobs, and claimed respectability in local courts. They
did this in the face of a growing imperial power that saw them as sexual deviants and racial others, even as it depended on their domestic labor to sustain the construction effort. The archive, read along the grain, documents this
clash.[56]

   The book takes a further step aside from U.S. imperial concerns by using
sources from the UK, Barbados, and Panama to locate West Indian women
as transnational subjects. These archives do not provide a simple counter to
the criminalization and caricaturization of Black women in sources created
by Americans. If anything, they show the overlapping racial structures and
realms of sovereignty that West Indian women were forced to navigate, such

as the colonial understandings of West Indian subjecthood by the British consul, and the racialized visions of honor enshrined in Panamanian legal codes.[57] Nevertheless, these archives open a window into understanding West Indian women as diasporic legal and financial intermediaries. They help shift the focus away from the perspectives of U.S. Canal Zone administrators and residents toward the mobility and aspirations of West Indian women and the relationships they cultivated.

This book is a history of West Indian women's labor of social reproduction as integral to imperial infrastructure, women's own survival, and the Caribbean diaspora more broadly. While the book's context is U.S. empire, its center is women's own experiences. The book follows the trajectory of "Silver" women, beginning in Chapter 1 with West Indian women's gendered freedom practices after emancipation and tracing their motivations and routes of migration to Panama—the rumors they heard, the ships they boarded, and the discrimination they found upon their arrival. It ends with the Canal's completion in 1914, tracing West Indian women's divergent paths in the aftermath of construction to the tenements of Panama, to other imperial ventures, and to the emerging Caribbean neighborhoods of New York City.

Over seven chapters, the book considers various aspects of West Indian women's lives thematically, reconstructing the webs of domination and transgression that shaped their intimacy, labor, and community building. The chapters move in and out of the Canal Zone, sometimes looking closely at the interactions between U.S. administrators and West Indian women, sometimes looking outward to Panama and to the islands, in an attempt to capture women's multiple sites of engagement with racial capitalism and to locate their experiences in Panama within a broader Caribbean context. Chapters 2 and 3 focus on the legal and moral conflicts West Indian women faced in the newly established Canal Zone, starting with a scandal in 1905 that categorized a recently arrived group of Martinican women as prostitutes and following the legal codes, marriage prohibitions, and criminal cases where West Indian women clashed with Canal authorities. Chapter 4 considers West Indian women's domestic and provisioning labor primarily through white American women's memoirs of the construction era, excavating West Indian women's attempts at labor autonomy in the American home through sources that routinely disparage them. Chapter 5 draws on British Colonial Office petitions to show how West Indian women in the islands mourned the passing of their kin in Panama and activated their economic entitlements as British subjects and inheritors. Chapter 6 uses municipal cases from Panama City neighborhoods to explore how West Indian women managed their lives in this new territory, where gendered and racialized understandings of honor excluded them from the benefits of citizenship. Finally, Chapter 7 looks past the construction era to show how West Indian women used strategies developed during the Canal construction to sustain subsequent Caribbean migrations.

A Note on Terminology

Throughout the book, I commonly refer to these women as "West Indian," despite the fact that, at the time, they would have identified themselves primarily by their individual island of origin. Women migrated from places with varied histories of emancipation and different constraints on labor migration. The term usually refers to the British West Indies, though here it also sometimes encompasses the French Caribbean since a significant early group of women migrated from Martinique. The great majority of West Indians in Panama indeed came from the British West Indies (particularly Jamaica and Barbados) and I base the majority of my conclusions on evidence from these islands. I try as much as possible to distinguish the origins of the West Indian women in this book and to consider how these differences affected their interactions and position within the Canal Zone. However, West Indians did follow certain general regional patterns that made their experiences intertwine, in particular the growth of U.S. capital in the Caribbean and the opening of imperial labor migration opportunities in the late nineteenth and early twentieth centuries. Women's strategies, whether from Barbados or Martinique, similarly correlated in ways that allow us to think more broadly of Black West Indian women's diasporic practices.

I use the term "Black" to underline the racial understandings that migrants faced in the Canal Zone, invariably cast as racialized Silver Roll workers and categorized as "Black" in official state accounts such as the U.S.

census. Within the Canal Zone, "Black" was almost coterminous with West Indian, while Panamanians were considered "natives." These categories speak to the "racial scripts" American administrators imposed on the region, but they significantly simplified the racial landscape of Panama, a place that had seen African and Afro-descendant forced transit, enslaved labor, and long-time residence since the early colonial period.[58] In Panamanian territory, West Indians continued to identify by their island of origin. The Panamanian census classified them as "foreigners." West Indian immigrants' Blackness, English language, and Protestant religion marked them as outsiders to the Panamanian body politic. By the 1920s nationalist xenophobia, the development of restrictive immigration laws, the further retrenchment of racialized discrimination, and the growth of a second generation encouraged the development of a less differentiated "West Indian" (or Afro-Antillean, in a direct translation of the Spanish) community identity that persists today. The events of this book precede the development of a more distinct West Indian–Panamanian identity but form the basis of the conflicts that followed.[59]

CHAPTER 1

The Land of Promise?

Emily Amelia Griffith must have sailed up to Colón in 1910 feeling a mix of fear and hope.[1] She was finally making her way to Panama to join her partner William after he had left, like many other Barbadians, to find work as a blacksmith on the Canal construction years prior. They were to be married in a Protestant church in Empire once she arrived. Emily Amelia traveled with her first child, a young toddler sick with "what old-timers . . . called the pox."[2] In Panama, she took her daughter to Gorgas Hospital, hoping the American doctors could stem the fever. The doctors put an ice pack on Emily Amelia's daughter, but it was too late. She died at Gorgas and was buried at the segregated Silver cemetery in Corozal. Emily Amelia's first moments in Panama were a mother's worst nightmare. She could not have known then that she would live many years in the Canal Zone. She could not have known she would have nine other children in Panama, though nothing could make up for the loss of her first. She could not have known that she would own property on Panamanian territory, in the neighborhood of Rio Abajo, founded by West Indian immigrants. In 1910 Emily Amelia might have felt her hopes for the future diminish as she came face-to-face with the ambiguous promise of life in Panama.

At the beginning of the twentieth century, two generations after the end of slavery, West Indians still found themselves in constrained conditions. Emancipation had not brought about economic autonomy from the plantation complex or freedom from the moral coercion of colonial governments. Migration held the promise of escape from the destitution and discontent of life in the Caribbean during a lingering economic depression. It held the potential for change. West Indians might have imagined that they could remake their circumstances and circumvent a lifetime of agricultural labor through migration. Some foresaw great riches in industrial projects like the Panama Canal construction, helmed by wealthy Americans who paid at least twice what you could make in the islands. Like Emily Amelia Griffith, some hoped to secure the welfare of their families and cement their withdrawal from the plantation. As Susan Proudleigh, the title character of Jamaican Herbert de Lisser's 1915 novel, explained, Panama "signified for them the land of promise, the land of their thoughts and dreams."[3]

But migration to Panama at the start of the Canal construction in 1904 did not mark an unprecedented break from the previous six decades, during which West Indians had attempted to negotiate and escape the limitations on their freedom after enslavement. West Indian women's move to Panama at the turn of the century was structured as much by the constraints and desires of British colonial island governments and American authorities in Panama as it was by the gendered freedom practices they had articulated in the wake of emancipation. Throughout the late nineteenth century, West Indian women divested from plantation economies and expanded their entrepreneurial labor, moving across imperial borders to sell their wares and services in transregional markets. They grew food, kept houses, took care of elders, and raised children, undergirding labor migrations with their work of social reproduction on the islands. They mostly ignored the attempts of colonial governments and churches to legalize their partnerships through marriage, remaining in cohabitation arrangements that provided them with physical and financial autonomy and delaying marriage until later in their lives. In essence, they made freedom and secured some modicum of material wealth by deploying flexible strategies of intimacy and market entrepreneurship on the margins of "free" labor across the Caribbean, while navigating colonial regimes that sought to define their economic and familial lives.[4]

Familiar with strategies of regional migration, West Indian women further seized on the promise and opportunity afforded by the investment of U.S. capital in Panama at the turn of the century. But the very act of their migration went against a colonial logic that actively discouraged their movement and devalued their labor, both on their islands of origin and in their destination. With few exceptions, the British Colonial Governments of the islands did not encourage West Indian women to migrate. Neither did the Isthmian Canal Commission recruit or officially hire West Indian women. It did not provide them with housing, food, or recreational facilities as it did for male laborers and white American women. Despite and because of this structural exclusion, West Indian women took on the challenges of migration mostly on their own terms. They paid their own passage, followed well-traveled migrant routes throughout the Caribbean, worked a variety of independent jobs, and openly lived with their romantic partners in illegal "concubinage." In the process, they suffered exploitation, disease, loss, and heartbreak. Because West Indian women moved outside of the direct purview of colonial authorities, their migration rarely obeyed the ideal of productivity and labor control that structured most Canal policy.

Like West Indian men contracted for Canal work, women too saw Panama as a land of promise and migrated there in spite of the active discouragement by British and American authorities. At the edges of imperial oversight over their uncontracted labor, they mobilized strategies of regional migration, social reproduction, and entrepreneurial labor to ensure their survival. These strategies relied on and subsidized the extractive labor economies of expanding imperial ventures throughout the late nineteenth- and early twentieth-century Caribbean. West Indian laundresses, cooks, and tavern and lodging-house keepers provided for the labor force of migrating West Indians who worked in the mines, on the plantations, and at construction sites across the region. The economic and social relationships these women built helped ease worker morale, lubricated the flow of material goods to otherwise isolated labor camps, and made imperial projects possible. The Panama Canal project heralded a new opportunity—one that would bring unprecedented amounts of capital to the region but which also brought intensified forms of imperial control and labor discipline. Migration to Panama did not produce the change West Indian women like Emily Amelia might have so fervently desired. Rather, West Indian women continued to navigate uneasily between reproducing empire and sustaining themselves and their communities—work that was often one and the same. Black women's freedom practices in the decades leading up to the Canal construction unfolded under the always contingent terms of imperial racial capital, which held out opportunities at the risk of disease, death, and discrimination.

Gendered Freedom Practices During the Era of Emancipation

After the end of slavery and apprenticeship in the British Caribbean, the meaning of freedom for West Indians was stifled by the disproportionate concentration of land among large plantation owners, the below-subsistence wages paid to workers, remaining structures of discrimination, continued legislative attempts at controlling the lives of free Black people, and a general economic depression after 1874 brought on by a decline in sugar prices.[5] British colonial authorities perceived the transition to free labor as a process of subjugating formerly enslaved Black workers by compelling their continued work on plantations, limiting their mobility, and encouraging a "proper gender order."[6] Their approach sought to foreclose routes to Afro-Caribbean land ownership, self-determination, and national sovereignty. Formerly enslaved people for the most part rejected these impositions and instead practiced multiple definitions of freedom, from escaping estate labor and fostering family ties, to accessing land and pursuing political rights.[7] They fiercely protected their freedom through work stoppages, uprisings, and everyday forms of resistance.[8]

Plantation labor declined in the nineteenth century as competition from European and North American beet-sugar producers disrupted the Caribbean monopoly on the trade, even though the demand for sugar had increased internationally.[9] Following emancipation, the British continued to coerce Black workers into plantation wage labor, such as with Barbados's notorious 1838 "Contract Law" and 1840 Masters and Servants Act, which limited internal mobility by tying workers to a specific plantation under a contract.[10] In 1839 Jamaican planters charged rents on estate grounds per resident able to work on the plantation in order to compel labor from all household members, including women and children.[11] After the British government established the

1864 Sugar Duties Act, reducing preferential duties for sugar from former British colonies, the price of sugar from the West Indies rapidly decreased. Agricultural work in the islands also became scarce due to a bad run of natural disasters affecting Caribbean islands during the time prior to the construction of the Canal, notably a series of alternating floods and droughts.[12] Many British West Indian planters suffered bankruptcy and abandoned their plantations, resulting in high unemployment.[13]

As European and U.S. foreign investors devised new ways to exploit sources of free labor in the late nineteenth century, regional mobility arose as a strategy of both colonial exploitation and Afro-Caribbean opportunity. Empires expanded beyond their formal borders into new territories and forms of production previously underexplored. West Indians departed the plantation and followed these new investments in cacao, gold, rubber, and bananas across the Caribbean basin. They joined multiethnic, polyglot populations in port cities and imperial borderlands, and moved across these spaces to bargain for higher wages and labor power.[14] Though propelled by the promise of employment and wages, West Indians practiced regional labor migration in ways unforeseen and often condemned by colonial authorities.

Women navigated regional migration through their own adaptive strategies, engaging in border-crossing market entrepreneurship and providing the reproductive and affective labor on which imperial labor schemes relied. Migration was not an individual act; rather, it was embedded in households bound by familial kinship and financial obligation—linkages maintained and managed by women. The port cities and borderlands of empire depended on Black women who supplied laundry services, sold foodstuffs, and ran boardinghouses. Their gendered practices of social reproduction and market entrepreneurship shaped the Caribbean migratory culture of the nineteenth century.[15]

Even before emancipation, enslaved and free Black women dominated the market trade and provided for the subsistence needs of individuals throughout the islands.[16] They sold food and sundry items in markets that on Sundays could attract as many as ten thousand people.[17] Enslaved men and women risked serious punishment to defend their right to market as they did in Antigua's 1831 Sunday Market Rebellion.[18] These higglers used their skills at hawking goods and creating dense commercial networks to escape enslavement and survive in cities.[19] Female slave mobility and market participation, however, were not uncomplicated liberatory acts. Rather, these actions were often institutionalized within the system of slavery, where enslaved people's mobile market activity served to subsidize slaveowners' schemes, while also providing a degree of sustenance and independence for enslaved people.[20] Black women had little choice but to make do within a system that exploited and marginalized them to produce colonial wealth. But within that system, they prioritized their welfare and that of their kin.

As freedom dawned in the Caribbean, the majority of Black West Indian men and women continued to work side by side in agriculture.[21] But by the mid-nineteenth century, women were pioneering the exodus from rural plantations to urban centers to work as market entrepreneurs. This increase in women's market activity accelerated the sexual division of labor.[22] Women worked in informal economies or as domestic servants for whites and the rising Black middle class in Caribbean port cities.[23] Their labor was highly visible in urban centers, where they dominated the markets.[24] Though Black women's entrepreneurship was still embedded in a colonial economy, it nevertheless marked a departure from British expectations about the appropriate transition to free labor, namely, their desire for a dependent wage labor force still tied to the plantation.

Higglers had to negotiate their everyday food and physical insecurity by adapting established strategies of survival, such as mobilizing across ports and urban spaces.[25] As the British traveler Charles Kingsley observed in St. Kitts in 1870, for example, Black women would pull up next to arriving steamers in boats filled with fruits and produce to sell to tourists—"the contents of these vegetable baskets often as gay-colored as the gaudy gowns, and still gaudier turbans, of the women who offered them for sale."[26] West Indian women were first at the scene of new arrivals and used multiple techniques to appeal to the tastes of tourists, such as wearing striking clothing. They capitalized on their market skills and mobility to survive in the period after emancipation and take advantage of new flows of travelers and capital through the region.

As early as 1851, the Jamaican traveler Mary Seacole applied these mobile entrepreneurial strategies on her journey to Panama, following her half brother Edward's departure:

Early in the same year my brother had left Kingston for the Isthmus. . . . Ever since he had done so, I had found some difficulty in checking my reviving disposition to roam, and at last persuading myself that I might be of use to him (he was far from strong), I resigned my house into the hands of a cousin, and made arrangements to journey to Chagres. Having come to this conclusion, I allowed no grass to grow beneath my feet, but set to work busily, for I was not going to him empty-handed. My house was full for weeks, of tailors, making up rough coats, trousers, etc., and seamstresses cutting out and making shirts. In addition to these, my kitchen was filled with busy people, manufacturing preserves, guava jelly, and other delicacies.[27]

Seacole, the daughter of a free Black Jamaican doctress and a Scottish soldier, traveled to Panama, Cuba, Crimea, and England with what she called "a view to gain." Throughout her travelogue-memoir, she presents herself repeatedly as an entrepreneur, always prepared to adapt to a new marketplace. While the locations changed, her strategy of "seeking authority . . . via her participation in the market" remained the same.[28] Prior to her departure for Panama, Seacole hired tailors, seamstresses, and other artisans to manufacture clothing and foodstuffs during weeks of assembly line production. This prominent Jamaican woman's commercial flexibility depended on the grueling labor of working-class Black men and women, who crafted the goods she sold for profit in Panama.

In Panama, Seacole initially helped her half brother establish his hotel in Chagres but branched out in several independent ventures, including another boardinghouse in Chagres, a women's hotel in Gorgona, and administering medicine to those struck down by cholera and yellow fever on the isthmus. As later West Indian women would also do, Seacole applied certain strategies throughout the Gold Rush to secure autonomy, flexibility, and profit: traveling as a short-term migrant, engaging in market entrepreneurship, and providing care services for West Indian workers. Seacole aligned herself with the opportunities enabled by the expansion of empire, capitalizing on the desperation of working-class Jamaican workers and the demand for migrant laborers across ventures in the Caribbean for her own gain. Yet she stood somewhat ambiguously in relation to the priorities of empire, at times critiquing the racial logics of British and American colonialism that would disparage Black women and exclude her from its benefits.[29] Seacole's search for economic autonomy affirmed the profit motive and extractive labor regimes of imperial ventures, even as she remained unsteadily at the margins of power. Though Seacole, who was born of free parents, educated, and middle class, is not representative of the working-class West Indian women who would subsequently travel to Panama during the Canal construction, her experience mirrors some of the strategies less-affluent women would take as economic opportunities opened up in the region—strategies that walked the line between the reproduction of imperial relations and the preservation of West Indian community and kin.

By the latter half of the nineteenth century, colonial authorities became increasingly worried about the problem of controlling free labor during the ongoing economic depression. In places like British Guiana and Trinidad, they foresaw potential labor shortages while islands like Barbados and St. Kitts faced overpopulation and potentially high unemployment.[30] In 1844 Barbados was the most densely populated island in the Caribbean. Though initially skeptical of immigration schemes to British Guiana and Trinidad, by 1864 the Colonial Government of Barbados was promoting emigration as the only practical solution to the unemployment and overpopulation of the island. These proposals gained further support after the decline of sugar profits. In 1894 the government established a commission to investigate "the best means of securing or encouraging the emigration of able-bodied families to other Islands in the West Indies where they may find permanent homes and be able to cultivate lands with easily marketable products."[31] The commission found that certain islands, such as St. Lucia with its plentiful land but low population, would indeed be suitable for emigration. However, by 1898, in their annual report they bemoaned the failure of this scheme and blamed it on working-class Barbadians, attributing it to "the temperament of the people, who, as a rule, prefer low wages and their own homes to higher wages and separation from their island."[32] They reported some small numbers of people leaving the island permanently but complained that Barbadians always sought to return after brief sojourns. According to these administrators, Barbadians failed to engage in emigration because they were naturally unproductive and tied to the land.

Barbadians *did* migrate, however. Between 1860 and 1890, they left for Suriname, St. Croix, Trinidad, and St. Lucia.[33] For example, the 1891 Trinidad census enumerates 33,071 British West Indian immigrants, of which 42 percent were Barbadians.[34] The Colonial Postmaster estimated that these emigrants sent back a total of £16,446 as money to their families, though scholars have suggested this obscures much higher amounts sent through unofficial channels.[35] The patterns in Barbados held for other islands in the Caribbean where regional migration similarly developed as a postemancipation strategy: Cubans traveled to Tampa to roll cigars, Grenadians and Vincentians to Venezuela to cultivate cacao, and Windward Islanders to British Guiana to mine gold.[36] Through these recurrent regional ventures, migration developed into what scholars have deemed "an integral part of Caribbean culture," a Caribbean "migratory tradition" as an adaptation to the conditions of postemancipation societies in the nineteenth century.[37]

Women made up a significant proportion of these early migrations, even outnumbering men at times.[38] Working-class women had an equal amount of "migration potential" as men of the same socioeconomic status as they also sought high wages and upward mobility.[39] Moreover, women often assumed sole or primary responsibility for the upkeep of Caribbean households. They looked for opportunities through regional migration to secure economic welfare for their kin or, while remaining at home, managed the mobile wealth of family members engaged in a household strategy of regional migration. Thus, West Indians did not reject emigration, which they in fact avidly engaged in throughout the period following emancipation. Rather, their movement was not the "right" kind of migration for the British, who decried the specific strategies West Indians used: short-term and return migration by multiple members of a household. Colonial authorities encouraged migration only if it followed their image of an appropriate gendered division of labor, in which a male head of household left to work for the entirety of a contract term and brought money back to support his domesticated wife and children and improve the financial condition of the colony. West Indian men and women certainly took to regional migration as a strategy, but not in the way colonial authorities envisioned.

In 1901 the colonial government realized another obstacle to the emigration scheme: Barbadians rejected long-term contract labor, seeing it as akin to slavery. According to that year's colonial report: "The Barbadian native, like every negro, is averse to being bound by contracts. They carry his mind back to the condition of the people before the days of emancipation, and he sees only in contracts a form subtly devised by the white man for replacing the yoke of slavery round his neck. Emigration under contract has more than once been tried with the Barbadian, and has invariably failed."[40] The report presented this discovery as further reproach to the Barbadian working classes for failing to emigrate, castigating their lingering memory of slavery. In fact, the report inadvertently displays the priorities and motivations of the Caribbean working classes. Though unemployment and low wages remained important push factors for potential migrants, working-class Barbadians valued their own definitions of freedom as much as they did monetary compensation. In short, Barbadians rejected British colonial ventures of emigration that promised wages but denied mobility and flexibility.

West Indians might have refused the "yoke" of a contract, but they nevertheless found ways to profit off of new imperial ventures. By the time of the French construction attempt in Panama in the 1880s, Jamaican women had forged and taken advantage of informal market routes between Kingston and Colón. In 1885 the City Council of Kingston had to prohibit the "custom" of women regularly bringing loads of laundry from Colón to be washed in the city. Captain Forwood of the Atlas Steamship Company and a member of the Kingston City Council observed that "an old woman is in the habit of taking down to Colón empty boxes and portmanteaus, and then returning with them full of dirty clothes, which when opened 'emitted such a bad smell that it was almost sufficient to knock a person down.' It was a regular business and he knew that as much as fifteen tons measurement of dirty clothes had been taken to Kingston."[41] While the council worried about the smell and potential disease, their concern shows the ways Jamaican women integrated the imperial waterways between British Jamaica and "French" Panama into their own commercial and entrepreneurial circuits.

Emancipation in the Caribbean was accompanied by a remapping of the relationship between capital, empire, and labor.[42] British and French colonial authorities sought to create a disciplined wage labor force by initially limiting opportunities beyond the plantation. By the late nineteenth century, imperial ventures funded primarily by U.S. capital expanded to borderlands across the Caribbean and South and Central America and sought to control a constant stream of mobile labor for new schemes of industrial production. West Indians followed these investments in search of economic opportunity while experiencing discrimination, violence, and labor exploitation. But they also deviated from the desires of imperial authorities and sought ways to advance their own priorities. West Indian women in particular functioned as the consummate border-crossers, integrating port cities like Colón into Afro-Caribbean market networks through their mobile labor in ways unforeseen to imperial administrators as did the laundresses of Kingston who so baffled the City Council. Women subsidized these early endeavors of global capital through their labor of social reproduction, providing temporary housing, laundry services, and foodstuffs at the edges of imperial ventures. Their long-standing mobile market practices would inform their engagement with the U.S. Canal construction as imperial investment reached its peak.

"Marriage Is the Exception"

A 1902 report in Jamaica's *Daily Gleaner* quoted a working-class Jamaican woman's opinion of legal marriage: "If we love each other, what need is there of marrying? If we don't we are able to leave each other."[43] For this woman, formal marriage seemed an undesirable constraint. Unlike what the church and colonial government claimed, marriage did not seem to her a matter of morality but one of practicality. Hers was a choice echoed by many working-class Black West Indians in the period after emancipation and preceding the Canal construction. Alongside the problem of free labor, colonial authorities also sought to solve the perceived moral degradation of formerly enslaved Afro-Caribbeans by fostering improvement and uplift.[44] Instead, throughout the late nineteenth and early twentieth centuries, working-class West Indians established and respected their own practices of partnership despite the forceful critiques and legal obstacles that politicians and clergy leveled. Though steeped in Victorian norms of the nuclear family promoted by the colonial state, working-class West Indians cultivated marriage arrangements that privileged autonomy and mobility and sustained wide kinship networks under matrifocal households.[45]

White missionaries and abolitionists advocated for legally binding, mo-nogamous, heterosexual, Christian marriage during slavery and continued to encourage it for Black West Indians after emancipation as the only appropriate context for reproduction.[46] They sought to establish the nuclear family with a male head of household as a measure of formerly enslaved people's "improvement" in freedom as well as a mechanism of labor division and control. But this was not the only and certainly not the dominant type of conjugal relationship available to formerly enslaved West Indians. Many engaged in common-law marriage—consensual, residential unions—or in non-coresidential unions, known in some of the islands as "friending."[47] Both of these types of relationships traditionally carried a set of commonly accepted, though not legally binding, childcare and financial responsibilities. They frequently resulted in long and stable relationships, bound as they were by affective and financial links among neighbors and kin in close-knit villages. The household functioned as a "cooperative unit" of labor, dividing production equally among men, women, and children of age.[48] Rather than wholly separate categories, these relationship strategies existed on a shifting continuum, where conjugal partners could leave or return to each other, or legally marry after some time. Their flexibility was precisely their appeal.

The unofficial marriage practices of Black West Indians presented a source of deep anxiety for British authorities after emancipation. Colonial administrators displayed an obsessive interest in regulating sexual behavior, concubinage, and illegitimacy in the Caribbean colonies.[49] This concern exemplified the British colonial government's approach to the transition to freedom, which attempted to curtail the movements and decisions of newly freed individuals while also ostensibly incorporating them into the larger colonial civilizing project. As many historians of the period have argued, emancipation not only affected men and women differently but it also transformed gendered practices and identities throughout the diaspora, defining a "new moral order" of expected behavior for the formerly enslaved.[50] The Caribbean was no exception.

However faithful these relationships were, the church and the British colonial state nevertheless consistently characterized them as immoral and pathological. The church attempted to refashion formerly enslaved people into lawful free subjects by enforcing patriarchal marriage, even excluding

Black women from financial church benefits when they engaged in "immorality."[51] In Barbados, Rev. A. Caldecott decried the failed efforts to increase sanctioned church marriage among the Black working class, claiming that "the greatest obstacle appeared to be ingrained in the Negro character, a reluctance to rise to the level of Christian marriage."[52] For Anglican clergy like Caldecott, the explanation lay in racial determinism, an innate biological refusal to "civilize." In Trinidad, the registrar-general acknowledged the legacies of slavery on contemporary marriage practices in 1891, insisting that "the dark stain of a former state of things be wiped out," yet he nevertheless believed this depended on a drastic change in the intimate practices of the working classes until "the home life of our people become what it should be, and must be."[53] In Jamaica, commentators in the public sphere frequently criticized the low rate and unenthusiastic adoption of marriage among lower-class Black Jamaicans. The Wesleyan missionary Rev. Stephen Sutton lamented that "marriage is the exception, and living in a state of uncleanness the rule."[54] For Sutton, as for many others, concubinage implied not only illegality, but uncleanliness both physically and morally. More sympathetic observers, such as the journalist H. G. de Lisser, suggested that "the simple truth is that no disgrace attaches to members of the labouring and peasant class who do not choose to get married."[55] West Indian men and women saw cohabitation as a legitimate, sufficient, and moral relationship practice. In a situation where Black Jamaican women worked in similar numbers as men on sugar and banana estates, owned their own provision grounds, and dominated the markets, concubinage became more of a "partnership rather than domination," according to the historian Patrick Bryan.[56]

The late nineteenth century also saw a transfer in the oversight of marriage from the church to the state. In Jamaica, an 1879 law assigned a superintendent registrar to each parish, who was responsible for publishing notices of marriage and conducting civil marriage ceremonies, albeit for a substantial license fee of ten pounds.[57] Similarly, in Trinidad, the Marriage Ordinance of 1863 addressed the "solemnization and registration of marriages," requiring that marriages only be performed in licensed places of worship and had to be announced to the registrar.[58] The following decade saw a profusion of morality legislation, particularly in regard to bastardy and illegitimacy, as these intimate matters came more fully under state supervision and concern.[59]

Marriage rates in the West Indies evidenced an initial boom following abolition, showing the desirability of marriage among at least some part of the formerly enslaved population.[60] In most islands, though, these peaks were followed by a leveling off to lower rates by the turn of the twentieth century. In Martinique and Guadeloupe, marriage rates increased immediately after emancipation but settled back to lower rates of 3.4 and 3.2 per 1,000 persons respectively by 1877.[61] Similarly in Trinidad, marriage rates rose to 9.9 per 1,000 after the abolition of apprenticeship in 1838, but they slowly tapered to 5.7 by 1860.[62] Statistical recording for marriage in Jamaica began in 1879 and indicated a rate of 3.7 per 1,000, which took a considerable jump to a peak of 7.4 in 1907–1908, during the early years of the Canal construction.[63] In Barbados, the rates hovered around 5.5 to 6.0 from 1890 to 1905 but would not grow past 7.0 throughout the rest of the twentieth century until the 1990s.[64] By comparison, the marriage rate in the United Kingdom did not drop below 13.0 per 1,000 persons between 1865 and 1905, meaning that for every year of this period, the rate was at least double if not triple that of the British West Indies.[65] Thus, while some West Indians embraced marriage after abolition, the rates remained comparatively low. The continued incidence of concubinage and accompanying high rates of birth out of wedlock in the islands plagued colonial administrators.[66] They celebrated the "improvements" evidenced by the rising marriage rates during their peaks while continuing to castigate the lower classes for insufficiently incorporating metropolitan values.[67]

These rates do not fully represent the attitudes of the West Indian middle class, which adopted church and legal marriage more enthusiastically than the working classes throughout the nineteenth and early twentieth centuries. Though there is no specific data on middle-class marriage for the period, scholars have shown how premarital chastity and church marriage became symbols of class differentiation.[68] This does not imply a clear binary between a Europeanized middle class devoted to traditional church marriage and gender roles versus an Africanized lower class tied to cohabitation and matrifocality. The size and precarity of the West Indian middle class likely meant that people moved between and among these types of unions, rather than committing to one based solely on class affiliation. According to some historians, working-class Jamaicans did "go to great lengths to marry legally, albeit in middle age after they had cohabited for several years."[69] Nevertheless, the middle class's adoption of church marriage reinforced the discursive links between certain state- and church-sanctioned relationship practices, respectability, and potential class mobility.

Divorces were extremely unusual. In Jamaica, marriage had remained under ecclesiastical law until the passage of Law 11 in 1879, which followed English law in allowing divorce.[70] There were only six recorded divorces in 1897 and two in 1899, with a slight increase at the turn of the twentieth century to about fifteen a year by 1907.[71] In the Leeward Islands (including Antigua, Nevis, St. Kitts, and the Virgin Islands), laws providing for legal divorce did not pass until the mid-twentieth century, so the nonexistent rates of divorce there rather reflect the extreme difficulty of canceling a marriage contract and help explain the continued popularity of common-law arrangements.[72] This suggests very little about the rate of actual separation among West Indians, but it does show a pattern of low legal involvement with the state regarding intimate relations. Cited causes for divorce were similar to those in Panama and in many places throughout the Americas: adultery and cruelty.[73] Given the low rate of divorce, it is more likely that both married and unmarried West Indians sought alternative or extralegal methods as a way to negotiate their relations rather than the state-legitimated avenue of divorce.

These precursors established common-law marriages and "friending" arrangements as long-standing practices in the islands that survived persistent attacks from the church and colonial state. For the most part, working-class West Indians ignored attempts by postemancipation colonial authorities to make them conform to official marriage, though initial spiking marriage rates show that some found it to be a "desirable ideal."[74] Even then, West Indians followed their own norms of respectability and commitment, often cohabitating for decades and forming families before seeking legal or church recognition, and defying characterizations of their nonlegal relationships as immoral. Nevertheless, West Indians practiced these arrangements within the context of state-backed projects supporting a Victorian ideal of monogamous, heterosexual marriage and a proper gender order that firmly upheld patriarchal authority. Black West Indians did not reject legal marriage outright, but neither did they passively conform to these norms. For West Indian women, withdrawal from the plantation, mobile market practices, and a general reluctance toward legal marriage all served as household and individual strategies to navigate the limitations of postemancipation colonial political economies. Women brought these same strategies to the Canal Zone, where they faced a new imperial power eager to police nonnormative labor and intimacies.

The Call from Colón

While part of larger Caribbean economic and migratory trends, West Indian women's move to Panama was also structured by the limitations set by U.S. authorities. Like the male laborers the ICC contracted, West Indian women hoped to gain higher wages and secure economic futures for themselves and their kin. Yet they were disquieting subjects for the Canal administration—their labor sorely needed but rarely acknowledged; their presence morally dangerous unless heavily surveilled and regulated. West Indian women thus had to fund their own forms of travel, mostly migrated without official contracts, and lived outside of company housing. The ICC did not encourage or support their migration, yet it depended on their everyday labor and services. West Indian women traveled on the margins of the Commission's regulation, relying on their kinship networks for support and on their previous practices of regional migration, entrepreneurial labor, and intimacy for survival.

Despite their earlier misgivings about contract labor schemes, in signing up with the Isthmian Canal Commission, West Indians fulfilled many of the hopes of the colonial administration to engage in wage labor, accept contracts, and ease the pressures of overpopulation through emigration. Yet the venture in Panama provided some new and specific benefits for West Indian immigrants—the promise of much higher wages, the potential for nonagricultural labor, and an escape from British colonial supervision. The lure of American prosperity and plentiful wages in the Canal certainly attracted many West Indians who, according to historian Velma Newton, "conceived of the move as a means of freeing themselves—even if temporarily—from plantation labour and the stigma of slavery attached to it."[75] Silver workers hired in 1907 were offered ten cents an hour for a sixty-hour workweek, totaling six dollars a week.[76] The promised gains were so high that West Indians imagined accruing enough money to return and buy land on which to build a house of their own. While some migrants must certainly have looked at the Canal construction with a dose of skepticism (and they certainly did after receiving the first reports of deaths), they nevertheless perceived it as a new, untapped opportunity with the promise of wealth that could secure their imagined futures.

Moreover, while Panama was seen in some ways as a promising new venture, it also fit in with established patterns of labor migration that Black working-class migrants had followed after emancipation. Barbadian men and women continued to migrate to Panama primarily as short-term laborers who sought to return to the islands before completing their contracts. Some West Indians integrated Panama into long-standing patterns of back-and-forth migration, evidenced by a 1907 cartoon in a Barbadian weekly in which a Black higgler named Janie explained her temporary absence from the market to her friend:

> No darling sweet love uh has bin down pun de Canal Zone
> Fuh look aftah Petah welfare as well as me own
> An uh now tek a bus back up fuh look fuh Aunt Jane
> Fuh bring sum money fuh she an uh den gwine back agen.[77]

As she explains, Janie had gone to Panama to look after her and her partner's welfare but also to save money to bring back to her aunt. She returned after her short stay "pun de Canal Zone" and planned to continue making round trips between Panama and Barbados to sustain her family. The newspaper's choice to depict a higgler as the main agent of this practice speaks to the common knowledge about West Indian women's migration to Panama and their financial practices rooted in social networks.

For historian Mary Chamberlain, the migratory response to the Canal construction represented "the centrality of migration within the ethos or culture of the island" rather than an absolute break from previous anti-emigration sentiment.[78] Not all men traveled under the yoke of a contract and, in fact, many followed well-trod migratory routes across the Caribbean.[79] Given their widely stated enthusiasm for emigration, it is not surprising that the colonial government in Barbados initially approved of the Canal venture, citing as early as 1905 the material prosperity it had brought to the laboring classes of the island.[80] They noted that, in the first year alone, 2,130 emigrants had left the island under contract and that these men sent remittances to their families.[81]

While almost half of all Barbadians who traveled to Panama did so with contracts, this was not the case for other islands that did not serve as official recruiting stations, such as Jamaica or Trinidad. It was similarly not the case for the overwhelming majority of West Indian women, who had not been recruited and received no prior offer of employment. Like West Indian men, they were driven in part by a financial imperative, but this came without the job security—or the yoke—of a contract. Nevertheless, as with previous regional migratory ventures, women saw the opportunity for jobs in domestic service, laundry, sex work, and food provisions. Martinican Margaret Pole succinctly explained it: "I can't make as much money in Martinique as I can here [in Panama], and I like it."[82]

Women likely learned of opportunities in Panama through rumor and by word of mouth, which circulated the image of Panama as a land of economic prosperity. Everyone knew of somebody who had left the islands in search of work on the Canal. Kinship and friendship networks served an essential role in transmitting information about the project and encouraging others to move. Some women migrated with sisters or friends, or knew someone who already lived in Panama. Though mostly geared toward men, advertisements in local newspapers placed by ICC agents also disseminated news about job opportunities in Panama to a wide audience, promising decent food, medical attention, free passage, and high salaries. Popular culture responded quickly to the Panama phenomenon, and songs about Canal migration and labor circulated around the islands, similarly giving weight to the myths and ambitions of West Indian migrants:

> Before me work fe bit a day
> Before me work fe bit a day
> Before me work fe bit a day Me

> wid come out a Merican cut
> Dem a bawl, oh, come out a Merican cut
> Come out a Merican cut, come out a Merican
> cut[83]

These songs bolstered the morale of men traveling to the Canal, who expressed their masculine pride and financial expectations, hoping to make their fortune on the "Merican cut."[84] Songs also passed on folk knowledge and myths about Panama throughout the islands. While they almost exclusively positioned Black men as their subjects, these songs also informed the migration of West Indian women who heard and shared them, perhaps also filled with a mix of pride, expectation, and apprehension.

West Indian men and women were drawn to the Canal project by the financial promise, a sense of adventure, an escape from colonial restraints, and the potential to work outside of the plantation. However, these motivations did not have the same meaning for men and women. Men's migration to Panama provided West Indian men the opportunity to perform a version of cosmopolitan masculinity enshrined in the symbol of the "Colón Man." This move could provide as much cultural capital as it did financial wealth. In their mythographies about the construction period, as literary critic Rhonda Frederick has shown, West Indian men cast themselves as affluent, "exemplary models of manhood" and "willing participants in modern capitalist projects."[85]

Some mythographies of West Indian women also cast them as aspirational for wealth and class mobility. Lisser's character Susan Proudleigh moved to Colón seeking to realize her ambitions for marriage and wealth after her family's loss of fortune.[86] Yet Susan is beholden to men's wealth and expectations throughout the entire narrative, first as financial support in Jamaica from her beau Tom Wooley, then as motivation to migrate from Mr. Samuel Josiah Jones, and finally, as the enigmatic source of her long-awaited riches, Mr. Mackenzie. Lisser's novel exposes the limitations on women's mobility and the reach of patriarchal power that conditioned the story of a woman trying to determine her own destiny.[87] The narratives of wealth and individual liberation that surrounded the "Colón Man" came with distinct restraints for West Indian women.

Throughout the decade of construction, colonial administrators heard grievances from West Indian migrants in Panama and occasionally admitted that these workers faced "harsh treatment by American overseers, who do not regard the black man as their brother."[88] Yet they continued to blame Black working-class migrants (rather than discrimination in the Zone) for any failure in raising the islands' prosperity, observing that "temptations exist outside the Zone to which large numbers [of Black men] succumb, with the result that they lose their health and fail to benefit pecuniarily by their sojourn in the Zone."[89] The colonial government, though ostensibly concerned with the well-being of the island's working-class residents, primarily cared about the financial health of the colony. They blamed working-class Barbadians for failing to fulfill authorities' expectations and instead pursuing their own agendas. The demands of colonial authorities and the promises of U.S. capital compelled West Indian men and women to migrate to the Canal Zone, but these migrants traveled in search of their own visions of freedom. West Indian women, in particular, migrated despite lacking contracts or other forms of colonial state support. Their migration followed the pull of American investment, but it challenged the organizing logic of colonial authorities who only imagined men as the subjects of migratory schemes and as the creators of wealth and prosperity for the islands.

Mail ships such as ones from the Royal Mail Steam Packet Company doubled as the means of transportation from the islands to the port of Colón and other Central American cities. Willis Abbot, in his 1913 account of his trip to the Canal, recounts his travel by Royal Mail Steamer accompanied by a "cargo of black ivory," by which he meant men sailing to Colón to work on Canal construction.[90] West Indians traveled topside, away from the passenger quarters that men like Abbott occupied. The trip lasted from five to thirteen days, during which the Black passengers were exposed to the weather and enjoyed few comforts, apart from modest meals.[91] These ships also brought West Indian women to the Canal, such as Mrs. Mary Couloote, who spoke of her travels from St. Lucia:

I come to the Isthmus of Panama 1903 I was a young girl I came with my sister on a ship by the name of la plata it live (leave) castries to jamaica then the ship left jamaica at 4pm o'clock the ship was going to the gulf of Mexico it started to roll it had a storm heavy brize water came into the ship I was to go down stairs to second class and stay their the sailor had chain around they waist and a pail emptying out the water when we reach colon they call every body name 5 men were missing from jamaica. . . . I and my sister whent to Pedro Miguel at my mother to live their a cuple years. I feel was to work, has to help my mother, for my brother was getting a small sallary at that time he was working at the Culebra cut.[92]

Mrs. Mary Couloote was not contracted, but she followed well-established paths of migration set by Black men and women before her. During the French canal construction, in 1885, the company had sent recruiting agent Charles Gadpaille to St. Lucia where he employed scouts to find good workers for the project.[93] Without a direct route to Panama, contracted laborers from St. Lucia traveled to Kingston by Royal Mail Steamship and then continued on to Colón in whatever boat they could find. In Kingston, they would have seen the crowds on the wharf next to the jail awaiting a ship or saying goodbye to their relatives. In 1903 Mary Couloote followed this same route, from Castries to Kingston to Colón.

Mary's trip became a harrowing sea voyage. A storm overtook the ship and five Jamaican men died as sailors frantically filled buckets with water and threw it overboard. Like Emily Amelia, Mary's entry into Panama was marked by death. Yet Mary persevered and eventually got a job as a laundress for two American bachelors. As Mary explained it, she migrated to the Canal to work in order to help her family, many of whom had also moved to Panama. Her brother worked for the Commission on the deadliest site of the construction, the Culebra Cut, where twice-daily dynamite blasts tore apart the rock and created landslides. Dangerous as it was, his salary was not nearly enough to support the family, and Mary felt an obligation to contribute. Her brother—the prototypical pick-and-shovel man—was not the sole wage earner of the family. Instead, Mary and her siblings traveled to Panama as part of a chain of family migration and all contributed to the household earnings.

Black women like Mary Couloote and Emily Amelia came to Panama from Jamaica, Barbados, Martinique, St. Lucia, Trinidad, and other Caribbean islands. The total number of West Indian women who traveled to Panama is hard to ascertain. The 1912 U.S. Census of the Canal lists that, out of 71,682 residents: 15,064 were white men, 29,650 were Black men, 4,459 where white women, and 8,775 were Black women.[94] This means that the population of the Canal Zone was 53 percent West Indian. The census only counts the men and women who lived inside the Canal Zone or worked for the ICC while living in Panamanian territory. The census thus highly underestimates the number of Black women who transited through the Zone. Nevertheless, it counts twice as many Black women as there were white women. The historian Michael Conniff calculates that there were around 20,000 West Indians on the Commission payroll in any given year, but "contemporaries estimated that only about a third of the West Indian community worked for the Canal at any moment." This suggests that the West Indian population in Panama and the Canal Zone combined could have neared 60,000, with women making up about a quarter of these numbers going by the Canal Zone proportions (putting the number closer to an estimated 15,000).[95]

The Canal Zone census shows a distinct predominance of Black male residents. The Barbadian immigrant population was 82 percent male, while the Jamaican population was 67 percent male. However, the 1917–1923 Zone death rates and the later Panamanian national census of 1920 show substantially more balanced sex ratios among West Indian immigrants.[96] By 1920, 9,425 British West Indian men and 8,278 British West Indian women resided in Panama City, making the population only 53 percent male.[97] Given that women rarely held Commission-sponsored labor contracts and were less likely to live in the Canal Zone, their population numbers in Panama were probably much higher than the Canal Zone census indicates.

What accounts for the difference between the male majority in the Zone census of 1912 and the balanced sex ratios of the Panama census only eight years later? The data disparity again emphasizes the skewed image of West Indian women that arises from looking only at U.S.-based sources and revises assumptions of such heavy male predominance in this era of migration. When viewing the period as a whole, it is clear that while men prevailed demographically, women migrated in much higher overall numbers than previously understood; they just did so through alternative routes and timelines less beholden to the needs of imperial projects. West Indian men traveling with contracts went directly to the Canal Zone, but many women bypassed the Zone altogether, landing in Colón and settling in Panamanian territory. Most men traveled in the first four years of construction, when American recruitment efforts were at their highest. Women, on the other hand, traveled in smaller but regular trickles after the first few years as their travel was not contingent on the offer of contract labor. Though the 1920 Panama census can only tell us about those West Indians who stayed after construction (rather than those who merely passed through or the total number of migrants), the balanced sex ratios nevertheless confirm the incompleteness of the Zone numbers. West Indian women were not a mere addendum to their male counterparts in Panama migration, even demographically. Their invisibility in the Canal Zone numbers is evidence not of their complete physical absence, but of their circumvention of imperial oversight.

Some women traveled in the wake of their husband's departures, hoping to be reunited in Panama. Often, if a West Indian husband was already working on the Canal, he would send remittances to his family back home. Nevertheless, these men's wages were usually insufficient to maintain one or more families on the island. Some women, like Martinican Julia Waugram, said they traveled to Panama "to help out" their husbands' income by doing small jobs on the side, such as laundering clothes.[98] Others, such as Naomy Etiene, whose husband labored on the Canal, contributed equally to the family income with her washing and ironing; the whole family worked to save money for their life together.[99]

Single women or women with absentee husbands would often travel to the Canal in groups with other women, usually neighbors or friends. Jane Ortancia, for example, migrated to the Canal Zone with her friend Jillui Richa. Upon their arrival, Jane moved in with Jillui and Jillui's husband, Theodiele, in a house the three of them shared.[100] Sisters and friends, such as Melanie Primeaux and Alcina Alcide, accompanied each other to the Canal and lived together.[101] Often they were young women, possibly seeking to live independently of their families' pressure for them to marry or settle down. Their movement occurred within tight-knit female networks that provided protection during crossing and support upon their arrival. Other women traveled with their children, such as Alfred Mitchell's mother who brought him along to the Canal Zone at age fourteen in 1904, the first year of construction. She worked to support them both and eventually found him a job as a water boy for the drilling gang in Bas-Obispo.[102]

Gold and Silver Housing

West Indian women had to pay their own way, acquire their own housing upon their arrival, and find employment without institutional support. White women's migration, on the other hand, was discursively and materially supported by the American authorities. After the Commission completed major sanitary works against the spread of malaria and yellow fever in 1906, it began to encourage white American women to migrate to the Zone. This was, in part, a measure to motivate and support skilled white American workers. As one of these early white American migrants, Rose Van Hardeveld, said, "The opinion had been expressed by our government that the wives and children were as necessary to the success of the job as the men were."[103] Many of the first white women who arrived were the wives of notable men such as Chief Sanitary Officer William C. Gorgas. The great majority of white women indeed came as wives to support their working husbands, to make the Canal Zone feel like home. Both the commission and white women themselves saw their domestication of the Zone as a crucial step in bringing civilization to Panama's jungle.[104] During his famous 1906 visit to the Panama Canal, Theodore Roosevelt commended white women's labor, saying "It is rough on the men and just a little rougher on the women. It has pleased me, particularly, to see, as I have, the wives who have come down here with their husbands, the way in which they have turned in to make the best of everything and to help the men do their work well."[105]

The Canal administration supported white women's migration more than symbolically. Commission authorities paid for white women's passage to the Zone. They provided free married housing and furniture in spacious, suburban homes. Quarters for married Gold workers were built on concrete bases with elevated wooden frames, screened from mosquitoes, and surrounded by manicured tropical landscapes and trimmed grass. The ICC built a female ward in ICC hospitals.[106] They fostered recreational activities, employing

Helen Varick Boswell of New York to build a network of women's clubs throughout the Canal Zone.[107] They expanded the offerings of Zone commissaries, encouraging women's consumption by offering linens, hats, fabrics, and other luxury goods alongside food, to the point that a journalist remarked, "It would take another article to relate the rhapsodies of the Zone women over the prices at which they can buy Boulton tableware, Irish linen, Swiss and Scandinavian delicatessen, and French products of all sorts."[108] With each of these incentives, the administration reinforced their commitment to white women's colonization of the Canal Zone. None of these services were made available to Black women.

In contrast, the ICC initially housed single male Black migrants in boxcars or old French barracks. Even after 1905, when the Isthmian Canal Commission began to build newer barracks, Silver Roll bachelors nevertheless received substandard housing that was subject to the whims and surveillance of the administration. For example, in 1908 the ICC forced Silver workers to eat at ICC mess halls by having them present a meal ticket in order to gain daily entry to their accommodations.[109] Workers without lodging checks were disallowed from the barracks and charged with loitering. Workers were also forced to shop exclusively at the commissary, using the internal currency system of a "commissary book" to buy anything from food to clothing. Silver workers, then, faced severe restrictions in their housing and living arrangements within ICC jurisdiction. By 1909 occupancy in ICC barracks had dropped by 40 percent as workers moved outside of the Canal Zone altogether.[110]

Married housing presented even bigger challenges for West Indians. Quarters were not guaranteed for West Indian couples, who often could not prove their marriages legally. By 1907 the ICC stopped building married Silver quarters creating fierce competition for the few remaining buildings.[111] The *Canal Record* of 1909 reported that there were only 3,056 "Negro" occupants of married quarters that year, including women and children.[112] Married Silver quarters were often crowded spaces. In the early years of construction, ten families could share a two-story building, such as in Folks River where a family could be housed in a room as small as 13 by 8 feet.[113] Bathroom facilities were built separately from Silver Quarters and were meant to be shared by as many as twenty-five families. The bath, some residents of La Boca complained, "does not seem to be a fit and proper one . . . especially for the opposite sex."[114] Official ICC photographs show houses built on stilts, to protect inhabitants from rats, insects, and other pests; prevent flooding from heavy rains; and provide natural air circulation.[115] The quartermaster's department declined to add screens to Silver married housing or schools, despite pressures from the sanitation department to prevent the spread of mosquito-borne disease.

The policy of housing ten families together changed after much protest from Silver workers who sought additional space, but these changes (along with general repairs to the quarters) only occurred near the end of construction.[116] Throughout construction, Canal authorities disavowed the effects of restrictions in access to food and recreational facilities for Silver workers and their families, commenting, for example, that "married Blacks live better than any other class" because "as a rule the women are good cooks and their food both in quality and quantity is much better than that they had at home as that of the married Whites is poorer."[117] By suggesting that Black workers had a better quality of life outside of ICC housing, administrators denied both their role in perpetuating racial exclusion and their obligation to provide for Canal workers. They passed off this responsibility to West Indian women who, unofficially but well-known to the Canal authorities, literally subsidized the labor force by feeding and housing them.

Indeed, most West Indians employed by the ICC did not live in its official quarters—23,411 out of 29,095 lived in privately owned housing in "native" towns on the Zone or in the cities of Panama (note that this figure does not account for the many uncontracted workers who also shared these spaces).[118] Beside the manicured areas of ICC-built infrastructure within the Canal Zone lay older local towns that predated the arrival of the United States. These towns would be eradicated with the ICC's depopulation order of 1912, but during the construction period, they provided the bulk of the housing for Silver workers. These areas remained under the legal control of the ICC. Owners had to pay rent or taxes on the properties, while the Sanitation Department regulated all construction efforts, such as the distance between newly built structures. However, given the population boom and subsequent housing pressure created by labor migration, the ICC had great difficulty in actually regulating residents of non-ICC property in the borderlands of the Canal Zone.

The streets of these parts of town were generally unpaved. Since there were no dedicated public spaces or recreational facilities outside the ICC-built areas, and houses were cramped, people lived outside, on the porches and in the streets of their neighborhoods, where they would talk, do chores, or pass the time. The houses were often built above swamps, so residents had to put down planks of wood to be able to walk across the area.[119] Domestic affairs did not take place inside the privacy of a home. The houses were too close to each other and often crowded with large families. Instead, child-rearing, laundry, and other domestic tasks took place outside, in porches and patios. The residents tried to liven up their rooms, crowding their belongings into the tight spaces and decorating with curtains, posters, and furniture. Harry Franck, a white American policeman, described a West Indian home disparagingly:

> They lived chiefly in windowless, six-by-eight rooms, always a cheap, dirty calico curtain dividing the three-foot parlor in front from the five-foot bedroom behind, the former cluttered with a van-load of useless junk, dirty blankets, decrepit furniture, glittering gewgaws, a black baby squirming naked in a basket of rags with an Episcopal prayerbook under its pillow. . . . Every inch of the walls was "decorated," after the artistic temperament of the race, with pages of illustrated magazines or newspapers, half-tones of all things conceivable with no small amount of text in sundry languages, many a page purely of advertising matter, the muscular, imbruted likeness of a certain black champion rarely missing, frequently with a Bible laid reverently beneath it. Outside, before each room, a tin fireplace for cooking precariously bestrided the veranda rail.[120]

Though Franck's distaste for the family's home is apparent, it is also clear that West Indians took care to make these cramped spaces their homes by enlivening them with furniture and decorations. Their homes show evidence of West Indian social activities such as going to church and watching boxing matches (the "certain black champion" likely to be the African American boxer Jack Johnson, who had won the world heavyweight title in 1908). The kitchen sat on the veranda to prevent fires from destroying these precariously built wooden homes. There, West Indian women would have cooked for their families and overheard the goings-on in the patios and streets of their neighborhoods.

Places like Rainbow City and Jamaica Town housed a multiracial group of workers in tenements, boardinghouses, and shacks, and catered to some of their needs with local businesses like Chinese convenience shops. These tenements were often owned by elite Panamanians—Ricardo Arias owned seven buildings in Gatún with a total of 109 rooms.[121] Some, however, were owned by West Indian women. Augusta Dunlop from St. Thomas, for example, owned a boardinghouse on land leased from the ICC in the town of Pedro Miguel that held at least four families. Despite the important service they rendered, women like Augusta faced consistent surveillance from the ICC. In July 1908, for example, Augusta was arrested after a visit from Sanitary Inspectors Brady and Espey, who saw two barrels of water in Augusta's house, one of which had yellow fever mosquito (*Stegomyia*) larvae. She was arrested, convicted, and fined ten dollars. After her arrest, Augusta wrote letters directly to Chief Sanitary Inspector Joseph Augustin Le Prince, claiming that Brady and Espey had a "spite" for her. She begged for pity as a widow with child. Her letters to Chief Inspector Le Prince were initially obsequious, telling him "I know with one word from you every thing is fix [*sic*], the great god will bless you and family."[122] Investigators blamed her for a number of violations, alleging that she had not secured the necessary permits to build her house from the Division of Municipal Engineering, that the house did not have enough closets, and that she had regularly failed to follow sanitary regulations. The assistant chief sanitary inspector, Herbert Canfield, characterized her as "an old and persistent violator of Sanitary Ordinances" and invalidated her, saying "Her police record is such as to cast extreme doubt upon her credibility."[123] Moreover, he claimed that "the grounds about her house are filthy" and that she was deservedly arrested, criticizing her personal and domestic hygiene to emphasize his point.

As the ICC began to mount a case against her, her letters to Le Prince grew more furious and she blamed Espey for drinking and keeping a woman at his office as well as intimating that Espey and Brady had shady real estate dealings in New Gatun.[124] She was overheard by several people saying "she would put [Brady and Espey] out of Gatun at any cost & stated she was not without white friends who was in good standing and would help her if she kneeded [sic] it."[125] The case became so notorious that Chief Engineer Goethals sent his personal investigator, T. B. Miskimon, to sort out the details and report back. Miskimon noted in his report that "this woman is a very suave talker, and carries a certain amount of conviction with her statements," though he also found evidence that Espey and Brady were in fact involved in less-than-legal real estate concerns.[126] Throughout all these interactions, Augusta used her contacts, "suave" manner, and knowledge of the neighborhood and the ICC to denounce what she perceived as an injustice committed by the sanitary inspectors.

The case ended with Augusta's arrest, a fine, and a personal letter from Chief Engineer Goethals, telling her that "the whole trouble has been caused by failure on your part to comply with the building and sanitary regulations."[127] Augusta paid her fine and moved away to Panama City. Augusta Dunlop is only one among the several West Indian women who owned boardinghouses in the Canal Zone and sustained the work of the ICC by sheltering West Indian migrants who could not, or would not, live in bachelor barracks. That the chief engineer had written her a personal letter showed a deep anxiety about the troubles this woman claimed—that West Indian residents of the Canal Zone consistently skirted the ICC's authority, and that a West Indian woman had enough power, resources, and support to present a valid claim against the Sanitary Department, one of the most powerful divisions of the ICC. Her house was later torn down following the depopulation order of 1912 for which she filed, and lost, a property claim.

The lack and low quality of Silver housing, along with the discriminatory segregationist policies that governed the Canal Zone, discouraged West Indians from residing there and effectively disallowed most West Indian women from official ICC housing. West Indians mostly opted out of this housing system by living in "native" towns within the Canal Zone or on Panamanian territory. In these towns, they lived in tenements or boardinghouses, some of which were owned by West Indian women. Women like Augusta Dunlop made the Canal construction possible by providing an important service of shelter, companionship, meals, and community to underserved Black workers whose needs the ICC could not fulfill. Even as she did so, however, she faced pushback from U.S. authorities, who characterized her as a troublesome and unsanitary person. Nevertheless, as her encounters with the police and Sanitary Department show, Augusta repeatedly challenged the dictates of ICC authority in order to maintain ownership of her property and run it in the way she wished.

* * *

In migrating to Panama, West Indian women acted against the wishes and limitations set by British authorities, who did not perceive them as productive labor migrants, and American officials, who almost exclusively contracted male laborers. Women traveled without the assurance of wages that a contract provided but also without the yoke of its constraint. Through kinship networks, gossip, and news from returnees, they learned of the high wages and high demand for their labor. The rapid increase in the male laboring population and the migration of white American women created a demand for female companionship and domestic work. As Silver worker Alfred Dottin griped, "I had to learn how to cook by force and wash my clothes because of the scarcity of women" in the earliest years of construction.[128] Black women who could clean, wash, cook, and nurture children could hope to double their salaries by migrating to Panama, making opportunity for themselves even as they were forced to carve out their own marginal spaces and contend with the Canal Commission's criminalization of their livelihoods and intimate practices.

Deteriorating conditions in the West Indies at the turn of the century, stemming from the depressed sugar industry and the resulting abandonment of plantations, inclined West Indians who saw their rural lives worsening to follow the ambiguous promise provided by U.S. capital investment in Panama. Though the depressed economic conditions of their islands under colonial government and the lure of economic prosperity in the Canal Zone pushed West Indian women to pursue emigration, it was as much their own traditions of household regional migration, mobile labor practices, kinship networks, and a desire for freedom that propelled their movement to Panama.

U.S. administrators did not entreat West Indian women to build the path
between the oceans, but these women nevertheless saw Panama as a land of
promise, informed by their own long-standing strategies of survival. The
clash between their traditions and the expectations of the Canal authorities
would soon become apparent. In the earliest years of construction, the arrival of almost three hundred Martinican women suspected of prostitution
to the Canal Zone led to a transnational scandal over the perceived moral
degradation these women would bring. In the face of violent backlash,
these women continued to express the desires they had clung to throughout
the nineteenth century, for the freedom to migrate, to work independently,
and to marry whomever and whenever they wished.

CHAPTER 2

"A Scandal on the Isthmus"

Clemence Gerald was born in 1879 in Martinique, a French colony still reeling from the aftermath of emancipation. Nine years earlier, Black men and women had led the Insurgency of the South, burning plantations and crying for revolt in protest against French colonial rule and the prolongation of forced labor.[1] While the establishment of the Third Republic of 1871 ostensibly led to full citizenship and representation for French colonial subjects, the Black working-class population of Martinique remained tied to plantations and plagued by poverty, compounded by a series of natural disasters that devastated the island, including hurricanes in 1891 and 1903, and the Mount Pelée eruption of 1902.[2] In this context, more than five thousand Martinicans left for the Panama Canal, drawn by the promise of work and financial gain. Clemence was one of those people. At the age of twenty-six, she heard from a recruiter, Mr. Lavenel, that there was "plenty of work" to be had in the Canal Zone. Clemence traveled to Panama in 1905, where she got a job as a domestic servant for the family of Mr. Davis, a white American Canal employee. She lived with her husband at Bas Obispo.

Two months after Clemence's arrival, J. M. Keedy, prosecuting attorney of the Canal Zone, knocked at her door. He had come to investigate the charge that Clemence, like the other three hundred or so Martinican women who had arrived on her ship, had come to the Canal Zone as a prostitute. Faced with this interrogation, she "became greatly excited, shed tears, and [was] palpably alarmed, fearing that [she was] to be returned to Martinique."[3] Keedy questioned her about her migration, her current job, her marital status, her morality. He did so in English, while Clemence might have only spoken French. Clemence had to swear an affidavit defending her honor in front of

Keedy and a municipal judge. Clemence could show that she was under the supervision of her husband and her American employer, which might have left the Canal authorities marginally more certain of her morals. Other Martinican women were not so lucky. If they were single, the ICC imprisoned them in a camp under police surveillance while they conducted the investigation. The women claimed they did "not lead an immoral life" and upheld their informal employment and common-law marriages as natural. Their affidavits voiced both a defense against the violent tactics of the interrogation and an assertion of their own visions of morality. Though Clemence was not herself detained, she saw her shipmates suffer under the Canal authorities and faced the coercion of growing U.S. power. Despite the hostility she faced in her early months in the Canal Zone, Clemence remained in Panama until her death in 1943 at Gorgas Hospital. She was buried in the segregated Silver section of Corozal cemetery, on the outskirts of Panama City.[4]

The year Clemence arrived, 1905, was a tumultuous time for the Canal Zone. The second year of the project had so far seen no construction on the Canal itself. The venture had become associated in the public eye with disease and delay. Hundreds of migrants hoping to benefit from the construction began to arrive in a region that lacked established services and infrastructure. At the end of the year, a scandal rocked the Canal administration—an article alleged that the U.S. government had paid for around three hundred Martinican women to travel to Panama as prostitutes. The report stoked criticism of the project stateside, fueled by media attention and frantic responses from Secretary of War Taft and other Canal managers. Congress called for a thorough investigation into the matter. The Canal administration responded by confining all the single Martinican women in a camp under police surveillance and submitting a lengthy report that included affidavits from the accused women, forced to defend themselves against the charge of immorality.

The report, produced in the earliest years of construction, encapsulates the confrontation between Black West Indian women's practices of labor, migration, and intimacy, and the racial gendered logics of the Canal administration, which mirrored in many ways the clashes West Indian women had had with postemancipation colonial states throughout the islands in decades prior. As with the critiques from British administrators, clergy, and journal-ists, the Canal administration's report is first and foremost evidence of how the U.S. imperial state categorized migrant West Indian women.[5] Suspicious of their entrepreneurial strategies and intimate practices of cohabitation without legal marriage, American Canal administrators evaluated newly arrived West Indian women on a spectrum of morality based on their marital status, level of patriarchal supervision, and forms of labor. The report, one of the few sources produced by the Canal administration to feature West Indian women's voices, configures women's "archival visibility" within a criminalizing and degrading logic that understood women as already potentially immoral.[6] It forced the women to account for themselves as either proper "laboring women" or "prostitutes," their responses structured by questions that sought to exonerate administrators from charges of corruption and establish a dominant vision of morality for governing the Canal Zone.

Canal investigators compelled these affidavits from women living under police supervision. They translated them from French and edited down the women's responses, highlighting only the material they saw as relevant to the investigation. But while shaped by the binaries set out by American administrators during the investigation (single or married, laboring woman or prostitute), the women's testimonies exceeded these limiting moral categories. In their affidavits, the Martinican women resoundingly rejected characterizations of their love and labor as deviant. They spoke about their motivations to travel for economic opportunity, their entrepreneurial work as laundresses or doing domestic odd jobs, and their relationships with men whom they declared were their husbands, even when they had not been legally married. Some even used the affidavits to outright criticize their treatment at the hands of Canal administrators. As the commission tried to discursively and physically contain these women, they instead affirmed their own visions of freedom—freedom to seek out work when and where they wanted, freedom to travel alone, freedom to express their commitment to a loved one without official approval.

These layered meanings, impossible to extricate from one another, condition each of the women's affidavits. Their expressions were distorted through the mirrors of the administration's taxonomies but not extinguished. To assume that these moral categories completely defined the women's utterances is also to commit an act of archival silencing. The women held to and expressed the patterns of labor and intimacy they had practiced throughout the decades after emancipation, seeking economic opportunity in entrepreneurial labor, depending on kinship networks, and maintaining flexible relationships that they defined as marriage. Though the report renders judgment on the women, it is evidence of a clash between two intersecting but separate understandings of morality and the ways each side translated this new encounter. As much as the investigation reveals about the anxieties of a newly established imperial administration in the Canal Zone, it also contains a parallel narrative of West Indian women maneuvering their precarious position in relation to an uncertain power.

The scandal animated debates about government profligacy, labor retention, sanitary regulations, and the moral role of the Canal administration. The Martinican women sat at the center of all these debates. Their arrival and the suggestion that they had come for reasons beyond the scope of productive labor created a crisis for the Canal administration about how to manage the Zone. The investigation and the women's internment were not so much the violent impositions of a fully assured imperial power as evidence of disquiet about the limits of U.S. hegemony in the Zone, particularly at the beginning of construction.[7] In congressional interrogations, policemen, quartermasters, middle managers, recruiters, and upper-level administrators worried about the gaps in their authority. They were asked to account for their labor practices and explain their role in fashioning a moral universe in the Zone. This media scandal provided a symbolic terrain on which to debate Canal administrators' role as moral arbiters of a new imperial territory.[8] Through their response to the scandal, Canal administrators configured a dominant morality that cast suspicion on West Indian women's labor as always potentially deviant, even as they relied on women's roles as companions, domestics, laundresses, and cooks. The administration would eventually reorganize its leadership and expand its power to further police "vice" and morality, with a focus on West Indian intimate practices.

Though it was the first and one of the last times the ICC actively recruited women from the West Indies for work on the Canal, the scandal revealed the project's reliance on West Indian women's domestic and intimate labor. Administrators spoke about the "crying need of them" as laundresses and household servants but also as wives and counterparts to Black male laborers.[9] Recruiters promised women good wages in Canal Zone hotels and homes, but among themselves they discussed the scheme primarily as a strategy for labor retention and hoped "we could get a better class of blacks if they could bring their wives."[10] Officials would later disavow this aspect of the scandal, but it was a central motivating factor for the venture and shows their initial understanding of the need for women's labor of social reproduction.

The investigation serves as a lens through which to understand the larger material and discursive context in which Black West Indian women entered the Zone—the hierarchies of power that structured the lives that unfold throughout the rest of the book. West Indian women's entry into the U.S. Canal Zone was marked by a scandal that judged their intimacies and labor with suspicion while also acknowledging the importance of their domestic and care work. In their affidavits, West Indian women expressed desires that echoed the practices they had developed in the immediate wake of emancipation—the desire to migrate and to gain financial wealth. Their arrival and domestic labor in Panama met with the administration's deficiencies in providing for the predominantly West Indian labor force. But their migration also circumvented the priorities of the Canal Commission, which sought to forcibly legalize their marriages and place women as domestics in American households under the watchful eyes of employers. Instead, these women presented the fluidity of their labor and intimacy as their strengths, reiterating that having multiple, independent jobs and living in common-law marriages were precisely their tried-and-true strategies for survival.

The Beginning of a Scandal

On October 26, 1905, the steamship *Floridian* arrived at the port of Colón carrying nearly three hundred Martinican women.[11] A month later, the *New York Herald* reported instead that the Canal administration had recruited and paid for "several hundred" Martinican prostitutes. The news reverberated throughout the United States and Panama, creating a scandal for the Canal administration, which was accused of mismanaging the Canal and facilitating vice. During the first two years of U.S. presence in Panama, the American public widely perceived the project as weak, mismanaged, and impossible to achieve.[12] Its initial phase required the Americans to amass a huge workforce, contain disease, repair the railroad, build facilities, and transport necessary equipment. Engineers had not even settled on whether to build a sea-level or a lock-style canal. During these early, unstable years, administrators were preoccupied with two main concerns: the technical aspects of construction and the management of Canal workers, both with an eye to fast completion of the project. Instead, they faced a host of issues that had to be addressed before construction could even begin—the spread of disease, the uneven supply of laborers, and the social conflicts raised by the large influx of immigrants to the Canal Zone. The investigation activated each of these concerns, forcing the Canal administration to account for their social management, sanitary regulations, and standards of morality.

A month after the women's arrival in Colón, Canal Zone governor Charles Magoon wrote to Secretary of War Taft about a rumor that Black women "had been brought here and distributed among men by our officials for immoral purposes" and "are now living with the men as concubines."[13] "I sincerely hope and believe that the rumor is not true," said Magoon, but he worried about an article that was soon to be published in the *New York Herald* denouncing the U.S. government for bringing prostitutes to the Canal.[14] Initially, Magoon, Chief Engineer Stevens, and Canal Commission chairman Theodore Shonts denied the administration's involvement but pragmatically stated the need for women to avoid the risk of further labor desertion among Silver Roll workers. Magoon noted that the practice was common in other ventures: "It is no doubt true that private contractors find it advisable, if not necessary, to supply their common laborers with women, and quite possible, if the practice is not permitted in the Zone, that it may affect the question of labor supply from the West Indies."[15] Despite its necessity, Magoon worried about the image this might give of the Canal administration. Though there was "no reasonable objection" to women traveling for employment as servants or laundresses, the migration of women for "immoral purposes" would "shock the public mind and be so repugnant to our citizens that it would seriously embarrass not only the agency but also the administration responsible for the acts of that agency."[16]

In late November, the *New York Herald* published the first national article addressing the issue, titled "A Scandal on the Isthmus of Panama." It cited several sources who questioned the morality of the Canal project, such as Rev. Thomas Wood of the American Protestant Chapel, who asked: "Are we to have a sewer of moral degradation because we want a Canal?"[17] An anonymous American man involved in the Canal construction worried about the condition of his family, saying that "the night they [the women] came it was awful, and since then I feel like I am living in Darkest Africa," and that he would send his family back to the United States if the women were to stay.[18] Both men made connections between the newly arrived Black women and the possibility that Canal society could slip into a state of moral degradation perceived as dark or African. During a second trip to Panama, Rev. Kilpin Fletcher of the Presbyterian Church told the journalist Poultney Bigelow of his surprise "that our government should have enlisted servants who spoke ONLY FRENCH seeing that the families on the Zone could themselves speak ONLY ENGLISH! Maybe Mr. Taft will issue another pamphlet and explain this polyglot family arrangement."[19] Fletcher sarcastically implied that the Martinican women could not possibly have come to work as domestic servants because they did not speak English; they had come instead to bring disorder to American families. Though on the surface the invocation of the French language seems merely a linguistic difference, any American administrator would have understood it to evoke the failure of the French construction attempt and thus a disruption of the Anglo-American project.

Wood's response in particular linked morality to hygiene and public health by using the word *sewer*. This association with contagious disease made these women, in the eyes of American observers like Wood, a potential cause for a repeat of the French disaster. Their sexualization, read as a French trait, made them potential carriers of viral and venereal diseases. These "French" women, then, were living symbols of the potential failure of the American imperial endeavor. Moreover, they represented a particular kind of Frenchness as colonial subjects who simultaneously embodied the French administration and the decadence of European empires. Having just managed to control what had until then been the deadly spread of disease in the Zone, the possibility of a return to this "disorder" was likely present in Zonians' minds.

This concern with disease was not limited to Black women. The reaction to their arrival has to be put in the context of an earlier incident involving another boat carrying Martinican migrants. In late September 1905, a month before the *Floridian* disembarked in Colón, the steamer *Versailles* arrived from Martinique with around 650 contracted West Indian men. Under recently approved Canal regulations, foreign workers arriving in the Zone had to be vaccinated against smallpox before landing. Though most disembarked, after hearing about the horrible working conditions in Panama from other passengers 140 of the Martinican men refused to submit themselves to vaccinations and demanded free passage back to Martinique. The steamship line refused this demand and appealed to the French consul. Eventually, the administration requested that the Zone police force the men to disembark, which they did "but not until nearly every one of them had been clubbed and several were bleeding from nasty wounds."[20] The men were eventually vaccinated and sent to Corozal to work. Though the American press reported on the incident, it did not generate the overwhelming government response the scandal with the women would—none of the men were interviewed nor was their personal character questioned.[21] Moreover, none of the men were imprisoned under surveillance by virtue of their marital status. So, while concern over disease was widespread, only in the case of Black women was public health seen as an issue stemming from personal intimacy.

The November 1905 *Herald* exposé of the women's arrival also quoted Henry Burnett, the ICC chief of labor and quarters, expressing the position of the administration about the incident: "We are then here to build the Canal. What have the morals of a lot of West Indian negroes got to do with it?"[22] Burnett's indifference displayed the general attitude of the American administration in the first two years of the Canal construction—the important thing was the work itself, and any social aspect would develop without administrative oversight. The women were brought to appease the laborers, who "won't work anyplace without their women."[23] As much as the project's primary purpose was building a canal, it turned out that "the morals of a lot of West Indians" had quite a bit to do with it.

A month later, Senator Benjamin Tillman of South Carolina brought the *Herald* article to the Senate's attention, denouncing the misuse of government funds, executive usurpation, and the immorality of the women's sponsored migration. Congress proceeded to make a public charge against the ICC for bringing the Martinican women to the Canal Zone for immoral purposes. At the time, the Senate had been hotly debating distribution of funds to the Canal construction and the *Herald* article further fed the already contentious argument on the Senate floor. A fight between Tillman and Senator Henry Cabot Lodge of Massachusetts ensued, drawing on long-standing concerns about the role of race, imperialism, and executive power in U.S. politics. Tillman, a staunch conservative and white supremacist, had only two years earlier delivered a speech on America's race problem, criticizing Roosevelt for granting privileges and rights to African Americans and warning that this would pose a great danger to whites.[24] Tillman and other Southern Democrats opposed America's new imperialist ventures, which they saw as an extension of Roosevelt's executive misuse of power that annexed even more undesirable "colored peoples" to the United States.

The Republican faction led by Henry Cabot Lodge was decidedly pro-imperialist and supported the 1898 intervention in Cuba, annexation of the Philippines, and the Canal construction. While Lodge repeatedly challenged Tillman and other Southern Democrats on Black voter rights, Southern Democrats criticized Republicans for advocating empire and nonvoting status for subject people yet supporting Black suffrage in the South during Reconstruction. The lines of race at home and abroad created contradictory positions for these parties, where they simultaneously sought enfranchisement for the nation's Black citizens while legalizing the second-tier status of its imperial subjects. The arrival of the Martinican women in Panama suggested to these senators that Black West Indians were not merely in the Canal Zone as temporary and transient laborers—they had come to build families and communities and, perhaps, to request political and civil rights from the American government.

Initially, the Senate abandoned its suspicions about the incident after Taft presented evidence, in the form of correspondence between Governor Magoon and Chairman Shonts, asserting that no one had arranged for the women's passage and that most of the women had jobs as domestics or in Canal hotels. Their reports argued that the women "as a class" were "neat, clean and industrious."[25] The administration presented the matter as an exclusive proposition—they *couldn't* be prostitutes *because* they were domestics. The

Senate accepted Taft's testimony and shelved any further investigation, but the distinction between "labor" and "prostitution" remained neither fully clear nor convincing to Congress and the American public.

Fashioning Categories of Morality

The matter did not die down. On January 4, 1906, Poultney Bigelow published a follow-up article, titled "Our Mismanagement at Panama," in the *Independent* that criticized the U.S. government's operation of the Canal project.[26] He traveled to Panama on November 29 by Royal Mail steamer, spending only two days in the Zone and leaving by the same ship on December 1 to New York. Bigelow's stay was short, but he used his time to speak to the managers of all the major Canal divisions, including the commissary, warehouse, railroad, and jail. He toured Colón, led by local American businessman Tracy Robinson. Robinson had been a "leading citizen" of the Canal Zone for forty years and owned a substantial amount of property in Colón, primarily tenement buildings that housed West Indian workers.[27] He often criticized the U.S. administration in the local press and became Bigelow's main interlocutor during his visit to Panama. Shonts and Magoon noted in their communications that Robinson had in fact been an impediment to progress in Colón since he rejected most proposals for sanitation that affected any of his properties.[28] While the news about the women's arrival had already been released and debated, Bigelow's article renewed public criticism of the Canal Zone project.

Bigelow was born in New York to a family with deep ties to American journalism, politics, and Panama. His father, John Bigelow, co-owned the *New York Evening Post*, and served as American ambassador to France during the Civil War and as secretary of state of New York. Bigelow Sr. had visited the Canal Zone during the French construction in 1886, when he wrote an extensive report on the conditions of the construction and made the acquaintance of Philippe Bunau-Varilla (a French engineer and later one of the main negotiators for the Canal deal), who would become his lifelong friend.[29] Bigelow Sr. became a staunch supporter of the Canal project and of Bunau-Varilla's interventions in Panama. Bigelow Jr. followed his father's interests in Panama but with the intention of exposing the commission's negligence of their laborers.

Bigelow's article denounced a number of failings of the U.S. administration in Panama, including unsafe housing conditions and unsanitary water and sewer treatment, but it focused mostly on the poor management of Silver workers. The article began with Bigelow speaking with a "well-dressed, self-respecting negro" who wanted to return to Jamaica because Panama did not meet his expectations. Throughout the article, Bigelow told of visits to West Indian homes and conversations with Black laborers, repeatedly highlighting their personal cleanliness and ability. The conditions of Black workers in Panama, Bigelow argued, were hampered by the extreme mismanagement of U.S. administrators who had encouraged unhygienic conditions, political promotions of white "tramps" over Black workers, and immorality. Among his many accusations was a doubling-down on the charge that "the United States authorities had imported at considerable expense several hundreds of colored ladies" for the purpose of prostitution.

With tensions already high, Bigelow's article proved to be the last straw. The scathing report was publicized in the American and Panamanian press as were Taft's public responses and Bigelow's follow-up reports for the *New York Times*, the *Washington Post*, and the *Los Angeles Herald*.[30] Along with major newspapers, the scandal was covered by local news in places as far-flung as Ocala, Florida, Roswell, New Mexico, and Barre, Vermont.[31] The press did not exclusively discuss the rumor of the women's migration. Rather, the focus was on the interpersonal conflict between the principal perpetrators within the administration, mainly Taft and Governor Magoon, and Bigelow himself. For example, the *Barre Daily Times* reported that Taft had "roasted" Bigelow as a malcontent, and the *Los Angeles Herald* said Taft was "flayed" by Bigelow's reporting.[32] Taft criticized Bigelow as a sensation-monger and noted that the journalist had only spent two days in the Zone. Bigelow responded with a letter to the editor of the *New York Times* where he defended his methods and reiterated "the maladministration and filthiness which flourish in this alleged paradise."[33] The men sniped at each other throughout the course of the investigation, with Bigelow characterizing their exchanges as an insurmountable rift in interpretation: "I saw a swamp that smelled bad to me, but [Taft] says it is eau de cologne."[34]

While not the main focus, much of the coverage mentioned the rumor about the women, such as the *Los Angeles Herald*'s report on the "revolting story" by which "the government has outraged decency by importing several hundred colored women to the Isthmus at the expense of the American tax-payer."[35] Magoon countered during a press interview in New York that "the stories concerning the 280 Martinique women now in the zone are discredited by the conduct of the women themselves," who had remained under police supervision and had not been convicted of any crimes. He further retorted, acknowledging the need for West Indian women's care work, "Can we dispense with female labor? It is as necessary there as elsewhere, and if we cannot dispense with it we must employ such women as we can get."[36]

The scandal regarding the women was embedded in the overall media narrative about the mismanagement of the Canal project. The press admonished administrators for transgressing moral boundaries in the name of the construction effort, whether by transporting Black women for sex work, promoting undeserving employees with political connections, or housing Black workers in disease-ridden swamps. The scandal gained intensity through back-and-forth disputes over the truth about conditions in Panama and the character of individual administrators. Whether the allegations were found to be true or not, the scandal placed Canal administrators under scrutiny and forced them to defend their governance of the Zone to the American public.

The increased media attention prompted a full Senate investigation of the matter, which was also covered in detail by the press. Congress requested oral testimony from Bigelow, Chief Engineer Stevens, Governor Magoon, and labor recruiter J. W. Settoon, among other Canal administrators, as well as affidavits from most of the Martinican women, every police investigator associated with the event, the church ministers listed in the *Herald* article, and the labor recruiter responsible for the women's arrival. While the press criticized Canal management widely, the investigation focused more explicitly on the women.

Before Bigelow's article, Taft had successfully denied to Congress the administration's involvement in funding the women's passage. At the start of this renewed investigation, however, new evidence surfaced; in Taft's letter to the president on January 10, 1906, he commented that he had just recently learned that the women *had* in fact traveled under the expense of the Canal's chief engineer.[37] Clearly worried about this new discovery, he added: "The evidence now submitted shows that without the knowledge of the Commission, but by order of the chief engineer, the passage of women from Martinique was paid, but that the women were carefully identified as the wives of laborers who had gone before to the Isthmus, or the daughters or sisters of such laborers; that every woman has a natural protector on the Isthmus, and that all were brought for needed legitimate domestic service and that not one was imported for purposes of prostitution or other immorality."[38] Now knowing that the women's passage was paid by the chief engineer, Taft focused on denying that they were prostitutes and on asserting that the U.S. government had fulfilled its duty in surveying, identifying, and categorizing the women. For Taft, having paid for the passage of the women was only defensible because they had male "natural protectors," implying the opposite—that "the condition of independence, whether it unleashed insatiable desires or brought misery and unemployment, led to prostitution."[39] For American administrators like Taft, the figure of the working woman symbolized social disorder and prostitution as an inevitable consequence of the incompatibility between work and the moral behavior expected of Black women, assuming a thin and permeable line between working woman and prostitute. Taft deflected blame from the Canal administration—they "were brought" for domestic service, and "not one was imported" for prostitution. But the possibility still stood that the women could be prostitutes, unless they were at all times controlled by one of their "natural protectors" or engaged in legitimate domestic service, which for the American administrators meant under the watchful eye of an upright white American family. The chance that they had come to the Canal alone, as many West Indian women did throughout the construction period, could immediately make them suspect.

Congress further interrogated Chief Engineer Stevens and the labor recruiter J. W. Settoon to apportion blame for the women's arrival in Panama. Settoon's interrogation established the discursive frames that shaped the later investigation of the women: Did these women have "natural protectors" in Panama? How many were wives? How old were they on average (because it was preferable that they be "elderly, settled women, who would be, or likely to be, good and reliable servants")?[40] What were marriage practices like in their home islands? And, most importantly, "were they laboring women or prostitutes?"[41] Settoon responded: "They were all sent there for the purpose of relieving the congestion of household service. There was an absolute dearth of it. The men were clamoring for their wives to come. . . . They were absolutely needed on the Isthmus in their capacities, just as we needed laborers on the Canal."[42] Settoon rationalized that the women were needed both for domestic labor and to appease the men. Though he affirmed in the investigation that he brought only "laboring women," Congress focused the vast majority of questions for Settoon on whether the women had husbands, brothers, or fathers who would watch over them, and on the morality of common-law marriage practices in the islands (asking, for example, whether men were faithful in these relationships). Clearly, Settoon's assertion of them as laboring women was not enough. For Canal administrators, the assumed slippage between a "laboring woman" and a prostitute had to be contained— by assigning these recently arrived women a male protector and gauging their moral practices. The focus on the women's intimate relationships highlights the administration's expanding concern with the social repercussions of the women's migration: What practices would they bring to the Canal Zone? What kinds of communities might they build?

Of the 295 Martinican women who had arrived, the investigation found that 126 were married, 51 were "living with men not married," 36 were "single working with private families," 48 were "working for ICC hotels," 10 were "single not employed," and 24 were laundresses.[43] The categories reiterate the understandings of morality among Canal Zone administrators. If women were established as legally married, the investigators did not record further information about their work, assuming these women to be under the umbrella of their husband's care. Similarly, those working with white American families or in a Zone hotel were safely assumed to be under moral supervision. The others lie less cleanly within this spectrum of morality and highlight the unruly process of taxonomy at work in the investigation.[44] Laundresses, though accounted for, did not work under the eye of an American employer. Fifty women admitted they were not legally married. These categorizations, rather than clarifying the moral hierarchy of the Canal Zone, instead flag the uncertainties that plagued these administrators. They were attempts at adjudicating the practices of West Indian migrant women, whose arrival had exposed the gaps in imperial power—the administration's urgent reliance on West Indian workers, their lack of social and moral authority over the Zone, and the miscommunication between administrative divisions. Fashioning "grids of intelligibility . . . from uncertain knowledge," in the words of Ann Stoler, was a corrective strategy to foreclose further criticism of the project and reassert imperial authority—to prescribe a moral standard.[45]

The women's migration was not organized in secret nor initially perceived by administrators as immoral. It was only as it was shaped into narrative form by the media and government response that the commission's recruitment of Black women from Martinique took on an association with corruption and obscenity. This association would shape the enforcement of morality legislation in Panama and the Canal Zone throughout construction that targeted West Indian women's intimate practices and regarded their independent labor with suspicion.

Investigating the Women

The investigation further produced 155 affidavits from the group of Martinican women. The affidavits are more representative of the U.S. government's growing anxiety over the matter and their desperate desire to delimit and categorize the social practices of West Indian women. Nevertheless, they also provide evidence of women's own understandings of their migration and labor. The great majority of the women affirmed that they had come to the Canal Zone for work and money, and that their lives were better there than in Martinique. They expressed their desire to participate in the economic opportunities that the Canal construction provided. They answered specific questions that sought to absolve administrators of immorality by proxy. Women stated that they were not immoral, that they lived with husbands, and that they enjoyed their jobs as domestics in American homes or ICC hotels—precisely the factors administrators wanted to establish.

In the process of presenting these affidavits as evidence, the commission narrowed the women's responses to hold meaning only within the categories of morality they had formulated throughout the investigation. They argued that the affidavits attested to the women's commitment to legal marriage, cleanliness, and industry. However, these same answers document women's defiance of the administrators' categories of judgment through women's accounting of their own practices. By calling their common-law partners husbands, West Indian women openly disregarded the administrators' concern with the legality of their marriages. By judging themselves to be moral while also holding an assortment of unsupervised odd jobs, they flouted the commission's desire to streamline their labor. Some women declared open criticism of the investigation and their confinement. They expressed bafflement at the expectations of legal marriage put forth during the investigation. The affidavits thus provide overlaid layers of meaning that simultaneously structured each other: the questions and categories imposed by administrators determined the women's answers, while the women's answers troubled the administrators' attempts at slotting them into neat moral categories.

Governor Magoon prefaced the affidavits with an explanation that they had been prepared by the prosecuting attorney of the Canal Zone J. M. Keedy, who visited the women, spoke with them, and "reduced their statements to the form of an affidavit."[46] The testimonies were heavily edited and likely translated, and they all follow a fairly routine structure: name, place of precedence and reason for migration, name of labor recruiter, current employment, and marital status. The affidavits use the same categories that marked the Congressional interrogations, attempting to locate each woman within parameters that evaluated their relative morality depending on whether they had jobs within American homes and legal marriages. Magoon questioned the reliability of the affidavits, describing how the women responded to Mr. Keedy's visits: "They became greatly excited, shed tears, and were palpably alarmed, fearing that they were to be returned to Martinique."[47] His comment rather shows the coercion in administrators' tactics, subjecting the women to a traumatizing interrogation under the threat of further policing and deportation. The women's responses indeed present a complicated historical trace; gathered under duress, they are primarily documents of self-preservation where women sought to not incriminate themselves. In his instructions to the chief of police, Magoon further questioned the trustworthiness of the women's testimony, arguing that "it will be difficult to secure admissions of wrongful and illegal action," among "people who do not consider such conduct as being reprehensible" in reference to the practice of "concubinage."[48] His is a preemptive admission of the difficulty of finding common meaning in the affidavits. The women would deem as natural and unremarkable what the administration would find to be reprehensible and immoral.

The investigation was not intended to express the women's views but rather was meant to present coherent proof of the administrators' innocence. Nor did it provide simple evidence of women's agency in the face of an imperial interrogation. When Maselle Present said "I am not living an immoral life," for example, she was likely answering a direct question from the attorney and had little option but to deny any immorality.[49] These women reacted to the scrutiny of an investigation that already assumed them to be deviant and forced them to defend themselves. Maselle's statement presents a paradox—it is a statement of self-defense overdetermined by the violent matrix of the investigation, but it is also an assertion of her own sense of morality. When she professed that she was not living an immoral life, she answered the interpellation of the imperial regime, but she also brought her own understandings of morality and respectability to that statement.

By far the most dramatic response to the media criticism was the confinement of all single Martinican women under strict police surveillance in a camp in Bas Obispo, where watchmen prohibited entry or exit to anyone after hours. In their affidavits, every unmarried woman mentioned this arrangement. One of them, Alfonse Ustach, expressed her clear displeasure: "I live in a camp with other single Martinican women, and a *watchman is over us all night*, who allows no one to leave or enter our quarters after 8:30 p.m. I am 69 years old. The morals of all the women in camp are good."[50] Ustach reiterated to Mr. Keedy that the women were all moral, suggesting that the interview process and the surveillance they were being subjected to was unnecessary. After a mere allegation in the press, the extreme response of the U.S. administrators in the Canal Zone to place women in a restricted camp under strict police supervision exposed their immediate assumptions about Black women's labor, their concern with imperial governance, and the violence of their techniques. If a woman could prove she had a "natural protector"—a male family member, preferably a legal husband—she could live outside of the camp. Yet the administrators who prefaced these affidavits continued to find the women untrustworthy for a variety of reasons. Almost any characteristic could imply the possibility of prostitution—young age, single status, an uncertain job situation.

The sharpest difference between the women's and the administrators' views was on the issue of marriage. Seventy-five of the interviewed women self-reported as single and sixty-eight as married. Thirteen did not explicitly state their marital status but were likely single since they resided at the camp. However, the numbers do not tell the whole story. Some women, like Louise Baya, stated they were *both* single and lived with a man "who is my husband," meaning most likely that they maintained a single partner but were not legally married, complicating the easy binary between these two states.[51] Cecil Daily avoided the word marriage, saying she "came here to join my man, with whom I lived in Martinique for seven years."[52] Every single one of the married women stated that they had been married for some time and had come to live with their husbands. Again, this does not mean that they were legally married. The American administration and the press obsessively discussed the prevalence of common-law marriage among West Indians as proof of their lack of morality and civilization in newspapers, interviews, and private correspondence. Magoon noted that the West Indian women in these arrangements "protested that they are not, as they term it, 'living in sin.'"[53] Though none of these outright protests made it into the affidavits, women's insistent categorization of their relationships as marriages shows their refusal of the association of concubinage with immorality. To them, living with a partner without a legal arrangement did not mean they were "living in sin." Regardless of the paperwork, they saw these as committed relationships that gave them the benefits of both companionship and relative freedom.

Magoon devoted much of his report to the understandings West Indians had about marriage and cohabitation. He highlighted not only how unreliable he found the women's voices but also how distressing he found these differences in West Indian marriage practices. The women resoundingly refused this reading of their partnerships, invariably using the terms *husband* and *marriage* to refer to them, even when they had not legally married. Antoinette Laonise expressed a deep devotion to her husband, telling Keedy: "If you send me back, he has got to go with me or I won't go."[54] And Leona Louis even retorted to the imposition of this expectation: "No one ever told me I had to have a husband."[55] To administrators, the prevalence of concubinage among the women seemed an insurmountable moral obstacle, to the point that they would soon criminalize this practice. The women, on the other hand, assigned no particular value to legal versus common-law marriage, expressing a variety of relationships as loving and committed, and contradicting the administrator's classification of legal marriage as the only acceptable practice.

The issue of morality was also clearly tied up with the women's employment. Most women cited the promise of a job as one of their main motivations for traveling to the Canal. Violin Feroline said "I came for work, and find plenty of it here" and Evelina Sovos noted that "It is better than I could do at home."[56] Except for a handful of women who were sick or injured, every single one of the women had a job. The investigation repeatedly mentioned that the women had respectable jobs as maids in American homes or in the Canal Zone hotels. Throughout their correspondence, the administrators approvingly highlighted that most of the single women worked for American families in a positive moral environment. The implication was that the best proof that they were honest laboring women was their placement in an American home or working under the supervision of the ICC. The administrators expected women to be under the oversight of a patriarchal protector (a husband, a family with a male head of household, or an ICC department) in order to assure their proper moral behavior. The married women were not asked to specify where they worked. Presumably, the interviewer did not bother to ask once he had established that a woman had a male protector. However, without prompting, they often mentioned that they did laundry or domestic service to help out their households.

The women described very different forms of labor that rarely followed the standards of morality that administrators had set out. Many described doing a variety of odd jobs, and characterized those jobs based less on stability or a moral environment than on their high wages and the ways they managed to support themselves and their families through wit, hard work, and flexibility. One woman, Ferdilia Capron, described it by saying, "I do any work that comes in handy."[57] The majority of them worked as laundresses, work that was usually done outside of American homes and with little external oversight. Policia Maria described this mobile labor as "working about as washerwoman from place to place."[58] Rose Mont Rose noted that, though she had started sweeping camp quarters, she had switched to doing laundry, "as I can make more money."[59] Few of them mentioned their American employers, though many instead discussed the kinship and relational networks that helped them find jobs—siblings and friends who had accompanied them on the trip or who worked alongside them. A few expressed their disappointment about the lack of employment and support in Panama that they had been promised; for example, Alexandria Piquot lamented, "I have not found all the work I could do."[60] As with the issue of marriage, the women's interpretation of their own labor remained incongruent with that of the investigators. Women did not view their flexible entrepreneurship as being at odds with their morality.

None of the women said outright that they were prostitutes. Nevertheless, it is possible that some of these women engaged in sex work as it was an avenue open to them for financial gain. Chief of Police Shanton reported to Magoon that his investigation had uncovered that "of the entire number which have arrived on the Canal Zone *not more than three or four* are common prostitutes."[61] This figure is questionable given that Shanton provides no evidence for this finding, and that the women did not openly characterize themselves as prostitutes. In Panamanian police records from the period, however, West Indian women often listed their employment as *oficios domésticos* (domestic labors), even when they also admitted to engaging in prostitution, which was legal in Panama.[62] Thus, some of the women could have in fact engaged in sex work and were just understandably hiding this from the investigators. Nevertheless, it is difficult to parse out how Shanton would have discovered this information or, rather, what evidence he used to ascertain that three or four of these women engaged in sex work, given the repeated misunderstandings administrators had about the nature and financial obligations of common-law marriages among West Indians. Shanton's finding is never mentioned again in the investigation or congressional interrogations.

The press and local ministers made much of the Martinican women's lack of English, but some, like Rose Mont Rose, explained, "I understand this because I speak English. I learned my English in Dominica."[63] Rose's response serves as a reminder that these Martinican women, like their French and British West Indian ancestors, likely engaged in transnational circuits of labor and migration before the Canal construction and had familiarity with multiple languages and imperial regimes. The women also reported to Mr. Keedy that they had "heard of the articles which were published in the papers of the United States respecting them and their morals."[64] Women's interaction with these investigators thus did not occur in a vacuum. Some might have faced interrogations in previous sites of labor migration where they were subject to similar suspicions of sex work, and had skills and rhetoric to contend with them. Others were aware of the larger battle over morality that shaped their investigation.

The Canal Zone administration expected all labor to be under their purview, and saw the arrival of independent female workers as an affront to the institutionalization of the project, even as they desperately needed the work of women. They proscribed moral behavior for women as a binary: they were either prostitutes or laboring women. The reality, as the women themselves explained, was much more flexible. The women told a story that only aligned sideways with the concerns of the Canal leadership. Rather than respectability, legal marriage, domestic labor in an American home, or male protection, the women sought economic opportunity, often choosing to work on their own, and lived openly without formalizing their marriages. For the women, maintaining their independence and mobility was the primary draw as it allowed them to seek various forms of employment in a male-dominated environment while providing for themselves and their families.

The affidavits as a group display, most of all, the anxieties of American administrators in controlling these women's social practices. They placed them under strict surveillance, interviewed each woman, and heavily edited their responses. Governor Magoon wrote an introduction to the report that tried to define these categories of judgment—what counted as legitimate marriage and legitimate labor—as narrowly as possible. Only legal marriage and domestic live-in labor in an American home or business would count. Anything else, he implied, suggested prostitution. Yet, in the face of this intensified policing of their bodies, relationships, and spaces, the women protested the moral judgments of U.S. imperial administrators, sometimes criticizing their confinement, like Alfonse Ustach, or reversing the blame onto the administrators themselves for failing to provide promised work opportunities. They consistently used their own definitions of marriage and respectable labor, subverting the inquiry process by insisting on calling their common-law partners their husbands and celebrating their own business acumen in holding multiple, entrepreneurial jobs.

*   *   *

Did American administrators recruit around three hundred Martinican women to the Canal Zone? Yes. Did they do so with the expectation that these women would provide sex work? They certainly did so with the desire that women would provide care and partnership for West Indian male laborers as well as domestic labor for the Zone community but not for the explicit purpose of prostitution. However, the scandal festered in the distinction between sex work and West Indian women's common-law arrangements, which administrators perceived as being separated only by a very thin line. Through their response to the scandal, Canal administrators coalesced an understanding of Black women's independent migration and intimate practices as deviant. Since Black women's labor was less practical, less productive, and thus less legitimate than other forms of contracted industrial labor, it became immediately suspicious.

The scandal sparked a defensive response from U.S. government officials. In his report to Congress after his famous visit to the Canal in November 1906, Roosevelt repeatedly cited Bigelow's article; one historian notes that "it was almost as though Roosevelt went to Panama specifically to erase the stain that his law-school classmate [Bigelow] had put on his enterprise."[65] It also set off a series of significant changes in the Canal administration. Roosevelt replaced many high-ranking officials and centralized authority over the Canal in one person. After this publicity disaster, the U.S. government and Canal administration became deeply invested in the social element of the Canal Zone.

Governor Charles Magoon was one of the first casualties of the incident. A few months after the Senate investigation ended, Roosevelt effectively fired Magoon through a Consular Reform Bill. Magoon subsequently became the governor of Cuba. In February 1907, Commission Chairman Shonts resigned to take a job in New York. In April 1907, Chief Engineer John Stevens followed him in a very controversial resignation, citing personal reasons. His precise motivations have never been disclosed, but his letter of resignation signals the exhaustion and stress the position had caused him, particularly over the public attacks from "enemies in the rear." Both Shonts and Stevens had been heavily criticized for their involvement in the incident, their mismanagement of funds and authority, and the lack of communication between different branches of the administration. By mid-1907, all three major positions in the Canal administration had been eliminated or the person had been replaced. Roosevelt hired Col. George Goethals, an army engineer with canal construction experience as the new chief engineer, chairman of the commission, and head of the Panama Railroad, uniting all positions of authority under one person. Unlike the prior two civilian chief engineers, Goethals had largely unchecked power and established a regime of military discipline (Zone policeman Harry Franck called him a "benevolent despot").[66] As an engineer, Goethals's priority was building the Canal, but, to him, the greatest challenge was "the necessity of ruling and preserving order within the Canal Zone."[67]

Soon after the rumors began to circulate, Magoon requested municipalities "where such ordinances do not exist, to enact ordinance prohibiting lewdness."[68] This became Ordinance 14, a local law that served "to prohibit and punish lewd lascivious cohabitation," that is, cohabitation without legal marriage. As we will see in Chapter 3, Ordinance 14 would become an expansive tool through which Canal administrators could police West Indian women's practices of intimacy, repeatedly seen as proximate to sex work. Prostitution became a prohibited practice in the Zone, adultery was discouraged, and vice became heavily regulated.[69]

As in other U.S. territories and corporate enclaves at the time, imperial power did not form a "monolith" in Panama.[70] Prostitution remained legal and common in the terminal cities of the Canal on Panamanian territory, Panama City, and Colón. As in other sites of empire, government officials hoped to curb prostitution while also depending on its existence. The system was "effectively repressed" in the Canal Zone in part because it could displace its vice to cities in Panama.[71] U.S. officials occasionally attempted to control vice in Panama, particularly the spread of venereal diseases, through deportations, the circulation of informative pamphlets, and pressure on the Panamanian government.[72] After construction was completed, prostitution in the terminal cities continued to create a series of problems for the U.S. administration.[73] West Indian women, in particular, "sparked debate among

U.S authorities, Panamanian politicians, and Afro-Caribbean labor activists" as to the correct response to the spread of vice.[74] The port cities of Panama functioned similarly to Limón, where West Indian women, including sex workers, could live and create communities generally undisturbed by the Canal administration. The affidavits from the Martinican women already give a sense of how, even under harsh scrutiny, they attempted to make their lives beyond the confines of the Canal administration.

The report, like much of the documentation produced by U.S. Canal authorities during the construction, primarily evidences imperial anxieties and concerns.[75] West Indian women appear as subjects of criminalization or sites of immorality. But women also intervened in this archive, puncturing imperial categories of morality and rendering visible the possibilities of their own self-determination. Even in the face of violent interrogations, West Indian women spoke of their own strategies of informal labor, their reliance on kinship networks, and their expectations of the responsibilities of common-law partnership. Throughout construction, West Indian women continued to build homes outside of the Canal Zone to avoid surveillance from Canal authorities and to access a wider variety of services that were denied Silver workers. They continued negotiating their common-law relationships amid the criminalization of "cohabitation without marriage" and the threat of domestic violence, seeking legal arrangements from U.S. courts, Panamanian police, and British diplomats. They continued working across fields of domestic and care labor that remained in high demand and sustained the Canal project. The events of 1905–1906, in the earliest years of construction, established the dynamic that would shape West Indian women's experience throughout the rest of the Canal construction period—a tension between American administrators hoping to contain immorality while depending on female labor, and migrant West India women seeking opportunity beyond the limitations of U.S. imperial authority.

CHAPTER 3

A Moral Battleground

In late 1905, soon after the arrival of Clemence Gerald and more than two hundred other Martinican women, the Isthmian Canal Commission made cohabitation between two unmarried people illegal in the Canal Zone with Ordinance 14:

> AN ORDINANCE TO PROHIBIT AND PUNISH LEWD LASCIVIOUS COHAB-
> ITATION
> Section 1. It shall be unlawful for a man and woman to live together as man and wife without being legally married. In order to convict under this section it will only be necessary to prove that the accused parties are habitually occupying the same room and bed.[1]

Though the text of the law made no mention of race or national origin, its passage had come amid the debates about West Indian concubinage surrounding the arrival of the Martinican women. The law effectively criminalized the intimate practices of most working-class West Indians, who indeed often chose to live together without legal marriage. It would further come to be used to punish women suspected of prostitution and those involved in interracial relations with white men. Section 1 of the law gave wide powers to the Zone police force, making the burden of evidence low and inviting surveillance of residents' personal living arrangements in order to prosecute "lewd and lascivious cohabitation."

Ordinance 14 was only one among a series of local laws used to police West Indian intimacy through regulations against interracial couplings, sex work and vice, sexual violence, and indecent conduct within ICC quarters. The enforcement of these laws subjected West Indian women in particular to extreme vulnerability and legal restraints under the assumption that they were agents of immorality and always in a state of sexual consent unless under patriarchal supervision. These assumptions extended throughout the Canal Zone legal system even in instances in which women were not the accused; in divorce proceedings, courts expected Black women to behave like powerless victims in need of a protector while, in cases of rape, the courts saw them instead as manipulative sexual predators. West Indian women thus appear primarily as agents of violence and disruption in sources created by U.S. authorities, which categorized Black women's everyday relationships as lewd and outside the moral norms of the Canal Zone.

These norms of morality were meant to uphold an idealized image of American cultural superiority and technical efficiency.[2] However, the Canal Zone of the earliest years of construction did not align easily with this ideal, beset as it was by engineering troubles, disease, and a diverse and rapidly increasing immigrant population. West Indian women lay at a particularly complex intersection of racial and gendered difference from this imperial vision. They provided informal labor, did not rely on ICC services, and fostered intimate networks outside the normative moral expectations of U.S. authorities. ICC administrators only uneasily tolerated their work of social reproduction, fearing the limits of their lack of influence over West Indian women. They saw Black women as having a natural "low degree of virtue," with little concern for productivity and accustomed to immoral practices from the islands.[3] The Canal administration thus built a discursive and legal apparatus that pathologized and policed West Indian women's behavior.

This apparatus manifested throughout the Canal Zone, from its criminal justice system—including its circuit courts, local laws and ordinances, and decisions by the chief engineer—to more informal encounters between West Indian workers and white upper-tier administrators or white American housewives. At each level, the system was buttressed by the commission's growing police and penal capacity as the ICC developed its regulatory functions and further erected the segregation of the Zone as a "hyper-American suburb."[4] The early years of construction saw the expansion of the ICC's deportation powers and its police force, a steady increase in arrests, and the use of imprisonment and forced labor at Gamboa Penitentiary.[5] As the dominant financial, political, and legal authority in the region, the ICC created an inescapable legal matrix for West Indian subjects that defined and regulated their movement, employment, and everyday life when traversing through the Canal Zone, even for women who did not officially work for the project.

Police investigations, court cases, and white women's memoirs nevertheless highlight West Indian women's insistence on practicing their vernacular understandings of love, intimacy, and morality, and the double-edged compromises they had to fashion to secure their everyday survival. West Indian women came into daily conflict with the ICC, white American residents, and their own lovers over the meaning of money, subjecthood, and heterosexual partnership. A few women loudly asserted their disdain for legal marriage and its constraints, even when faced with judgment from employers or police. Others deployed imperial authorities' own categories of morality to defend their partnerships, regardless of legality, positioning themselves as its ultimate arbiters. For example, they mobilized discourses of abject victimhood in front of white bosses to access financial support from delinquent spouses, forcing white Americans to recognize the responsibilities between partners in concubinage and leveraging the potential violence of Canal authorities to secure their earnings. For those middle-class West Indian women who had undergone legal church marriage, the Canal Zone courts offered a way to divorce from abusive husbands by presenting themselves as helpless victims at the mercy of the judicial system.

Black women's marginal status in the Canal Zone made them subjects of suspicion, but it also provided a window of possibility for their edgewise engagement with imperial authorities. Their strategies were structured by the legal and moral standards of the ICC, the practices they had brought from the islands, and the labor and sexual economy of the Canal Zone. Their longtime engagement with the British colonial government on the issues of marriage and bastardy throughout the nineteenth century had prepared them to confront state projects of morality. The discrepancy in gender ratios among West Indians in Panama gave them a level of clout in managing their interpersonal relationships. Their domestic labor gave them access to the intimate spheres and confidences of white employees and administrators who they could sometimes turn to for aid. Their work alongside the official contracted force opened the opportunity for their use of the same legal system that was often positioned against them. The moral conflicts of the Canal Zone were thus made and remade in the interactions between Black women, U.S. residents, and imperial authorities, as the ICC sought to bring the labor force under its vision of morality and women sought to safeguard their financial earnings, physical safety, and intimate relationships.

Regulating "Lewd Behavior" in the Canal Zone

In the early decades of the twentieth century, U.S. colonial officials, medical personnel, and corporate administrators dealt with the intimate lives of their new subjects across imperial territories in many different ways. In Costa Rica, for example, the United Fruit Company paid lip service but, according to historian Lara Putnam, "put little effort into paternalist social engineering" regarding morality.[6] In Chile, the Braden Copper Company actively attempted to reconfigure notions of proper masculinity and femininity at the El Teniente Mine in order to stabilize a permanent labor force.[7] In Puerto Rico, U.S. officials sought to protect "gente decente" from prostitution and civilize the population. They encouraged monogamous marriage by establishing legal divorce, a move that was immediately popular with Puerto Rican women.[8] The administration of the Canal Zone shared some of these tactics, while diverging in others; it was part military base, part enclave economy, part American colony. Canal Zone officials regularly expressed their anxiety about West Indian women's sexuality and paid more than lip service to these concerns by enacting legislation that criminalized interracial relationships and cohabitation without marriage. But American administrators ultimately saw West Indians as a temporary labor force and felt no urgent need to provide for their sustenance or moral education in the form of dedicated social engineering. The policies of the administration during construction regarding West Indian intimacy were aimed at maintaining productivity. The ICC and white Canal Zone residents tolerated West Indian women to the extent that they provided for Silver laborers or worked for white Americans. Any perceived deviation from the goal of efficient construction rendered them threats to the coherence of the American project.

To the great consternation of U.S. authorities, West Indians continued to practice the relationship patterns they had followed in their home islands once they arrived in the Canal Zone. Both American authorities and white residents of the Zone pointed to West Indian relationship practices as signs of racial and moral deficiency. White Americans imagined Black West Indian women as straddling a murky boundary between wage labor and prostitution that positioned them as always potentially criminal. Though administrators relied on the labor that women provided in support of working men and white families, the ease with which West Indians could leave and restart relationships deeply troubled U.S. authorities. They understood the prevalence of common-law marriage as evidence of West Indian women's lack of respectability and proximity to prostitution. Cohabitation without legal marriage thus became a disputed battleground between West Indians and the Canal administration who criminalized the practice they disparagingly called "concubinage." In the face of expanding American legal and military power in the Zone, West Indian women nevertheless found ways to love in the same arrangements they always had.

Even in sympathetic portrayals, American commentators and authorities found West Indian immigrants "hopelessly unmoral."[9] West Indian women, who lived and worked on the outskirts of the ICC's authority, faced particular surveillance and suspicion of immorality, even when there was no evidence of wrongdoing. In a 1915 letter from an anonymous white American "wife" to General Goethals, for example, she complained: "In regards to the colored women that collect wash in the bachelor's quarters, it is disgraceful the way in which they are allowed to carry certain matters to a point far beyond respectability."[10] She went on to say that the men had good morals and asked Goethals to intervene in the matter, with the suggestion that Black women needed to be separated from unaccompanied white men. While the white men ogled Black women at work, the letter writer saw the women as the guilty party, lacking respectability by their mere presence and labor among white bachelors. The letter writer expressed no concern for the safety of these Black women, seeing them only as sexual temptresses rather than potential victims of sexual aggression. Other white American residents repeatedly referred to West Indian marriage practices and associated them with vice and degeneration, placing particular blame on Black women. Rose Van

Hardeveld commented that "the West Indian woman still had her new man every few months and bore numerous children to poverty, disease, and filth."[11]

Accounts from white Americans show the complex tensions that arose between West Indian understandings of their intimate relationships, based on long-standing cultural practices of flexible cohabitation without legal marriage, and those of the emerging legal and political system of the Canal Zone in the early years of construction, which upheld state-sanctioned white heterosexual marriage. Governor Charles Magoon reported on West Indian women's interpretations of marriage as follows: "The distinction which they make between relations which are sinful and relations that are proper is that when a woman cohabits with a man—living with him for a short period and not intending to be married to him, but to pass from him to another whenever they feel inclined—such relation is sinful; when a woman takes up her abode with a man, intending to establish permanently the marital relation, to be faithful to him and to deny herself to other men, such relation is not sinful, even if the civil or religious marriage ceremony has not been performed."[12] Upon their arrival in Panama, these West Indian women empathically expressed their moral code to American administrators, making careful distinctions between the relationships they perceived as proper or not. Their system, based on cohabitation, duration, loyalty, and intention, had less to do with established religion and official marriage ceremonies. These relationships came with unspoken but distinct expectations of faithfulness, integration into networks of kinship, and financial support. Women held the right to leave these relationships "whenever they feel inclined" if these expectations were not fulfilled. The women used the language of sin to affirm their philosophy, giving it the righteous heft of Christianity. For Magoon, on the other hand, West Indian women's distinction between "proper" and "sinful" relations seemed baffling given what he saw as the inherent immorality of the practice—a sign of West Indian women as primitive subjects.

In an attempt to curb practices of cohabitation among West Indians, the Canal Commission enacted Ordinance 14 early in the construction decade, during the scandal with the Martinican women. It sought "to prohibit and punish lewd lascivious cohabitation" and allowed police to persecute "concubinage," explicitly criminalizing the everyday relationships of most West Indian residents of the Zone. Anyone found living without a marriage certificate could be fined twenty-five dollars and sentenced to thirty days in jail unless they married before their case went to trial, in which case, they could avoid prosecution.[13] Thus, the law essentially forced legal marriage on anyone found cohabiting. It served the purpose of imposing compulsory monogamy on Zone residents and pathologizing any refusal to follow this norm.[14]

As cohabitation without marriage was mostly prevalent among West Indians, the ordinance was clearly designed to give the police broad power to intrude on West Indian relationships. The law was often enforced to charge West Indians with "lewd and lascivious behavior." Two hundred people were arrested under this ordinance during fiscal year 1908–1909 alone, the highest number of arrests made under this charge during the construction decade.[15] Most years had fewer arrests, with an average of ninety. However, the number of arrests does not tell us the actual number of people who faced surveillance and police intrusion under this charge as many likely avoided outright arrest by opting for legal marriage. Indeed, as the Southern Baptist clergyman Rev. F. Moss Loveridge explained, by 1908 "the enforcement by the Commission of the law forbidding cohabitation of persons not actually married has resulted in many of the negroes having the marriage ceremony performed."[16] On one occasion in 1908, the municipal judge issued 264 marriage licenses in the span of five days.[17] During the construction decade, arrests for "lewd and lascivious cohabitation" were almost always divided equally between men and women, making it one of the few crimes for which women were charged at the same rate as men (West Indian men, given the demographics, usually far outnumbered women in Zone arrests for any crime).

The number of arrests under this charge gives us only a partial portrait of the policing West Indians faced. In 1907 there were 1,206 cases for disorderly conduct (the largest category of arrests overall), 332 for disturbing the peace, and 650 for violating sanitary regulations.[18] Annual reports noted that West Indians made up the majority of "the criminal business before the courts" across all crimes.[19] West Indian women faced significant arrests only in "quality of life" offenses, rather than any violent crime.[20] Any of the above charges could have been used to police nonnormative intimate behavior among West Indians alongside Ordinance 14. Thus, the ordinance was only one among a series of legal mechanisms that served to surveil West Indian intimacies. Charges specifically under the ordinance began to decline in

1914, with the end of construction and the formal expulsion of most West Indians from the Zone.

Along with prosecuting unlawful West Indian concubinage, administrators also used the broad powers of Ordinance 14 to police interracial relations, which the Isthmian Canal Commission defined solely as "cohabitation and immoral conduct of white employees with native and colored women."[21] There was no specification for the unimaginable interracial relationship between a Black man and a white woman. The law thus doubly targeted Black women's sexuality, both as part of their common relationships with West Indian men and as the perpetrators of immoral interracial conduct.

American residents used Ordinance 14 to censure what they perceived as immoral interracial intimacies involving West Indian women. For example, in a 1913 complaint, a white American woman named Anita Seaman denounced two white women and four Black West Indian women for consorting with white policemen.[22] The police investigated Seaman's allegations and chose to focus exclusively on the West Indian women while ignoring the two white women she had also accused. The West Indian women were all subsequently punished for cohabitating with white men.[23] Only one of them, Carmen Ellis, a twenty-six-year-old "light St. Lucian," was "known in Gorgona as a common prostitute," according to the report.[24] C. M. Grant, a fifty-five-year-old Jamaican woman who owned a restaurant on Second Street in Gorgona, had been seen with William Platoo, a steamshovel cranesman, who visited her regularly. An informant had seen two different white American men enter the room of Rebecca Smith, a thirty-eight-year-old Jamaican who also owned a restaurant on Second Street. Her eighteen-year-old daughter, Sybil Isaacs, who lived and worked with her, also had a relationship with a white American, a machinist named Harry Buschman. Both older women were business owners and, in Grant's and Isaacs's cases, were known to have only one consistent relationship, with men who visited them regularly— hardly substantial evidence of prostitution. The accusation was based solely on hearsay and white American witnesses. However, these women's jobs in restaurants and saloons—sites often associated in the Zone with drinking, gambling, entertainment, and prostitution—and their role as independent businesswomen, placed them in a precarious position in the eyes of the Canal administration.

The investigation memo concluded that there was not enough evidence to prosecute any of the women for prostitution but that the facts were "sufficient to recommend the deportation" of all the women.[25] Though the ordinance makes no mention of a disparate burden of proof, in application the law favored white men, who were given no punishment for this crime while the Black women faced deportation. The men, who all pled guilty to the charge of interracial cohabitation, were merely ordered to cease relations with the women from Gorgona or face unemployment. The women, "on account of their general reputation and previous bad conduct at Gorgona" and not because they were found guilty of prostitution, were ordered to leave the Canal Zone within less than a month.[26]

There was no direct evidence that any of these women worked as prostitutes except the word of an informant, yet the slipperiness of this category for Canal authorities was justification enough to deport them. In both Anita Seaman's and the police's view, interracial cohabitation almost necessarily implied a relationship of prostitution. West Indian women were preemptively assumed to be engaging in immoral conduct and disrupting white society. However, deportation did not always mean the end of West Indian women's interaction with the Canal Zone. In one 1911 case, ten Jamaican women were arrested under suspicion of crossing into the Zone on payday for the purpose of prostitution. They were sentenced to fifty-five days in jail for the crime of vagrancy. Upon their release, they were barred from the Zone and ordered deported not to their country of origin but to the country of transit from which they had entered the Zone—Panama. From there, they could have easily continued their border-crossing work.[27]

While these Gorgona women were ordered deported for interracial relationships, other West Indian women managed to subvert these ambiguous regulations of intimacy. A statement from Sergeant William Rutherford, district commander at Ancon Central Station, to his chief of division on August 10, 1913, reported the arrest of white American foreman James W. Lord and a Black St. Lucian woman named Silvery Henry for disorderly conduct.[28] On August 8 at 10 P.M., Rutherford received a complaint about "disgraceful" interracial acts in a room in Ancon (room #7, house #11). According to his statement, "I went to the room and looking through the slats in the door I saw Lord lying across his bed dressed only in B.V.D. under-clothing which was unbuttoned from top to bottom, the woman, Silvery Henry, was sitting in a chair engaged in picking 'crabs' from the man Lord's privates." The case contains an ambivalent relationship to this moment of intimacy—a disavowal of Silvery's actions through a joke about "picking crabs," paired with the voyeuristic attraction of the policeman as a Peeping Tom looking through the slats onto a private scene. Rutherford characterized Henry's actions as "picking crabs" to avoid asserting any sexual element in the scene. The crime was cited as disgraceful or sexual conduct within ICC quarters. Both participants were found guilty and fined—$25 for Lord and $10 for Henry, both of which Lord paid.

Though the Black woman in this case was identified, we know little about Silvery Henry, and the report positions her as a sexual accessory to Lord. Nevertheless, there is something extra in the report, an aside that provides a glimpse into the intimate possibilities of a Black West Indian woman in the Zone. Rutherford ended his report noting that "both defendants left the District Court Room and went in the direction of the Ancon Post Office walking side by side," characterizing Henry and Lord as romantic partners in crime. A handwritten note in the margin provides a coda to the case: "Lord moved from ICC quarters and is living in private room elsewhere 8/15/13." Since the criminal charge was explicit that they had engaged in sexual behavior "within ICC single quarters," it seems possible that Lord and Henry moved to a private room to continue their relationship outside of ICC surveillance.

White anxiety about the dissolution of racial and sexual boundaries in the Zone informed the criminalization of these acts.[29] Silvery Henry's partnership with Lord shows that criminalization did not deter all West Indian women from pursuing interracial relationships. To assume that West Indian women had no say in these matters would be to both deny them sexual agency and ignore the relative economic independence they had in the Canal Zone. Nevertheless, West Indian women had to contend with raced and gendered hierarchies in maintaining interracial relationships with white American men, who firmly held the economic, political, and social authority in the Canal Zone. Relationships between Black women and white men in the Canal Zone always involved a highly imbalanced power dynamic that repeatedly fell into the realm of sexual and economic exploitation backed by the legal regime of U.S. empire. Silvery Henry's choice to stay with Lord was perhaps another Black woman's complicated act of self-preservation.

As James Lord's involvement with Silvery Henry and the Gorgona women shows, not all white employees in the Zone followed the letter of the law regarding interracial relations. In another 1906 case, the ICC investigated the involvement of Police Sergeant J. P. Cooper with a Jamaican woman living in Bas Obispo named Beatrice Hayworth. In his report to the governor, the physician B. W. Caldwell blamed Beatrice for soliciting and being "obscene and vulgar." He further admonished the relationship: "Such practices encourages poor respect for the law in the minds of those inclined to break its principles. Society is robbed of the protection the law intends to afford it. Its purity is threatened and by countenancing such actions, society loses its best traditions and becomes demoralised. License becomes rife, and that purity of a community with which we who are on the Isthmus wish and hope to surround our homes and our families becomes nothing but the filthy atmosphere which prostitutes and rogues breathe."[30]

The problem, for Caldwell, was, on the one hand, the loss of confidence in police officers seen consorting with women he perceived as inherently criminal and, on the other, the general attack on (white) society's purity by interracial sex. Caldwell, a high-ranking ICC medical official, saw this relationship as the precipice before the end of society itself. It is hard to overstate how seriously Caldwell presented this charge, fearing that society would become demoralized and fall apart. The ICC's lack of enforcement against Sergeant Cooper thus far had threatened to normalize these relationships until such "license becomes rife." Caldwell's fear stemmed in part from Cooper's legal protection of Hayworth, who had escaped prosecution multiple times due to Cooper's intervention with local judges. Like Silvery Henry, Beatrice Hayworth found a difficult path to secure her personal safety at the side of a white American man. Her association with Cooper protected her, for a time, from the daily violence of male-dominated canteens and from the persecution of the Zone's legal system, even as it also invited more scrutiny into her life.

The wide powers of legal tools like Ordinance 14 to intrude into the private lives of Canal residents meant that West Indian women faced frequent surveillance by police and administrators, who assumed them to be the main perpetrators of "lewd cohabitation" and who often suspected them of engaging in sex work. The sources do not account for the everyday coercion Black women must have faced as Canal police enacted Ordinance 14 and forced

West Indians into legal marriage to avoid punishment. They only show the more extreme cases that resulted in arrest or deportation. Nevertheless, Ordinance 14 served the express purpose of policing Black female sexuality and punishing interracial relationships. It functioned as one part of a larger project of imperial governance that sought to contain immorality, perceived as stemming from Black women's sexuality, within the newly formed enclave of the Canal Zone. Black women faced limited choices when the eye of the ICC turned on them. Even their attempts at finding safety through interracial relationships with white American administrators or police officers proved dubious as these could initiate further inquiry into their lives.

Consent and Sexual Vulnerability in the Canal Zone

The criminalization of Black women in the Zone also stemmed from a legal understanding of their excessive sexual appetites and constant state of sexual consent. The complex issues of consent and agency within a context of the exploitation and degradation of Black female sexuality are amplified in the series of rape cases that came before the Canal Zone courts during the construction decade, which were almost exclusively rapes of women of color. Between 1910 and 1912, sixteen rape cases came before the Second Judicial Circuit. Only four of the perpetrators were convicted; all four were West Indian men.[31] Yet the courts often found West Indian women as much the culprits of the rapes on their own bodies. Responding to a request for information, the Third Judicial Circuit judge, Thomas E. Brown, stated that "the crime of rape, or attempted rape, is essentially one of the most difficult to prove. On the Canal Zone it is of course a matter of common knowledge that women of the West Indian class are of a low degree of virtue, and there arises therefore a sort of moral presumption in the majority of cases that there would be no necessity for the use of force."[32] In the understanding of the criminal justice system of the Canal Zone, Black women by nature could not be raped since they existed in a constant state of consent.[33] Rape was defined by the courts as only being true under a limited set of circumstances such as "where the female is under the age of thirteen years," when there was documented evidence of lunacy, or when the female resisted but was overcome by violence.[34]

These were the grounds on which the courts saw the case of Barbadian William Wait's rape of eleven-year-old Keturah Lewis.[35] In her statement, Keturah explained that she was sent to Wait's room to deliver some clean clothes her mother had washed for him since Wait was a boarder in a residence run by Keturah's mother. Wait took her by the hand and put her in his bed. When she refused, "he do it by force."[36] In his statement, Wait instead said she was "playing with him" and consented to the sexual relations. Moreover, he persisted in characterizing her as an overly and improperly sexualized woman, despite her age, saying "It seems she like it the first time and return to him."[37]

Because Keturah Lewis was under thirteen years of age, this case was initially considered a rape by the Canal Zone courts. Wait was found guilty and given the minimum sentence for rape, which was five years' imprisonment. His lawyers appealed his case to reduce his sentence, hinging their complaints on the perceived precocious sexual development of the young girl, essentially arguing that it was not rape because Wait had misjudged her age. Colonel Goethals agreed to pardon him, explaining: "It appears, however, that the girl with whom the offense was committed was of such physical development as to lead Waits to believe that she was more than thirteen years of age; that the offense was committed with the command of the girl, and with the knowledge, and apparent consent of her parents; and after the offense was committed he expressed a willingness to marry the girl, but was unable to do so because of the refusal of her father to consent to their marriage."[38]

Ultimately, after serving three out of five years of his sentence, William Wait was granted a pardon due to the mitigating circumstances raised by the courts, mainly, that eleven-year-old Keturah Lewis looked more physically developed than thirteen and had given her "consent." The pardon came directly from the highest authority of the Canal Zone and reiterated a characterization of West Indian women as oversexed and immoral. Even in a circumstance involving a very young child, the top leadership saw it right to intervene and reassert the always assumed sexualization of a Black girl. Keturah emerged as a consenting agent only to the extent that she allowed and essentially *requested* ("with the command of the girl") sexual assault on her body. The blame, in Goethals's eyes, was on Keturah for encouraging the act and her parents for refusing to properly marry her to her abuser. This response was not unique to the Canal Zone—the banana zone in Puerto Limón, Costa

Rica, experienced a similar pattern of cases of coerced sex involving prepubescent Brown and Black girls.[39] As in Limón, West Indian women's vulnerability to rape and the Canal administration's sexualization of Black women structured these women's attempts at maintaining intimate, sexual, and financial relationships in the Canal Zone. The threat of Black women's sexuality was perceived as extreme to the point that an eleven-year-old girl could be portrayed as a sexual temptress rather than the aggrieved party in a rape case.

These cases represent only a small percentage of the sexual violence that Black West Indian women faced. Most women likely did not report rapes or attempted rapes to the Canal Zone courts, knowing these were not legally considered rapes or correctly assuming that the U.S. courts would judge them as seducers and refuse to punish the perpetrators. The courts found West Indian men to be culprits in thirteen out of the sixteen cases but never persecuted a white American male for sexually assaulting a Black woman, showing the racialized understandings of criminality that also structured Black men's lives. Though these encounters are not archived, it is not unlikely that domestic servants were coerced into unwanted sexual relations by their white employers. The Canal Zone courts provided little avenue for redress in cases of rape and, judging by the low number of cases heard in these courts, West Indian women understood that. As with instances of domestic violence, West Indian women likely resorted to other means to find some sense of justice and lived with the trauma of sexual violence. The Canal Zone court's negation of Black women's sexual autonomy by assuming their constant consent to rape goes hand in hand with other forms of surveillance and policing to which they subjected Black women during this period. In positioning Black women as oversexed, consenting deviants, the Canal Zone courts contributed to a discourse that pathologized Black intimacy.

"No Truck wid 'usban's"

As the stories of Silvery Henry and Beatrice Hayworth show, though West Indian women were constrained by the legal and discursive violence of Canal Zone authorities, they nevertheless found ways to assert their financial and reproductive agency, even if this required making ambiguous alliances.

To secure their physical, financial, and emotional safety, West Indian women often relied on the same sources of power that denigrated and exploited them—the white administrators, bosses, and housewives that mediated their relationship to the ICC. Local police reports and white American memoirs presented West Indian women as symbols of Black inferiority, but these documents also reveal how women leveraged their labor mobility and appealed to informal authorities to negotiate for greater physical and financial autonomy. West Indian women repeatedly fought for their safety and independence, even at times explicitly reasserting their commitment to cohabitation without marriage as wanting "no truck wid 'usban's."

White American observers often commented on West Indian relationships with bemused judgment. Foreign correspondent and travel writer Albert Edwards told of a Jamaican couple who visited Colonel Goethals during his notorious Sunday morning "court," where he personally arbitrated minor conflicts among Canal Zone residents: "The first callers were a negro couple from Jamaica. They had a difference of opinion as to the ownership of thirty-five dollars which the wife had earned by washing. Colonel Goethals listened gravely until the fact was established that she had earned it, then ordered the man to return it. He started to protest something about a husband's property rights under the English law. 'All right,' the Colonel said, decisively. 'Say the word, and I'll deport you. You can get all the English law you want in Jamaica.' The husband decided to pay and stay."[40] Edwards's story shows the West Indian man as intractably uncivil and bound by his colonial relationship to the British Empire. The story works on several registers to legitimize American authority in the Zone—by suggesting that American law was more common sense and liberal than English law, by presenting West Indian men as uncivilized subjects in need of didactic authority, and by positioning West Indian women as subjects in need of saving from West Indian men. It further shows the tensions among competing patriarchal visions between West Indians and the Canal authorities. "Under English law," the West Indian man alleged, he could beat his wife and maintain ownership over joint property. As a Black immigrant under a racist and segregated U.S. regime, he invoked the power of a British colonial relationship against the authority of the ICC to maintain control over his personal affairs. Goethals rejected this appeal, portraying it as a backward practice incompatible with the modern system of the Canal Zone. The American authorities wielded the law in favor of a wronged West Indian woman—only they held the legal and moral power to correct intimate relations and enforce reciprocities. The story positions a white American man as a savior of the Black woman from the patriarchal authority of a Black man who sought to subdue her, disavowing the system's own investment in Black women's dispossession and their extraction of her care labor.

In the story, a West Indian and a white American man interact about a barely mentioned woman. The West Indian woman served a merely symbolic purpose—as a subject discussed by the men around her. The anecdote was meant to suggest that West Indian men misunderstood how to properly manage their wives, with the implication that the Canal authorities had to teach them. While much of the administration characterized Black women as potential prostitutes, some white Americans positioned them instead as helpless victims of their husbands' abuse to reify racist tropes of backward Black men. These discourses positioned Black women in a paradoxical space—powerless and silenced unless they were able to demonstrate proof of their own culpability.

Yet the story also hints that the West Indian woman in question had earned money through her own work, that she was unwilling to hand it over to her husband, and that she defended that right to the highest authority on the Canal Zone. It highlights the continued links between intimacy and economy in West Indian partnerships and how they came into conflict in the Canal Zone, where women had ample opportunities for independent labor. Though the story shapes the scene as being essentially about an exchange of masculine power (from the immoral Black West Indian man to the lawful white American man), it also shows a West Indian woman successfully claiming her financial autonomy in front of the administration and maintaining ownership over her earnings. Rather than the enlightened imperial governance of the Canal's chief engineer, we could read the story as evidence of one Black woman's persistence in securing her wages. Though only the men speak in the story, "the fact was established that she had earned [the money]" through her own labor. The story makes no claim as to who, exactly, brought the case in front of Colonel Goethals, leaving open the possibility that it was the West Indian woman looking to protect her earnings. Nevertheless, the woman's ownership of her wages was only secured by appealing to the patriarchal power of Colonel Goethals's personal court, in some ways affirming the authority of the white American protector.

Given the financial precarity of traveling to and working in the Canal Zone, it is no surprise that many sources make clear the significance of economic support in a West Indian partnership. These financial relationships often depended on the white American bosses who managed the labor and wages of West Indians in the Zone. At times, West Indian women took advantage of these hierarchical relationships by appealing to the authority of white American employers in order to gain concessions from their West Indian partners. One white American boss recounted his dealings with the personal problems of his Black staff, describing the letters he received from the wives of his workers.[41] In these, West Indian women complained about not receiving child support from his employees, such as in the following letter from Ellspeth Graham:

> Respectful Sir:
> In the large trubel of my hart I write to you. I am a fair young maden of twenty-one (21) summers what has suffered grate wrong from one Cyril Thelan works for you. I born fo him two (2) suns, aged ate and ten yrs old. They are his and he don't help me no more since he took up with that Sophy Andrews lives in Chorillo. My honer was torn assunder and I need a comisary book for he hasn't given me one (1) fore one month. Make him come to time and the Lord Jesus help you forever.
> Your obedient servant.
> Ellspeth Graham.[42]

The letter reveals that West Indian women like Ellspeth considered child support their prerogative, even when they were likely unmarried and had no legal right to it under U.S. law. When they could not find legal recourse through the courts, West Indian women sought the authority of white American bosses to put pressure on their male partners for economic support.

Ellspeth addressed herself to this man in deferential terms, calling herself his "obedient servant." She used dramatic, romantic, ultrafeminized language, positioning herself as a "fair young maiden" and saying her "honor was torn asunder." She characterized Cyril as an immoral villain, for he is the one who left her for another woman despite his obligations. She asked not for money but for a commissary book, which she could use to buy food and households goods, suggesting that Cyril had neglected his family's basic needs. Unable to compel Cyril through other means, Ellspeth instead used a number of rhetorical strategies to appeal to the masculinity, paternalism, and authority of his white American boss.

For West Indian women like Ellspeth, honor and integrity did not require official marriage. Ellspeth saw herself as a religious, moral woman and Cyril as the culprit in breaking the unspoken requirement of supporting his children. She understood their common-law arrangement as requiring a certain commitment. For West Indian women, living in cohabitation did not necessarily lack the obligations and benefits of partnership. As another West Indian woman named Loralia explained it, "I'm not married, but I hasn't been overlooked."[43] Ellspeth sought to leverage white patriarchal power to invoke these obligations and ensure survival for her and her children. Though petitioning a white American boss through the use of deferential language, Ellspeth nevertheless reaffirmed her own understanding of relationship obligations and forced American authorities to validate this understanding.

Despite judgment from white Americans, some West Indian women asserted their independence from the perceived burden of legal marriage. Upon quitting her job, a West Indian domestic servant named Mary told her white boss, Elizabeth Parker, that "she couldn't work anymore because she was 'making a baby.' [Parker] asked her if her husband had a job and she said, ''Usban'! 'uh! Hi don' 'as no truck wid 'usban's.'"[44] Parker expressed her surprise and amusement at her maid's audacity to flout conventions, but her story also gives us insight into West Indian women's position in the Canal Zone regarding the subject of marriage. Evidently, Mary did not feel a moral, financial, cultural, or legal imperative to marry. Mary quit her job to prioritize her reproductive choice. She might have had another partner or a wide network of neighbors and kin who could help her—the archive does not record the collective practices of West Indian women who likely aided each other in these situations and could have supported Mary at this time. Either way, she categorically wanted nothing to do with a husband.

Interestingly, the phrase *no truck with* means literally to want no exchange, business, or trade with, once again highlighting the inextricability of financial and sexual relationships for West Indian women. While Parker immediately assumed Mary would need a man to support herself and the baby, Mary responded in clear terms that she did not depend on the earnings of a husband. Mary's decision reflects the low rate of marriage among West Indians in both the islands and Panama, but her use of the phrase *no truck with* further suggests that Mary saw herself as financially independent from a husband. West Indian women like Mary did not see the need for official marriage in a situation where they could easily acquire both jobs and companionship. A Jamaican woman named Agnes, working as a domestic servant, similarly told her boss that she "regarded the marriage tie as a species of slavery to which she would by no means submit," echoing the desire for freedom West Indian women had expressed as their priority since the period after emancipation.[45]

West Indian women like Agnes, Silvery Henry, Ellspeth Graham, and Mary faced judgment and accusations of immorality from white bosses and Canal authorities. In different ways, these women defied imperial understandings of their relationships and intimacies as immoral, or even unusual. They called on Canal authorities to honor the obligations of common-law relationships on moral grounds and affirmed their financial independence within those relationships. Like Mary, some loudly asserted that they did not even need husbands. Alongside the continued low rate of marriage among West Indians, these examples evidence the prevalence of vernacular understandings of intimacy, love, and sexual and financial autonomy among West Indian women through the construction years. Despite aggressive attempts to force them otherwise, working-class West Indian women chose "friending" (non-coresidential unions) and independent employment over legal marriage and its attendant expectations of re-creating American-style heterosexual normativity. To defend these practices, West Indian women had to develop temporary, uneasy alignments with Canal Zone authorities. Nevertheless, as these sources show, the criminalization, surveillance, and

everyday violence West Indian women faced from the ICC and its white employees did not stop them from pursuing their own visions of safety and
freedom.

Legal Marriage and Divorce

For middle-class West Indian women who came to the Canal Zone legally
married or who chose to marry after their arrival in Panama, the ICC's power
to grant divorces gave them a narrow avenue for protecting themselves from
intimate partner violence and to secure sources of subsistence. In this process, they, too, had to contend with the administration's characterization of
West Indian women as immoral as well as with the relocated West Indian
middle classes' "culture of respectability."[46] As in the late nineteenth-century
Caribbean, divorce was quite uncommon among West Indians in Panama.
The Canal Zone Circuit Court heard only eleven divorce cases involving West
Indians for the decade of construction. Nevertheless, this small sample of
cases provides insight into middle-class West Indian women's experiences
with marriage and interactions with the Zone courts. Even for these legally
married women, the choice to seek divorce occurred within an overall context where concubinage and West Indian relationships remained a contested
moral battleground. By seeking a divorce, these newly single working women
potentially opened themselves up to the ICC's surveillance and risked losing
their sources of income and community support. To forestall these possibilities, West Indian women presented themselves before the Canal Zone courts
as victims of amoral husbands who had violated the social contract of marriage, at the mercy of the court's benevolence.[47] The eleven divorce cases show
how West Indian women mobilized discourses of victimhood in suing for
divorce, positioning themselves as destitute wards of the courts, in order to
escape severe abuse and gain crucial financial support from their partners.
By distancing themselves from the lewd working-class Black woman, one who
engaged in concubinage and independent labor outside the home, these
women carved out livelihoods and safety for themselves. The process of le-
gitimating their status as moral single West Indian women required reinforcing imperial notions of proper and improper Black femininity.

Some West Indians married in the Canal Zone, and these weddings were often extravagant affairs. An American man invited as a guest to the wedding of Jamaicans Mose and Mariah commented that these ceremonies required a lot of money "in order to do it up brown, as a 'wedding' and not just a marriage."[48] Mose and Mariah, like many West Indian couples, lived in a common-law relationship for thirty years and raised a family before saving enough to have an official ceremony. West Indian men at weddings dressed in black suits and silk hats, with large bridal parties of young women in white dresses, while the brides wore sweeping lace and satin gowns. People would stand on their balconies and in doorways to watch the festivities parading through the neighborhood.

This perhaps suggests one of the reasons for the generally low popularity of marriage: In order to "do it up brown," West Indians had to save much of their income for both legal fees and festivities. Though the phrase "do it up brown" generally meant to do something "just right" or to its greatest extent, in the context of Black Jamaicans, it had the added suggestion of color and caste difference. Though this concern might not have been present for the white American commentator, working-class Jamaicans who traveled to Panama retained some of the class and color distinctions from the island that echo in this phrase. The early decade of construction had little in the way of a visible West Indian "colored middle class," but, as in the islands, it was these West Indians who were more likely to pursue legal or church marriage and "do it up brown."

Most British West Indian immigrants voiced allegiance to the Church of England, but only "a small proportion of this number [were] actually communicants."[49] In 1908 there were twelve Black Episcopal congregations in the Canal Zone as well as some Methodist, Salvation Army, and Southern Baptist missions within the Zone and in the adjacent cities. Many of these had been built during the French construction and repaired by the ICC as segregated Black churches. These churches had auxiliary features such as Sunday schools and youth groups, and required a membership tax of around twenty cents silver each week.[50] French West Indian immigrants often practiced Catholicism and could instead attend services in churches across Panama. Though churches dotted the Canal Zone, most clergymen agreed that the majority of West Indians did not interact with these institutions. Rev.

Loveridge admitted that "not over 3000 are directly touched by church work," though a bigger proportion had indirect engagement with it.[51] This says little about religious belief among West Indian immigrants, but it does suggest that only a small proportion of the immigrant population—likely the artisan middle class, which was predominantly Jamaican—stuck to church sacraments like marriage. Members of this West Indian middle class often held higher-paying jobs with the ICC, were legally married, and sent their children back to the islands for private schooling.[52] For example, middle-class ICC schoolteachers Georgina and Gervaise Harry both worked in the segregated "colored" schools, married in 1899 at All Saint's Church in Kingston, and sent their son, also named Gervaise, to school in Jamaica and later to the UK. Gervaise Jr., born in Panama in 1910, eventually became a doctor and was listed in the *Who's Who* of Jamaica.[53] He would later return to the isthmus to attend a medical conference in 1952 where he precipitated a wild-cat strike by West Indian hotel workers who protested his exclusion from the segregated Washington Hotel.[54]

Official records have little to say about women's participation in the churches of the Canal Zone, but the recollections of West Indians suggest some women embraced church values, attended church events regularly, and were central in transmitting religion to their children. Middle-class mothers dressed their children in knickerbockers, long stockings, and Eton collars to take them to church on Sundays.[55] Throughout novelist Eric Walrond's semi-autobiographical stories, mothers constantly serve as conduits of religion and respectability, such as in his title story "Tropic Death" where Gerald's mother had "rooted religion into his soul."[56] The church served an important social role for West Indians in Panama where, as the activist and diplomat George Westerman explained, "there were no other agencies to fill its place" as a center of West Indian cultural life.[57] It also continued to serve a role in transmitting notions of morality, respectability, and class status that informed the intimate practices of those West Indians who chose to legally marry.

The Canal Zone civil courts were only available to Canal Zone residents and ICC or Panama Railroad (PRR) employees, which excluded many West Indian women. The Panamanian state would not recognize divorce until Law 17 of 1911 (and even then only under limited "necessary" circumstances of abuse, alcoholism, etc.), which was later extended to all voluntary divorce in the nation's first Civil Code of 1917.[58] Before 1911 the Catholic Church had authority over marriages, so Panama's institutions provided no opportunity for West Indians seeking divorce. There was no significant change in the patterns of West Indian divorce from the nineteenth-century Caribbean to the early twentieth-century Canal Zone due to both persistent West Indian practices and lack of access to the courts. Thus, what this small sample of cases shows is one strategy among many that West Indian women, particularly middle-class women, used to negotiate their autonomy and safety in the Canal Zone.

The eleven divorce cases come from the First and Third Judicial Circuits, with only one from the Second Circuit. The judicial system of the Canal Zone had been organized following a letter from Roosevelt to the secretary of war sent on May 9, 1904. The letter authorized the Isthmian Canal Commission "to make all needful rules and regulations for the government of the zone and for the correct administration of the military, civil, and judicial affairs."[59] It granted the Isthmian Canal Commission legislative power stemming directly from the Executive Branch and provided for the protection of "life, liberty, and property." The ICC then created a system consisting of municipal courts for small claims and three circuit courts. The First Circuit served the areas surrounding Colón and the Third, based in Balboa, sat close to Panama City. Both courts, then, were adjacent to the two cities in Panama with the largest West Indian presence. The act also created a Canal Zone Supreme Court, made up of the three circuit judges. The decisions of the Canal Zone Supreme Court were final as neither Congress nor the U.S. Supreme Court had authority over it. At least one of the parties in the suit had to reside in the Canal Zone or work for the ICC or PRR, but many of the participants in these cases, including defendants and witnesses, lived outside of the Zone.

The civil code of the Canal described the mix of legal precedents that the courts drew from in their decisions on divorce. Divorces were generally considered under U.S. law. Nevertheless, "Marriages celebrated in [any foreign country not U.S. territory] may be annulled in [U.S. territory—i.e., the Canal], and the spouses may be separated by divorce, for causes which authorize dissolution and divorce, according to the laws of the State where the marriage was contracted."[60] Canal Zone judges had to sort through a variety of legal traditions in making their decisions—Panamanian civil law, U.S. common law, and the laws of the foreign states from which laborers arrived.[61] In practice, however, most American courts used the precedent in which men could divorce their wives if the women had committed adultery but not vice versa. Women often had to prove adultery aggravated by another factor such as cruelty or financial abandonment. The court granted divorces *a mensa et thoro*, meaning "from bed and board," which legally distinguished the couple as being apart, but neither party was allowed to remarry until the other died, while the man remained financially responsible for his ex-wife.

Divorce was not altogether common among either white Americans or West Indians in Panama. The typical white American divorce case occurred when a Canal worker requested a divorce on the grounds of "desertion," claiming that their wives had left them by refusing to move to Panama. White American men were the predominant claimants in divorce cases. Desertion had a well-established precedent in U.S. divorce cases, particularly in the early twentieth-century U.S. West, where men sued for divorce at an unusually high rate during the era of settler expansionism.[62] In comparison to the number of divorce suits that involved white Americans, there are relatively few cases involving West Indians, which makes sense considering the divergent marriage rate between these two groups. Among those, however, the scant documentary record suggests that West Indian women were far more likely than white American women to sue for divorce.[63] West Indian claimants never sought divorce for desertion. Instead, these women usually advanced divorce suits on the grounds of financial abandonment, violence, and adultery. The first cause was the most oft-cited but was always accompanied by other reasons. This does not necessarily mean that financial abandonment was the number one reason West Indian women actually desired divorces. Rather, this was the reason West Indian women chose to highlight to the courts in order to secure a divorce.

In front of the court, women invariably said they sought legal separation primarily because they perceived their husbands as shirking their most important duty in a marriage—providing income. West Indian women were also more likely than white American women to cite domestic violence as a reason for seeking a divorce and frequently included vivid descriptions of the abuse they endured at the hands of their husbands.[64] The few West Indian men who sought divorce did so out of sexual jealousy, accusing their wives of adultery or sexual insults. Except for two dismissals due to death and residency status, the circuit courts of the Canal Zone granted every divorce requested by a West Indian, regardless of gender.

Annie and Helon Sparks moved to Panama in the early years of construction from Jamaica and Trinidad, respectively.[65] They met in Panama and married in St. Luke's Church in Ancon, then a small wooden chapel, in December 1908. In her petition for divorce four years later, Annie complained that Helon had a difficult temperament and frequently became violent and abusive toward her. One day during June 1910, while Annie was in the second trimester of pregnancy, Helon became extremely violent and repeatedly beat and insulted her and gave her a black eye; the police rushed into their house and separated them. Two months later, with the baby's birth near, Helon decamped to Limón, Costa Rica, taking all the couple's money. He returned to the Canal after neglecting Annie for two years and got a new job as a station engineer but still refused to support his wife and child. The proceedings were not documented, but the judge granted the divorce due to Helon's "cruel and inhuman treatment" and ordered him to pay all court fees along with $100 in child support to Annie.

Eugenia Peters had similar complaints to those of Annie Sparks.[66] Eugenia, from Martinique, and Arthur, from Trinidad, also married in St. Luke's Church in Ancon in 1910. Afterward, Arthur got a job as a Canal Zone police officer. Throughout their married life, Arthur repeatedly beat Eugenia, but it was not until January 1913 that Eugenia reached a breaking point. One day, Arthur beat Eugenia so badly that he caused severe abdominal pains and Eugenia was forced to seek medical assistance she could not afford. Arthur then deserted Eugenia, taking all their money, and leaving her in an empty room with the rent due. Soon he was living in open concubinage with another woman who was pregnant with his child. He objected to Eugenia's complaints only on a technicality—the fact that they lived in Panama City rather than the Zone. But the court overruled him because his job in the Canal Zone police force qualified him for residence. Though Eugenia had reasonable cause for action, the couple settled out of court. The divorce was granted and Eugenia received a monthly $10 alimony payment as well as a large part of the court fees from Arthur.

Though Arthur was adulterous, this alone was insufficient grounds to request a divorce. The women also had to emphasize Helon's and Arthur's physical abuse and financial neglect. Both women presented themselves as victims of cruelty for whom only the court could provide the security they needed. Their petitions included the same description, almost verbatim: "Her life has been reduced to one of misery and wretchedness too intolerable to be borne, she consequently feels that she owes it to herself to seek the protection of this Honorable Court." Both women employed the same lawyer, Grenadian Valentine E. Bruno, who (along with Barbadian Walter H. Carrington) commonly represented West Indian residents of the Canal Zone and clearly understood this as an efficient legal strategy in presenting women's claims to the courts.[67] Through their lawyer, both Eugenia and Annie appealed to the judge as a paternalistic protector, characterizing their lives as intolerable and hopeless without this support.

West Indian women were not necessarily destitute after these separations, but they presented themselves as such to a court that was otherwise keen to see West Indian women as illegitimate or immoral. Annie, for example, survived what was probably a very challenging two years with a newborn child and without spousal support while Helon was in Limón. She likely relied on social networks or found a job to help support her family during this trying time. However, women like Annie rarely spoke of their own economic endeavors. This strengthened their case based on necessity and distanced them from the moral concerns brought forth by independent Black female labor. She received the divorce and alimony she requested by seizing on the opportunity of Helon's return to the Canal Zone and presenting herself as impoverished and helpless.

Both couples had been married in Panama at St. Luke's Church and both were relatively well off in comparison to their West Indian compatriots in the Zone. Helon worked as a station engineer and Arthur as a police officer—jobs that carried higher status and significantly higher salaries for Silver Roll employees than regular "pick and axe" men. Black policemen, for example, made between $40 and $50 silver a month. This suggests that West Indian couples who chose to legally marry and divorce in the Canal Zone were part of a small but growing West Indian middle class that had migrated to Panama. These educated, upwardly mobile West Indians remained attached to

Christian traditions. Policemen like Arthur Peters often had experience in the British army or in the local police forces of their island.[68] They were thus more invested in a West Indian "culture of respectability," whether stemming from their class standing in the islands or from their newfound status in the Canal Zone.[69]

To be clear, West Indians in middle-class jobs maintained a delicate position; by 1908 the administration had transferred all these jobs to the Silver Roll and demoted many skilled West Indian station and railroad engineers.[70] Even Black police officers were subject to the racial discrimination of the Canal Zone; the head of Civil Administration noted that "we do not give them the same police powers that we give white policemen."[71] This further contextualizes the small number of divorce cases and the expectations of femininity that structured West Indian women's marital relationships. Black women in this stratum had to negotiate the fragile margin between middle-class respectability and working-class immorality. They had to contend with both the conservative values of the West Indian middle class and the desire to establish themselves in the Canal Zone as respectable to avoid the persistent criminalization, exclusion, and job insecurity West Indians faced.

From the court's perspective, women's spousal obligations required only that they take care of children and remain faithful. Richard Lewis is one of the few West Indian men who initiated a divorce during this period and the earliest West Indian divorce case in the archive.[72] His complaint shows what a West Indian man thought constituted grounds for divorce as well as the possibilities West Indian women sought in Panama. Richard and Felicia married in Jamaica in 1899, but he left for Limón a year later. He sent remittances to her throughout the years but never returned to Jamaica; instead, he moved to Panama to find more work. Five years later, Felicia also moved to Panama with her six children (one of whom was fathered by a different man in Jamaica) but did not contact Richard. He heard of her arrival and went to confront her. On his visit, Felicia told him she did not travel to Panama to be with him, and that she had a child from another man. Presumably, Felicia moved to Panama in part because she had been left alone with several children to raise and sought job opportunities. By traveling to Panama and remaining indifferent to Richard's demands, Felicia's migration also expressed her departure from any expectation that she settle down or depend on a husband who had deserted her. Five years after Richard abandoned her in Jamaica, Felicia took matters into her own hands and migrated to find a better life for her family. Richard requested a divorce and asked for custody of his five children, noting that his financial contributions to Felicia meant he was fulfilling his duties.

Richard died at Colón Hospital before the case went to trial and the children stayed with Felicia, so it is impossible to know what the state's response to his claims would have been. However, considering how much he had invested in the divorce, he probably had good reason to think that her alleged adultery would be enough to grant him the divorce and custody. Stories like Felicia's point to the great difficulties West Indian women faced; though Richard sought the divorce, it was Felicia who had been abandoned with a large family, little financial support, and no knowledge of her husband's whereabouts. It was Felicia who migrated with six children to another country without the official promise of a job. Moreover, this shows how Richard positioned Felicia as an indecent woman—one who, left to fend for herself in Jamaica, chose to be an adulterer—thereby reinforcing the Canal court's ideas about the natural indecency of Black women.

Though the women never cited abuse as the sole cause of divorce, violence was present in every case and often in extremely aggressive forms. In Annie and Eugenia's cases, as in many others, the women detailed these abuses to the court to decry men's immoral behavior and garner the sympathy of the judges. By emphasizing their husband's abuse, they also showed the necessity of the divorce they were requesting and distanced themselves from criticisms of West Indian immorality. However, West Indian women were not deferential to this violence outside of the courts. The cases show that women would often respond to spousal abuse with verbal insults, hurled objects, or the powerful weapon of gossip. Despite their physical, economic, and legal disadvantages, West Indian women used strategies at their disposal to deal with this abuse when it became unbearable or, as in the case below, to deal with the daily violence of some long-term partnerships.

The 1912 divorce of Courtney and Mary Black is both the longest and most unique divorce case of the decade of construction—the single instance where the participating West Indian woman refused to build a defense based on her victimhood.[73] The Blacks' numerous complaints and cross-complaints build a complex story of adultery, abuse, and deceit. Courtney and Mary were married at Gatun Catholic Church in 1910. From their various conflicting affidavits to the court, the story can be reconstructed as follows: According to Courtney, about a year into their marriage, he arrived home one day to find Mary in bed with another man. Mary acknowledged her guilt and apologized. Courtney forgave her and they continued to live as husband and wife for some time. Either because Courtney could not afford to support her in Panama or because she requested to go back, Mary eventually traveled back to Jamaica. Mary said that, during her time away, she received no more than five dollars of support from Courtney and that he tried to dissuade her from returning. She nevertheless returned to Panama and got a job in Gatun as a domestic servant for the family of Captain Johnson, settling down independently of her husband. Mary found a job in Panama to support herself, assuming that Courtney would not provide support after refusing to send remittances to her in Jamaica. As Courtney had neglected his marital responsibilities and was no longer present in her life, Mary started relationships with one and then another West Indian man in the Zone.

Courtney did not visit Mary until several months after her return to Panama, when he confronted her with accusations of adultery. To these, Mary responded that she "intends to do what she likes." In his witness statement, Courtney's brother Charlie Black corroborated this story, adding that Mary was unrepentant about her actions and had told him "her skin was hers and that she intended to do what she was pleased to do with it."[74] Mary brazenly expressed her independence and bodily self-determination, defying Courtney's attempt to malign her reputation and control her sexuality. Interestingly, these words came not from Mary directly but through Courtney and his brother in front of the court. Thus, they could easily have been fabricated by these men in order to present Mary as a shameless adulteress as proving this was essential to Courtney's case. Nevertheless, assuming that Mary expressed something akin to these words, the case attests to at least one West Indian woman's bold declaration of sexual autonomy.

Meanwhile, Courtney had also begun a relationship with a neighboring woman, Evelyn Davis. Mary went to Evelyn's house to confront them, but upon her arrival Courtney began to beat her while Evelyn insulted her. Mary tried to resolve the situation by asking Courtney for a divorce. At first, Courtney "left in disgust" and ignored her, repelled by her simple request. She then visited the district judge at Ancon and told him of the situation, but he refused to assist her. Mary could not leverage her husband's adultery into a divorce and was left with little recourse.

After continued pressure from Mary, Courtney eventually brought his own divorce suit to the First Judicial Circuit Court at Ancon and was granted a trial by the same judge who had earlier denied Mary. Courtney hinged his complaint on Mary's unladylike conduct, positioning her as an oversexed deviant. Both he and his brother emphasized the sexual impropriety of her behavior. Courtney further accused Mary of annoying him at his workplace. In these divorce cases, West Indian men often complained about the effect of their wives' nagging on their work. Canal courts were sympathetic to this argument from male laborers, wishing above all to maintain productivity. Courtney complained that Mary visited him at work every day, repeating that she "wants to be free" and demanding a divorce.[75] Courtney presented Mary's repeated voicing of her desire for independence as evidence of her disruptiveness, coarseness, and lack of respectability.

Even though Mary was denied a hearing by the same judge, she persevered in voicing her complaints to Courtney, wearing him down in public until he gave in to her demands for a divorce. The judge eventually ruled in favor of Courtney, deciding it would be "unsafe and improper" for Courtney to continue living with Mary because of her adultery and "cruel and inhuman treatment" of him.[76] In most other cases brought to the Zone courts, a husband's financial neglect of his wife was considered justification enough to grant a divorce in favor of the wife. In the Blacks' divorce, however, Courtney built a story around Mary's unladylike behavior—her loudness, her verbal abuse, her continued fighting and nagging, and her adultery—that took precedence over his faults. The court decided in favor of Courtney as he was considered the victim of Mary's loose behavior. But though Mary was found responsible, she nevertheless received her wish—the divorce she had long sought.

It would be easy to position Mary as an exceptional case in contrast to other West Indian women in these divorces because she distinctly voiced her independence. The difference lies in the narratives these women presented to the courts to characterize their different legal circumstances. It is possible that the words of Mary Black echoed in the experiences of other women throughout their quotidian interactions with their husbands and lovers. They, like Mary, often left their husbands and found independent jobs. They might have expressed similarly bold statements in interpersonal conversations. However, in front of the courts, most West Indian women amplified a narrative of victimhood in order to strengthen their case. The courts requested proof of neglect and misery, and the women gave it to them. Mary Black, on the other hand, was accused by Courtney of precisely the immoral behavior that the courts found so distasteful in West Indian women. She did not have the opportunity to present a narrative like that of Annie Sparks or Eugenia Peters; instead, she chose to acknowledge her choices and assert her independence. In the end, Mary Black's statement is not just evidence of one woman's forceful conviction but rather a window into the possibilities of what other Black women *did not say* to the courts. In a context where Black women were considered naturally immoral, middle-class West Indian women usually chose to de-emphasize their pursuit of autonomy and highlight their dependency on patriarchal systems (their husbands, the judges) as a strategy of survival. Outside the courts, however, women likely used a variety of tactics; like Mary Black, they might have publicly admonished their husbands, pursued other relationships, relied on their community for support, and worked multiple jobs.

Mary's strategy differed from that of other West Indian women in divorce cases. Unlike them, she did not garner the sympathy of the judges, even after her initial testimony regarding Courtney's physical abuse, and avoided the defenses of victimhood or destitution. This was in part because Courtney vigorously characterized her as the guilty party—a brazen adulterer. But in her primary goal of divorcing Courtney, Mary succeeded. She repeatedly pressured her husband to accede to her demands for freedom in public spaces, forcing him to initiate the divorce proceedings. Though she had to accept a degree of humiliation in a public court to do so, Mary's strategy ultimately served her desires and allowed her to "do with her skin what she pleased."

Mary Black's case reveals the double bind West Indian women faced before the Canal Zone courts. Annie Sparks and Eugenia Peters had to present themselves as victims, unproductive and helpless, to win their divorce suits. They had to reinforce, at least rhetorically, that they were passive subjects, first to their husbands, who had failed to care for them, and then to the American courts. Mary Black, who did not follow this strategy, was unable to get the courts to recognize her request for divorce. Instead, her assertiveness made her out as the guilty party in this suit and she was only able to gain the divorce she sought after her husband brought it to the courts. Black women in the Canal Zone only received recognition as agents before American courts when they provided proof of their own oversexualization, immorality, and assumed criminality.[77]

*   *   *

The criminal justice system of the Canal Zone criminalized West Indian women's intimate behavior, put them at risk of surveillance and deportation, excluded them from legal protection, and forced them to find alternative routes to safeguard their survival. The handful of divorce cases show that this system prompted West Indian women to account for their sexuality and powerfully controlled the context in which utterances about intimacy and independence circulated, even for middle-class West Indian women who were legally married and thus ostensibly not a moral threat. Neither class nor legal marriage shielded West Indian women from the prejudices of U.S. empire. This chapter accounts for the discriminatory conditions that structured Black women's everyday life and labor in the Canal Zone. However, it has also shown how West Indian women found ways to skirt and, at times, disturb the moral taxonomies of U.S. imperial governance. Beatrice Hayworth, Silvery Henry, and Mary Black—among many other West Indian women left unrecorded in the legal archives of the Canal Zone—threw into relief the incompleteness of the American project and the arterial nature of its imperial rule.[78] These women continued to live as they chose; they kept common-law partnerships without legal marriage and pursued financial gain through entrepreneurial labor, despite the persecution they faced for these practices. Many more West Indian women did this than an archive of criminalization can fully capture. Their lives nevertheless remained deeply embedded in structures of racial capitalism. West Indian women continued to serve as the social reproductive forces of the Canal endeavor, and their strategies of survival often depended on the same institutions that criminalized them. Their practices did not dismantle the powerful monopoly on violence and policing held by the United States in Panama, which still deported, arrested, and disparaged West Indian women. But West Indian women's collective efforts fostered a parallel vision of morality and autonomy that cast doubt on the reach of imperial hegemony.

CHAPTER 4

Labor in the Domestic "Frontier"

The cover of *Maid in Panama* depicts a West Indian higgler as a "mammy." Her skin is an exaggerated ink-black, her body and breasts are large, her face round, and she wears a servant's apron. The higgler walks across an open field carrying a tray of tropical fruits on her head, with a background of palm trees, a placid river, and fluffy clouds. The higgler on this cover introduces a 1938 edited collection of short autobiographical stories by white Americans, primarily white women, reminiscing about their Black workers and servants during the Canal construction. During that decade, Black West Indian women provided the domestic and intimate labor that sustained American imperial colonization of the Canal Zone. Their work in homes, river laundries, boardinghouses, and kitchens took place beyond the purview of the Canal administration and mostly went unremarked in official sources, but their consistent presence in memoirs like *Maid in Panama* belies their importance to Canal Zone society. West Indian women's domestic labor subsidized the Canal Zone endeavor as they provided services in the gaps that the ICC could not fill during its earliest years, such as feeding and housing West Indian workers, providing entertainment, and laundering the clothes of thousands of employees working in the heat, dust, and humidity of Panama. West Indian women built a provisioning economy in the orbit of the Canal Zone that made the construction effort possible.

Their portrayal in memoirs like *Maid in Panama*, however, obscures as much as it reveals. Memoirs by white American women remain one of the few sources that speak at length about Black West Indian women's labor in the Canal Zone. In their recollections, white women are overwhelmingly concerned with the Black West Indian women who work for them, from their

Figure 2. Cover of *Maid in Panama*, illustrated by Anne Cordts McKeown. Sue Pearl Core, *Maid in Panama* (Dobbs Ferry, NY: Clermont Press, 1938).

maids to the local higglers and laundresses of the area. These memoirs privilege the perspectives of white women, who frequently insult and misunder-
stand the West Indian women around them. The authors associate Black
women with racial and sexual excess, uncleanliness, and barbarism. They
rhetorically attempt to put Black West Indian women in their place by ridi-
culing and disparaging their labor.[1]

In the U.S. South, the mammy served as a nostalgic fiction that erased
the violence of slavery, hiding it underneath the veil of a happy slave.[2]
Though they were not enslaved, the image of the Black higgler in the Canal
Zone similarly romanticized the "happy" relationship between white American employers and "primitive" Black workers.[3] The West Indian higgler-
mammy effaced Black women's work and Americans' dependence on it.
Though ostensibly a tribute to "mammies," higglers, cooks, and maids, memoirs like *Maid in Panama* rather served to cement and justify Black women's
inferior position in the Canal Zone, naturalizing their role as servants. The
mammy furnished visual proof of the need for the "civilizing influence" that
white Americans provided to their "backward" servants during the construction era. As historian Tara McPherson has argued about mammies in the
United States, the Black West Indian servant served as the symbolic ground
where the white American woman in the Canal Zone "elaborates the details
of white female subjectivity" as an agent of U.S. imperial expansion.[4]

Most West Indian women workers did not answer directly to the Isthmian Canal Commission. Nevertheless, the stricter modes of discipline that
organized contracted labor on the Canal reverberated in the Zone home,
where West Indian female workers faced informal regulation from their primarily white American female employers. Bosses and clients criticized West
Indian women's cleaning and cooking techniques, sought to control how
servants spent their personal time and money, attempted to underpay them,
and trivialized their work. U.S. empire in Panama thus came into being not
only in the halls of the Canal administration but also in the white American
home, under the eyes of white American housewives marshaling ideas of
"proper" domesticity.

Yet white women's attempts at dictating Black women's experiences in the
Canal Zone unwittingly provide a record of how Black women transgressed
and rejected their employers' standards of civility and proper labor. Reading

these memoirs against the grain, Black women emerge not as compliant servants and satisfied mammies, but as mediators and entrepreneurs, negotiating their relationship with their bosses to receive better pay, assert their sexual autonomy, and control the conditions of their labor. The West Indian women in this chapter did not engage in overtly political action or organize as workers during this period; they did not strike, or make legal claims to the ICC about their employment.[5] Nevertheless, West Indian women made significant choices to protect their earnings, time, and privacy. They took their time doing their work, expected employers to finance their startup costs, and rebuked their bosses' incursions into their personal lives. Though these strategies—what Stephanie Camp has called "everyday forms of resistance" in the context of the U.S. plantation South—could be seen as merely individual expressions, their outsized importance in bosses' accounts confirm their centrality to both bosses' and workers' interpretations of their labor and the workspace.[6] West Indian women's labor resistance was never simple. Even as they rebuffed their employers' demands, their work in Canal Zone homes, laundries, and streets sustained the racialized labor hierarchies of the construction project. Nevertheless, West Indian women sought to extract whatever benefits they had as uncontracted laborers in the Canal Zone—the chance to receive pay in gold, to leave jobs at will, to transit through segregated spaces, or to be their own bosses. West Indian women pursued ways of making freedom and profit for themselves and their families that challenged the structures of racial capitalism in the Zone and troubled the nostalgic project of memorializing American empire in Panama.

West Indian women's labor practices in the Canal Zone developed in a dialectical relationship with the white American bosses who provided their main source of wages and employment. They had to contend with the demands of these employers, who required servants to learn "American" ways of cooking and cleaning and to behave subserviently. West Indian women's attempts at wearing what they liked at work or asking for higher pay, for example, could come with the threat of unemployment, a loss of earnings, or potential violence. White women's memoirs never outright portray the insecurity Black West Indian women faced in their Canal Zone workplaces. The white memoirists instead position themselves as benevolent household managers and West Indian women as their easygoing, if sometimes troublesome, servants. The threats West Indian women faced nevertheless lie at the margins of every story and structured these women's everyday lives and work in the Canal Zone.

These memoirs also show how labor relations between Black female workers and white female employers produced understandings about race, gender, and nation in the growing transnational migratory labor economy of the Canal Zone. These authors elevated white women's presence in the Canal Zone as an equally important part of the American imperial endeavor in Panama alongside male administrators, portraying their uniquely feminine role in taming and civilizing the domestic sphere. They articulated these notions of white womanhood in direct relation to their Black West Indian employees, who served as the physical representation of the frontier. West Indian servants, laundresses, cooks, and nannies were the uncivilized and childlike raw material to be shaped by white women's interventions. In the aftermath of construction, when these memoirs were published, Black domestic servants became the symbolic vessels for the gendered political meaning of womanhood and American empire—the contented mammy proof positive of the success of white women's imperial endeavor.

White women in the Canal Zone, as in other contexts, were not bystanders to the project of imperialism but rather played an active role in maintaining its racialized hierarchy.[7] Some attention has been paid to white American women in the Zone, and scholars argue that they were key in importing middle-class values to the Zone and that they "defined their identity through the distinctions they discerned between themselves and those who served them."[8] This scholarship has focused on the white women themselves, not taking into account the historical context of their writings or the constant presence of Black women in their narratives. While American memoirists emphasized the narrative of the domestic sphere as a racialized frontier they had tamed; West Indian women rejected the colonization of their time, independence, and bodies.

White women upheld Panama as a wild domestic frontier to control their maids' movements and sustain white American supremacy in the Canal Zone. But the memoirs also expose these tactics as a fantasy of imperial control. The hidden subversions of West Indian women problematize the nostalgic, nationalist spaces these American women disseminated.[9] Their labor extended far beyond the limited scope of the American home that white women represented in their memoirs. West Indian women asserted their occupational mobility and economic self-determination to their bosses, developed their own businesses networks, and used a repertoire of entrepreneurial practices they had brought from the West Indies and adapted to their situation in Panama to secure earnings. They often worked as semi-independent contractors or independent businesswomen, sidestepping white employers' authority and defining their own economic landscapes. They sometimes circumvented the roll system, forcing customers to pay in gold currency. Their work as higglers, laundresses, boardinghouse keepers, and domestics sustained white Americans and Silver workers who did not receive appropriate provisions from the Canal administration, but it also supplied their own communities. Women provided wages that supported West Indian families in Panama or were sent as remittances back to their kin in the islands. West Indian women's entrepreneurial labors turn our eye to the alternative economies at work in the Canal Zone—parallel to the construction efforts but in service to women's own financial futures and that of their kin.

Working in the Canal Zone

The official records of the Canal administration rarely recorded West Indian women's presence or labor. The available data, though incomplete, nevertheless contextualizes their association with the field of domestic labor. According to the census, only 285 American women worked in the Canal Zone.[10] On the other hand, the census counted 3,274 women from Barbados, Jamaica, St. Lucia, Martinique, Grenada, and other West Indian islands as workers.[11] The most common category of labor for women was domestic service. The census lists 3,206 foreign-born women as "Laborers, Domestics, etc. (not employed by the Isthmian Canal Commission or Panama Railroad)."[12] Eighty percent of these domestics were West Indian, with a handful of Panamanian women.[13] This demographic concentration hints as to why residents of the Canal Zone associated West Indian women with the domestic trade. Zonians would have likely read a Black woman at work in domestic service or higglering as West Indian. Likewise, a Black woman in the Canal Zone might have been assumed to work in domestic service.

However, the number inevitably underestimates the number of Black women actually at work in the Canal Zone—of all the Black women resident in the Zone (which itself underestimates their total population numbers), the census only accounts for 47 percent as employed. The census does not include the many Black West Indian women who did temporary and piecework in American households, providing cooking, cleaning, and laundry service to several families during flexible hours, or the women who walked across Zone towns bringing food to workers and residents. It does not account for the West Indian women who did not reside in the Canal Zone at all and fell by the wayside of population assessments. The majority of West Indian women in the Canal Zone for work are thus not included in the census at all. Some West Indian women did indeed work for the Canal Commission (the census counts forty-six individuals) as hired laundresses, cleaning staff in hospitals and hotels, or as teachers for the segregated schools that serviced West Indian children.[14] These positions were relatively few; the great majority of West Indian immigrant women worked in private or informal domestic service and were not individually recorded as ICC employees. The census's inadequacies highlight the importance of looking beyond the statistical records to understand the centrality of West Indian women's labor to the everyday operations of Canal Zone society and women's own relationship to their work.

Maintaining a white American household in Panama required a massive amount of work, and domestic servants, laundresses, and household help were in high demand. They found their jobs by applying directly to American housewives—by word of mouth or through newspapers and posted advertisements—since there was no central recruiting station for this work. Domestic servants in the Canal Zone not only had to cook, clean, wash, and perform childcare but they also had to do this in an environment of incessant rain, mud, and dust from dynamite blasts, rampant ants and bugs that proliferated in the humid climate, and a low or difficult to acquire supply of basic necessities. The work of a domestic servant in the Zone, then, was not only constant but required a nimble adaptability to the often-unanticipated domestic disasters that befell them.

Many Black West Indian women provided domestic labor as semi-independent contractors, hiring out their services as laundresses to American housewives and businesses in the Zone. Others sold food, provisions, and small trinkets door-to-door as higglers. West Indian women also combined several jobs; as one woman, Ferdilia Capron put it, "I do any work that comes in handy."[15] Scholars of the Caribbean have shown that Black women's enterprising market activity was not a new phenomenon. In fact, enslaved and free Black women had dominated markets during the period of slavery, from New Orleans, to Kingston, to Antigua; they were known as higglers in Jamaica and Barbados and *marchandes* in Dominica, Trinidad, and St. Lucia.[16] By the mid-seventeenth century, white shopkeepers and merchants felt so threatened by Black women's market dominance that they endeavored to bring it under state control. In Barbados, there were several efforts to link higglering to criminality in 1668, 1708, and 1733.[17] The practice did not become officially legal until 1794.[18] In 1831 the colonial legislature of Antigua attempted to shut down the Sunday market, dominated by female traders, and faced a rebellion.[19] Despite consistent attacks on their attempts at self-sufficiency and survival, West Indian women continued to dominate the market trades throughout slavery and after abolition, fostering Black economic independence from the plantation.[20] Throughout the West Indies, higglers would sell prepared foods like bread, fritters, pepper sauces, cassava, and grater-cake for a few farthings as well as cold beverages and small household items out of their small shops that opened out on well-transited public lanes. Susan Proudleigh, the title character of De Lisser's 1915 novel about a Jamaican woman's migration to Panama, established and ran a small food stall in Kingston, "a little shop" which she "stocked with the things she knew would sell."[21]

A good cook in Jamaica earned only twenty-four shillings a month or around $6.[22] Meanwhile, maids in the Zone earned approximately $12 to $15 per month, so moving to Panama could easily mean doubling their pay.[23] A typical "pick and shovel" man earned ten cents per hour doing backbreaking labor which, on an average of ten hours a day, would mean approximately $24 to $30 a month.[24] This means that a West Indian maid could significantly add to a household economy, earning about half a male laborer's income. West Indian laundresses often set their own prices and could reportedly make as much $6 in one *day*, equivalent to a Silver laborer's weekly pay.[25] For comparison, a white Gold Roll nurse earned $50 a month.[26] West Indian women could rarely hope to make Gold Roll wages or be hired in equivalent skilled positions. Nevertheless, Panama held good opportunities to increase their income. Even when not employed by the Isthmian Canal Commission, a laundress could potentially replicate a white laboring woman's earnings through her work. Moreover, Black women negotiated higher wages throughout the years they worked in the Zone. A journalist noted a complaint he heard from a white American woman, reminiscing that, "in the earlier days . . . it was possible to get servants for very low wages," but that Black women kept demanding higher salaries as the construction era went on.[27] At first, some maids received as little as $5 silver a month. But by 1908, it was impossible to hire a West Indian servant for less than $10 a month, and "many get $20 if they are good cooks and help with the baby," meaning they could make the equivalent of a Canal laborer's monthly salary. The journalist guessed that West Indian women had finally "developed a capacity for work and management equal to that of servants in the States," and had internalized American values of productivity.[28] More likely, West Indian women learned to manipulate the high demand by white Americans and low supply of their labor to extract higher wages from their employers.

In the Canal Zone, migrant Black women worked as in-house domestic servants, sold prepared food to workers and produce to white American housewives, and hired out their laundry services. Despite the insecurity they faced there, the Canal Zone offered an urgent demand for their domestic labor and substantially higher wages for their services than they could get in the islands. This not only provided the motivation to move but it also created a labor dynamic that held particular advantages for West Indian women. They were often able to turn down jobs, quit abruptly, or find new employment. American women's memoirs display the clashes that arose when white bosses' assumptions about appropriate labor came into conflict with West Indian women's own expectations.

Memoirs of the "Frontier"

Sue Core's *Maid in Panama*, Elizabeth Parker's *Panama Canal Bride*, and Rose Van Hardeveld's *Make the Dirt Fly!* narrate the nostalgic memories of white American women who lived in the Canal Zone during the era of construction.[29] All three narratives evince a deep preoccupation with the presence and labor of Black West Indian women. Black women served as the locus of concern for white American women for two reasons. First, they represented symbols of racial difference within a feminine sphere in the male-dominated environment of the Canal Zone. They provided a mirror for white women to work out their gendered and racialized anxieties about how to maintain proper standards of domesticity and femininity in a context where these notions had been thrown into disarray by the challenges of the early years of construction. In their memoirs, white women narrativized themselves in specifically gendered and racialized ways. They were the bringers of domesticized civilization to the edge of the frontier, a border marked by Black West Indian women.

Second, West Indian women's indispensability to the official Canal project and their self-reliance presented a symbolic threat to the project of American imperial domesticity.[30] West Indian women's independent labor and successful navigation of the chaotic Canal Zone frontier jeopardized the romanticized, coherent narrative of American dominance of Panama in which white women were invested. By defying American notions of productivity and respectability, Black West Indian women called into question the basis of American sovereignty in the Canal Zone, which depended on the characterization of Black and Brown subjects as uncivilized and unable to prosper without American aid. The memoirists find narrative ways to contain the perceived threat of Black West Indian women's difference by casting them as primitive and premodern. The memoirs show how the project of producing racial difference and upholding racial ideology in the Canal Zone depended on white women's practices of domination in the home. Through the rhetorical device of nostalgia, they produced themselves as pioneers of civilization and West Indian women as the problem to be solved.

The stories these white women told relied on emphasizing racial difference and celebrating white American's technical dominance over their perceived uncivilized servants. But the Panama Canal Zone of the construction period is, like McPherson notes about the American South, "as much a fiction, a story we tell and are told, as it is a fixed geographic space."[31] The memoirs were all published decades after the Canal's completion. The authors' concern with the presence and mobility of their West Indian servants betrays a deep anxiety about the political changes of the postconstruction period and the ambiguous triumph of the Canal enterprise. The memoirs showcase the nostalgic stories these authors told themselves—that they tamed the wild jungle and successfully brought civilization to their backward West Indian domestic workers. They also betray the tenuousness of these fictions.

In the United States, the Canal was widely perceived as an achievement of American technological and military might, and its completion was celebrated in events such as the Panama-Pacific Exposition of 1915.[32] Growing unrest in Panama after the end of construction called this triumphal narrative into question, disrupting notions of the Canal as an undisputed success. Throughout the 1920s and 1930s, West Indian workers organized a series of strikes to protest layoffs and the precipitous drop in wages that followed construction.[33] The economic depression following the completion of the Canal also fostered the growth of nationalist political parties in Panama. Marixa Lasso argues that, during the 1930s, a combination of anti-imperialism and anti-Black racism brought together by nationalist, middle-class politicians inspired a new notion of Panamanian-ness.[34] It was during this period that the Canal Zone began to be strongly associated with imperialist intrusion within Panama. Though the Canal Zone was always a contentious and conflicted space, by the 1930s Zonians had faced massive labor strikes, Panamanian nationalist fervor, and a growing hostility toward American imperial presence. In response, Core, Parker, and Van Hardeveld wrote memoirs of their time in Panama as nostalgic souvenirs of their civilizing project, catalyzed by a felt sense of crisis and criticism.

The massive popularity of frontier nostalgia in the 1950s also powerfully shaped the memoirs. At the time, Westerns dominated publishing, television shows (*Gunsmoke*, 1955), and films (*Davy Crockett*, 1955). By 1959 Westerns accounted for around 24 percent of prime-time programming.[35] The narratives drew inspiration from the early stories of James Fenimore Cooper and repeated the same tropes of the lone white frontiersman dominating the "noble savage," usually through superior technology. These women invested themselves in a feminized version of the frontier narrative, locating themselves on the home front in what Parker called "the Battle of the Maids and Houseboys."[36] The authors used the trope of the frontier to reaffirm a coherent narrative of successful conquest by replaying that encounter as one between white and Black women, where white women civilized their unwieldy

Black servants. The women saw their interactions with maids as a symbolic struggle of civilization against the encroaching jungle of Panama. In their first encounters with West Indian women, these authors cast themselves as lone pioneers with superior intellect and technology and Black women as savages to be dominated.

Rose Van Hardeveld, author of *Make the Dirt Fly!*, was a homesteader originally born in Alsace-Lorraine. Her Dutch husband, Jan Van Hardeveld, had naturalized and claimed eighty acres in Logan County, Nebraska. Although Rose was an immigrant, she portrayed herself repeatedly as an American woman and felt kinship with other white women in the Zone. As a homesteader, she would have already participated in earlier American colonization efforts throughout the West as a project of bringing civilization to an untamed territory, asserting white geographical supremacy, and displacing indigenous peoples.[37] She moved to Panama in late 1906 at the age of twenty-nine to accompany Jan, who had gotten a job with the ICC and been assigned married quarters. Rose and her husband lived in House #1 in Las Cascadas with their four children.[38]

Rose Van Hardeveld comments extensively on Black women within the first few pages of her book. On her first outing alone to the commissary shop, Van Hardeveld met two Black women who she referred to as "Fuzzy-Wuzzys," after a Rudyard Kipling poem: "Two black women in ragged dirty dresses had come in and were jabbering at the Chinese, but he paid no attention to them. I was reminded of Kipling's 'Here's to you, Fuzzy Wuzzy' when I glanced at these two black faces with their hair standing up in a stiff fuzzy brush."[39] Kipling wrote the poem of the same title in 1892 as a celebration of imperial might. The poem gives sarcastic praise to Sudanese Beja warriors who won a battle during the late nineteenth-century Mahdist War, only to eventually lose the war and come under British imperial control. The poem traffics in a tone of humorous condescension. It refers to the Beja warriors as having an "'ayrick 'ead of 'air" and calls them "big black boundin' beggar[s]." The poem reduces the fighting Beja to "Fuzzy Wuzzys" and revels in their loss—"Our orders was to break you, an' of course we went an' did." Van Hardeveld had all these themes in mind when she saw the two Black West Indian women. She read these women as adversaries and, through the poem, compared them to Black soldiers bound to lose a colonial war, despite their temporary advantage. As in the Kipling poem, the primary identifier of the Black "other" was their hair of "stiff, fuzzy brush."

It turned out, however, that the "jabbering" Black women were multilingual, and helped the newly arrived Van Hardeveld negotiate with the Chinese salesperson, who only spoke Spanish. They served as intermediaries and translators, showing their competence in the face of Van Hardeveld's inexperience.[40] It was precisely this that compelled Van Hardeveld to characterize the two women as losing warriors in a colonial war. Van Hardeveld saw the women's easy understanding of the rules and customs of Panama and her own reliance on them as a threat to her natural authority. To call them "Fuzzy-Wuzzys" reset the stage for Van Hardeveld, placing the women as the Beja warriors and herself as the representative of the empire, meant to eventually win the war for dominance. Van Hardeveld continued to rhetorically denigrate Black women by referring to them throughout her memoir as "Fuzzy-Wuzzys." Though she manifested anti-Black racism repeatedly throughout the memoir, she saved particular distaste for Black women, such as the one who often sat near the local cantina about whom Van Hardeveld said, unprompted, "She reminded me of a fat spider waiting for someone to devour. She often smiled and nodded at me in a friendly way, but I hated her."[41]

Both the women at the shop and the woman at the cantina occupied spaces that epitomized the Canal Zone as a contact zone of clashing encounters defined by asymmetrical relations of power and miscomprehension, translation, and heterogeneity.[42] Van Hardeveld was particularly compelled to establish the inferiority of the Black women she encountered in interstitial, public spaces where she (and the Isthmian Canal Commission as a whole) lacked overwhelming power. The commissary, staffed by a Chinese man who spoke no English, and the cantina, typically a gathering space for workers and women looking for entertainment, drinking, and sex, were spaces that threatened the idea of a cohesive, homogeneous space contained by the laws and morality of the Canal Zone. Van Hardeveld saw Black women, who so easily traversed these spaces, as enemies, even when they offered their knowledge to her.

Elizabeth Kittredge Parker's memoir contains less overtly imperialistic tones, but she similarly positioned Black women as ignorant workers desperately in need of training by white women. Parker, the "Panama Canal Bride," was a recent Wellesley College graduate from Dover, Maine. She arrived in the Canal Zone on February 13, 1907, following her fiancé, Charlie, whom she married on the day of her arrival. Charles Liebermann Parker, from Washington, DC, served in various roles in the Quartermaster's Department throughout construction, including as superintendent of labor, quarters, and subsistence in Gorgona. Parker met her first maid soon after her arrival, during her wedding breakfast: "As we sat down to our wedding breakfast, I was aware of more contrasts—the long table on the narrow screened porch, thick white china, plated silver, *pâté de fois gras*, champagne, roast turkey,—all served awkwardly by a little Jamaican maid in a gingham dress."[43] Parker first met this young West Indian woman inside her own newly established home and immediately after her wedding. Thus, her encounter was less plagued with anxiety than Van Hardeveld's commissary conversation and instead served to reaffirm her dominance of a domestic American space. The extravagant array of furniture, silverware, and food seemed to her harmonious, with the awkward maid as the incongruent outsider. The rest of her memoir reiterates this contrast and finds Parker attempting to maintain the standard of civilization she presumes stands against the encroaching otherness of West Indians and the Panamanian jungle.

Later, Parker relates a conversation with a friend who was trying to find a new maid. Her friend, Kay, says about West Indian women that "they seem so stupid, but when I tried to do without one, I decided they weren't so dumb after all. We have to realize they've never seen the inside of a civilized home before. They've always cooked on charcoal braziers, washed their clothes in the river, and used gourds for dishes."[44] Parker and her friend Kay both agreed that West Indian women provided an invaluable service and admit that they had misjudged their maids' skills. However, they also undercut these comments by simultaneously characterizing West Indian women as uncivilized. They associated Black women with nature (gourds, the river) while positioning themselves as masters of the civilized, technologically advanced home. As in Van Hardeveld's encounters, Parker and her friend designated West Indian women as uncivilized precisely in the moments when their dependence on Black women's work became most explicit.

Sue Core, the editor of *Maid in Panama*, worked as a fifth-grade teacher in Ancon Elementary School in the Canal Zone for thirty-three years, from 1919 until her retirement in May 1952.[45] Themes of jungles and frontiers abound in many of her works. Though her books never circulated widely in the United States, her teaching and writing continue to be fondly remembered in ex-Zonian circles, such as the online group "Canal Zone Brats."[46] *Maid in Panama* contains a collection of stories submitted by Canal Zone old-timers that chronicle their experiences with Black workers, but primarily domestic servants. In it, Americans relate humorous anecdotes about the intriguing differences they perceived in their servants, emphasizing at every turn the hierarchy of civilized whites to raw Black workers, such as in a story titled "The Millinery Art": "Another trial was the raw, inexperienced household servants who were the best to be had, then; brawny and cheerful, but appallingly ignorant black women fresh from the bush country of the various island hinterlands from which they had come. Training and teaching them the habits and customs of American households was almost as much a job as the digging of Culebra Cut itself."[47] By listing white women's trials, the narrator of this story elevated white women's domestic and social labor to that of the men building the Canal. They, even more so than the men, were responsible for rearing the Canal from its infancy—the mothers of its civilization. The infancy did not just refer to the Canal project but also to the raw state of the landscape and the servants, who originated in the bush country. The story presented Black women as prehistorical, from a hinterland in the infancy of development, and thus requiring training from white American women. Their brawn went hand in hand with their ignorance; their physical appearance was again presented as evidence of their lack of civilization and lack of femininity. Nostalgic remembrances like *Maid in Panama* attempted to fix Black womanhood to natural servitude by positioning Black women as ignorant, inexperienced, and wild. In this representation, Black women were barely considered human but rather as animals "fresh from the bush."

The majority of the stories in *Maid in Panama* give short accounts of language mishaps or mistranslations. In uncannily similar narratives, a Black maid given an order by her boss humorously fails at her task by misunderstanding a key word. For example, Mabel the maid, after being asked to "put the flowers in water to keep them fresh," dunked rose buds face down in a bowl of water, to the great dismay of Mrs. Brown. These stories suggest the domestic frontier as an area that *required* intervention because of West Indian maids' ineptitude. Maids were repeatedly shown as uncivilized, unable to use technology, understand correct English, or interpret social cues that seemed natural to American housewives. Though they might seem mostly silly or humorous, it is really these stories that center the collection—everyday mishaps between maid and boss provided the commonsense justification that West Indians were naturally inclined to be servants and required instruction. Moreover, the stories all obscure any force white bosses exerted over Black maids—not a single maid was shown to be punished or reprimanded in the stories for any of their mistakes. Core refers to the relationship between "white boss and colored worker" as one of "mutual exasperated tolerance," erasing the implied power dynamics by implying symmetry between the two women.[48] The dynamic these authors present is one of benevolent maternalism, where white female bosses struggle to train childlike and inept Black maids as the frontline of the battle against the dangerous and disordered frontier.

The increased criticism the Canal project faced in the 1930s and 1940s and the popularity of frontier stories explain the emergence of these various memoirs, but it is the labor relation between white American women and West Indian workers during construction that structures the narratives they tell. These authors used the genre of women's memoir to assert their importance alongside men in crafting and perpetuating the project of American progress. To do this, they positioned themselves as frontierswomen, and Black women as the raw material that they dominated discursively and spatially. The stories repeatedly contain Black women within white American domestic spaces, where bosses could reiterate their powerful notions of a superior Western civilization and their maid's infant-like inferiority. However, the stories also belie a deep anxiety about Black women when they stepped outside of the boundaries set by their bosses as this questioned the narratives of successful dominance white women sought to perpetuate in their memoirs. Black women often resisted white women's project of containment by taking advantage of the high demand for their labor and their mobility.

"The Battle of the Maids and Houseboys"

Live-in domestic servants had to negotiate a difficult position while working in the Zone. In exchange for guaranteed housing and the semblance of

respectability and job security that came with working for an American employer, domestic servants faced increased surveillance and a constant demand
on their time and labor. They were subject to the whims of their employers
and to specific rules about time off, recreation, dress, and behavior. They also
had the closest relationship to white American families, assisting them in
their everyday lives, seeing their moments of frustration and difficulty, cooking their meals, and taking care of their young children.

For white American employers, "the battle of the maids and houseboys"
involved limiting the movement, choices, and self-expression of domestic
workers in order to instill American ideals of cleanliness, respectability, thrift,
and productivity. They perceived any attempt at self-determination by West
Indian servants as an affront to their authority. By working slowly, quitting,
refusing to do certain work, or choosing to prioritize their personal desires,
West Indian women consciously and unconsciously made bosses' dependence
on them visible and rejected impositions on their freedoms.[49] For example,
Miriam, one of Van Hardeveld's first maids, "treated us with condescending
tolerance."[50] Though she lived within walking distance from her bosses'
house, Van Hardeveld complained, "Miriam, fat and dignified, made the trip
in twenty or thirty minutes" whereas it should have, in her opinion, only
taken five.[51] Miriam ignored her boss's understanding of timeliness, working at her own pace while understanding her work's vitality to the maintenance of her boss's expectations of life in Panama.

Another West Indian maid, Rose, similarly contested the recriminations
from the lady of the house that her cleaning was slapdash. After Mrs. Johnson "remonstrated gently" with her about this, Rose responded, "You cyan't
have every t'ing, you know. You never gits good biscuits and clean corners
from the same maid!"[52] Mrs. Johnson remembered this as an amusing and
placid encounter, where Rose answered in an "unabashedly acquiescent"
manner. Mrs. Johnson's story effaces the hierarchical power she held over
Rose, instead reiterating fictions of the amiable and happy maid, submissive
in her servitude. In fact, Rose did not "unabashedly acquiesce" to Mrs. Johnson but rather rebuffed her boss's complaint and refused to improve her house
cleaning. Rose reiterated her own skill with cooking good biscuits and presented that as sufficient labor. She might have been purposefully avoiding the
onerous work of cleaning, especially for a finicky housekeeper like Mrs. John-

son. Without knowing Rose's precise motivations, we can nevertheless see her attempt at managing her boss's expectations. West Indian women across the Zone likely relied on these everyday strategies to control their own labor.

White American women's memoirs are deeply concerned with even minute aspects of West Indian domestic servants' intimate lives. For example, Mrs. Morrison spoke about her first "girl," Jasmine, a young woman from Barbados, saying:

> What Jasmine knew about the ways of white folks could have been incorporated on the point of a needle without undue crowding. However, be it said to her credit, she was willing. So much so that she became practically one of the family, and stayed with them for fifteen years.
>
> One of her lady's earliest memories of Jasmine harks back to the first Sunday she was with them. A day or so before, one of her boys had upset a bottle of red ink on the kitchen table, and his mother, having nothing else handy, grabbed a sponge lying near, and mopped it up. The sponge, being brightly crimson, was tossed into the garbage pail. Not to repose there unblossomed and unseen, however. On Sunday morning Mrs. Morrison spied it gaily and triumphantly decorating the hat of Jasmine as she went proudly off to church.[53]

For white American women, managing the household meant keeping some version of order. As scholars have described for the nineteenth-century British imperial context, it meant maintaining clear boundaries between order and disorder.[54] Cleaning, anthropologist Mary Douglas explains, is "not a negative movement, but a positive effort to organize the environment . . . making it conform to an idea."[55] Mrs. Morrison perceived the sponge as a used and dirty item after cleaning up the red spill and saw her disposal of it as a positive act of cleaning. Due to Jasmine's assumption that the sponge had other uses, the narrator implicitly characterized her as part of the disorder, an "Other" that needed to be organized into the boundaries created by this housewife. Jasmine did not conform to the ideas of order and civilization that her white employer espoused, instead repurposing Mrs. Morrison's discarded sponge as a fashionable accessory.

The story repeats the myth of domestic servants being "one of the family."[56] This phrase obscures power dynamics and positions the domestic servant as an always conditional, unequal member. Jasmine could never gain the benefits of actual family. The phrase here serves not to incorporate Jasmine but to infantilize her, positioning her as an ignorant childlike figure (what she knew could fit "on the point of a needle"). The myth of the family, as Anne McClintock has argued, serves to sanction social hierarchy within a presumably organic, ahistorical institution that placed men as patriarchal leaders of naturally subservient women and children.[57] The image of the family guaranteed "social difference as a category of nature" that could be extended to legitimize exclusions in nationalist and imperialist projects.[58] In the case of Jasmine, her boss granted her status within the family only by characterizing her as uneducated, ultimately reinforcing that she was only part of the family in the sense that she was a subordinate. The comment serves to emphasize that Jasmine was *not* family so she did not qualify for its benefits, and that only white Americans had the power to designate others as insiders. Positioning maids as one of the family is, like the frontier, a tenuous fiction built by white women to maintain the racial hierarchies of the employer-domestic relationship.

As with other encounters in the memoirs, the white woman saw a Black woman's clothing as a particularly significant site of contention. Mrs. Morrison rhetorically tried to undercut Jasmine's joy in her new garment by positioning her as a fool. Yet the story ends with a hint of jealousy in the narrator's last phrase; though she was making fun of Jasmine, it is ultimately Jasmine who proudly displayed her new accessory on the way to church while Mrs. Morrison is left in the awkward position of spying on her maid. A story about a sponge might seem inconsequential, but it implies that American women saw small domestic battles over keeping order, both in terms of cleanliness and in terms of social hierarchy, as supremely important in conquering the Canal Zone. More importantly, it shows how a domestic servant like Jasmine endured these attempts at control, physically rejecting the unspoken laws of cleanliness in the American household and prioritizing her own appearance and church community. Jasmine did not confront her employer outright (though we can leave open the possibility that she was indeed trying to slyly provoke her boss). Nevertheless, Mrs. Morrison perceived Jasmine's inversion of the sponge's value as a threat to her authority within the American domestic realm.[59] Jasmine—like Miriam, Rose, and other West Indian women—worked against fictions of being one of the family by prioritizing her own needs and desires, thus questioning the supposedly natural state of her servitude and the ideals that governed the American home for white women.

Like Jasmine, many Black West Indian working women promoted their own sense of respectability and pride through their dress, ignoring white women's aesthetic sensibilities. White American women consistently mentioned the clothes and appearance of the Black women around them in their memoirs, always noting these as markers of cultural difference and disparaging West Indian women's self-presentation. Nevertheless, West Indian women wore colorful and elaborate clothing, even while performing the difficult labors of domestic service or higglering, and thus embodied their own ideas of dignity and self-determination.

Parker remarked on the clothing of the first West Indian higgler she encountered: "The basque was tight fitting and around her neck, she wore a gay kerchief. Another was perched on her proud head, intricately folded—its ends standing up like two little birds about to fly from their nest."[60] The comments about clothing, though sometimes positive, were always used by these white women to mark cultural difference. In this scene, for example, Parker expressed surprise at the Black woman's elegance and pride in her clothing. Parker showed this same surprise at the juxtaposition of her new Black maid Sarah wearing a crisp white apron upon first seeing her next to the foie gras, thereby implying there was a contradiction between Blackness and propriety.[61] In both cases, Parker expressed curiosity, not disdain. Nevertheless, she found elegant, neat clothes unusual and unexpected when worn by Black women. The clothing was notable to her only because Black women had donned it, as most white women's clothing went entirely unremarked.

Every mention of Black women's clothing in these memoirs occurs as white women observed Black women at work. As such, their remarks were always enmeshed with understandings about proper behavior and proper labor. For white women, Black women's often extravagant clothing was proof of their banality, indulgence, and poor economic sense, which also manifested in their labor practices. Van Hardeveld made this connection explicit when discussing the washerwoman she had hired: "She was a Barbadian girl named Princess Brown. She came dressed in a bright pink silk dress with a straw sailor hat pinned to her hair. Without removing any of her finery, or losing any of her dignity, she sat in a chair beside the tub of clothes and began a leisurely rubbing between her hands; although she remained several days, she never accelerated her pace nor finished the tub of clothes."[62] Van Hardeveld went on to fire Princess Brown, though she continued to face the same issues with her successors, commenting that, "with the whole Isthmus teeming with black women and girls who should have been glad to obtain work, we could not find one person that was efficient or dependable."[63] Van Hardeveld suggested that Black women's exuberant clothing and self-presentation was representative of their laziness and implied a certain underserved pompousness in Princess Brown's demeanor. Van Hardeveld and other white American women thus portrayed Black women as their opposite—vain, whereas white women were Spartan; lazy and slow, whereas white women were hardworking. Princess Brown defined the pace and style of her work for Van Hardeveld, thwarting the white woman's attempt at efficiency. Princess prioritized maintaining her finery and dignity over completing the laundry work on her boss's time line. Perhaps Princess came from a slightly higher social class in Barbados and was unused (or averse) to doing manual labor, perhaps she chafed at Van Hardeveld's expectations, perhaps she merely wanted to look fabulous. Whatever the case may be, the story makes clear that Princess Brown was less than concerned with a white woman's opinion.

White women in the Zone failed to perceive what the elegant dresses and headpieces might have meant to Black West Indian women, materially and symbolically. Rather than deference to the labor hierarchy between Black and white women as the predominant framework of their lives, Black women's exuberant clothing displayed an assertive commitment to public expression. That is, while white Americans tried to contain Black women's movement and expression, these women were instead "able to define their own version of freedom that included self-determination and personal pride" through their clothing purchases and display.[64] Moreover, they emphatically occupied both public spaces and private American homes, despite attempts to discipline their behavior. This was not merely banal consumption and personal ostentatiousness but a representation of Black women's investment in the "rituals of status and self-presentation" they had brought with them from the islands.[65] White women's obsession with Black women's clothing further reiterates its importance, at least to their own understanding of their relations with their workers. For white women, their maids' colorful clothes were both a marker of their cultural difference and an affront to the standardized norms of civilization the Canal project tried to promote. But the clothes represented the material fruits of these women's labor, particularly in the early years of the Canal Zone, when fine cloth and dresses were not easily acquired. The rules of consumption during construction instructed white women to be thrifty and resourceful, to make do without the fineries of life stateside. Black women instead flaunted colorful, extravagant clothing while also performing hard labor, defying the easy categorizations of frontier life in which white women were invested.

Mobile Market Entrepreneurs

Black West Indian women functioned beyond the fictionalized frameworks of subservient nostalgia that white women remembered. The same stories, read from the perspective of Black women's experiences, show how these women used their position as flexible, uncontracted labor to cultivate financial and spatial self-determination within the racialized labor hierarchies of the Zone. Though the ICC ostensibly provided food and laundry services to Canal Zone residents, it was in fact West Indian women who filled the gap in the high demand for both. This labor directly served white Americans, but it also provided for West Indian needs. As higglers, boardinghouse keepers, and laundresses, West Indian women engaged in entrepreneurial practices adapted from the islands that fostered commercial and social networks in the Zone in the service of other West Indians. Their market strategies of mobility and flexibility were a "visible everyday negotiation" of the insecurity of the Canal Zone; that is, they were strategies meant to secure livelihoods for themselves and their families while vulnerable to the lack of legal protection and the consistent assault on their independence by Canal administrators and white American bosses.[66]

White American women such as Rose Van Hardeveld repeatedly disavowed the labor of West Indian women, arguing that American women did
most of the housework themselves "because they could not bear the messy
negress around."[67] White women were in fact heavily dependent on West
Indian women's labor. In one instance, for example, Parker despaired about
her ruined dinner party after the commissary informed her they were out of
leg of lamb. Back in her house, she saw Marie, a Martinican higgler, coming
up the path: "Much to my joy, she had a beautiful Spanish mackerel in her
basket. Wonderful, I thought. At least, we can have a fish course! Sarah [her
maid] could fry fish beautifully. I gave a sigh of relief." Her dinner party was
saved by the provisions and service of two West Indian women.

Higglers like Marie appear as crucial interlocutors for these white women,
given that they provided many of the daily foods the commissary could not
stock and often served as their primary connection to the world outside of
the American home. Already a common practice in the islands, higglering
translated easily to the Canal, where American commissaries struggled to
keep up with the demands of the ever-growing towns. Van Hardeveld complained about the difficulty of getting to her local commissary, which was located in the town of Empire two miles away. Though she could reach it by
train, "it meant lagging around in the heat for long hours, and the trip had
to be made almost every day."[68] Moreover, commissaries, which in the early
years refused to import foodstuffs from Panama, offered a very limited supply of food.[69] Even if Americans made a trip to Panama, "one could buy every
possible kind of food" only "at terrible prices!"[70] Meals in the early days often meant basic canned staples and, even after more commissaries opened
throughout the Zone, they were, Van Hardeveld recalled, "not much more
than a shed, but gratifyingly accessible to me after these long months of
having to travel long distances for food or do without. There were staples
and canned goods, including milk, onions and potatoes and once in a great
while a few pale shrunken cabbages."[71] American women traveled or sent their
maids to the commissaries early to line up and acquire perishable goods
like meat, fish, and vegetables before they inevitably ran out. More likely,
they acquired their fresh food from local higglers.

Higglers traveled through American neighborhoods, selling food to the
housewives who would otherwise have had to travel quite far to the commis-

saries where the range of goods was limited, but they also provided for their own underserved communities. Commissaries were segregated and stocked few of the foods that West Indians enjoyed. Later, in response to protests by West Indian workers, the ICC began importing sweet potatoes, yams, and codfish.[72] Meanwhile, the mess halls served West Indians three meals a day for nine cents each, but the food was often inedible and the mess hall offered no seats for the workers. According to a food supplier from Omaha, "The only difference I could see between the way they fed those negroes and the way I feed my hogs is that the food was put on a tin plate instead of a trough."[73] Amos Clarke, a West Indian Silver Roll worker, described the work of higglers as an essential part of his morning routine: "In those days, there were no restaurants. In the morning, two women of color would approach our place of work each one carrying a tray with hot coffee, bread and butter, selling them for ten cents." Clarke credits two Jamaican women for his sustenance, Mariam Cunningson and Caroline Lowe.[74] Lowe remained in Panama her whole life and lived to be over one hundred years old.[75] In the same act, higglers like Cunningson and Lowe fed the Canal's workforce, made some money for themselves, and sustained their own communities—a practice of survival and care inseparable from the structures of racial capitalism in the Zone.

Unlike the ICC commissaries, higglers had no official provider and depended on the produce grown on their small, independent plots or gathered from trustworthy farm contacts. From her porch, Rose Van Hardeveld could see a West Indian home at the edge of "the jungle" where "wild lemons, oranges, and other luscious fruit, rice and cassava grew in well-cared for profusion around the hut."[76] West Indian women like Augusta Dunlop in Pedro Miguel owned land where they grew ackee, breadfruit, guanabana (soursop), mango, papaya, and yucca.[77] Unlike white Americans, many of these West Indian women would have been familiar with the produce that grew in the tropics and could re-create their agricultural practices from the islands. Higglers like Marie, Mariam Cunningson, and Caroline Lowe likely created complex commercial networks in the Canal Zone, using their farms and business relationships to provide an indispensable service.

White women's dependence on Black women's market labor is obvious in another *Maid in Panama* story.[78] The author tells of her daily vegetable vendor, an older Jamaican woman she calls "the Hoo-Hoo lady," due to the energetic cry she gave in the mornings to make her presence known, which sounded "somewhat like the call of a cookoo in the jungle." As in Van Hardeveld's memoir, the narrator made an easy and naturalized analogy between a West Indian female worker and an animal. Like many West Indian women, the "Hoo-Hoo lady" held multiple jobs to support her large family—she sold vegetables "up and down Ancon Blvd . . . on the days that she doesn't wash clothes for her two or three customers."[79] The returns from individual items were small—each tomato was ten cents, a small bag of green beans fifteen cents—but they could add up.

The narrator noted that, despite the difficulty of her work trekking in the humid tropical weather to different homes carrying a heavy load, "Hoo-Hoo" always seemed serene because she had become "inured to [the] disappointment" that must have been an everyday part of her job when customers did not buy her products. The story highlights the woman's skill at selling her wares—the narrator even noted that she could not control herself from buying something every time the saleswoman came around.[80] The story was meant to celebrate the "Hoo-Hoo" lady's commercial prowess, though ultimately it traffics in the same stereotypes white women memoirists reiterated about West Indian women—their animalistic nature, their hardening to emotion. However, the scene also reinforces the fact that this West Indian woman worked energetically, that she had a large family whom she supported financially, that she worked multiple jobs and had several steady customers, and that her products were essential and enticing for white Americans. Rather than the placid "mammy" of the *Maid in Panama* cover, the story of the "Hoo-Hoo" lady tells us about a businesswoman who knowingly exploited the market need for her goods by white American residents, carving out notoriety as a local merchant.

Higglers had to negotiate prices with their customers, who were occasionally reticent to pay the amounts these women could demand. Van Hardeveld tells a story of marines buying from a higgler: "[They] bargained long and loud for a luscious pineapple, which the taller of the two reached up and took from the tray on her head. They pretended they were going without paying for it, as the price seemed too high. 'De H'Americanos, dem too rude,' the vendor told the universe, with a sullen face. The boys threw a coin and called, 'Keep the change,' as they went on. The vendor's face beamed as she exclaimed,

'De H'Americanos, dem too sweet!'"[81] Van Hardeveld does not quite recognize any of the higgler's dexterity in this scene, seeing her instead as a buffoonish character, a fool whose quick change of heart depends entirely on the patronage of her American customers. The marines could have stolen the pineapple and left the higgler unpaid with impunity. Since West Indian women had few legal avenues to pursue small claims of robbery against white Americans in the Canal Zone, a higgler would have had to bear the cost of the theft. Higglers likely had to rely on different techniques to ensure payment; this woman, for example, loudly lamented the Marines' behavior until they paid up. West Indian women faced consistent belittling from customers but used their cunning to haggle with them and eventually receive payment (as suggested by this story, even higher pay than the pineapple commanded). Americans may have established the racialized standards of labor value in the Canal Zone through the roll system, but Black West Indian women consistently evaded the absoluteness of that system by manipulating American desire for their services and valuing their own work above the prices Americans expected. Beyond merely responding to American demand, these higglers cultivated their own plots of land, provided food for West Indian communities, and supported their families with the profits of their labor. Their market practices likely expanded Americans' tastes for Caribbean produce and foodstuffs with which they were previously unfamiliar.

Many West Indian women worked independently and contracted out their various services as domestics and laundresses to American housewives. Some women would even ask American clients to provide the start-up costs for their business, as in this story where a housewife describes her first interaction with a new laundress: "Kate, first wash woman I had on the Isthmus, outlined for me during our initial conference, the various purchases I should make to start off our laundress-lady combination. She enumerated soap, starch, blueing, clothes pins, ironing board, iron, washboard and tub. Kate was a particular lady of definite convictions, and gave me careful instructions as to the exact brand of each commodity which she preferred. Wishing to please her, I made careful note in order not to make a mistake in their purchase."[82] The narrator narrowed in on the importance of the "laundress-lady combination," a crucial labor relationship in the Panama Canal Zone where steam laundries were uncommon and dirt abounded. White women complained repeatedly about the extreme difficulty of doing laundry. They often characterized the activity as a symbolic cleansing of pristine white clothes and tableware of the dirt and uncleanliness of Panama. The narrator recounted the story in a humorous tone, reversing the authority between her and Kate and highlighting the absurdity of the white American lady having to do work for the laundress. Yet she did indeed provide these numerous implements for Kate, who then used her employer's capital to set up an independent business in the Canal Zone.

In the early years of construction, the Canal Zone only had one machine-washing facility, in Cristobal. Laundry was collected daily by the district quartermasters and sent back within a week. In 1912 the company reported serving 7,260 employees monthly, so clearly many of the over seventy thousand residents did not rely on the commission laundry facilities for their needs.[83] Personal household machines were virtually unheard of at the time, so most laundry had to be done outside without the aid of electricity. Most West Indian women who contracted with American families washed clothes in backyards using tubs and soap provided by their bosses. Others, who did not have patrons, did laundry at the river: "One of the familiar sights of this hamlet is the village washing place, a pool near the railroad tracks, formed by the swirling of the water in the Frijolita River at a point where it is turned at right angles to its previous course by the interposition of a bank of clay and rock. The method of washing clothes among the lower-class natives and the West Indians can be observed here."[84] These river laundries were meeting grounds for the women who would get together to work and pass the time while doing this difficult and monotonous task. These spots indeed became familiar sights to Americans, who often remarked on the community of laundresses in the press and disseminated images like the color illustration below (Figure 3) in popular publications about the Canal. The image identified the Black laundresses at Taboga as subjects of racial curiosity, noting that "Taboga, site of the Commission sanitarium, is the most picturesque point readily accessible from Panama City. The laundry place is the gathering point for the women in the village."[85]

The Black laundresses are depicted in a jungle distant from the urban environment of the Canal Zone and thus the civilizing force of the American

THE WASHING PLACE AT TABOGA

Figure 3. F. E. Wright, "The Washing Place at Taboga," 1913, watercolor. Willis John Abbot, *Panama and the Canal in Picture and Prose* (New York: Syndicate Publishing Company, 1913). Photographic insert between pages 152 and 153.

home. The illustration used an impressionist technique to dissociate the women from the technological feats of the Canal, relegating them to a hazy, separate world, while still asserting an anthropological gaze on their bodies and labor. The topless woman in the background serves not as an object of sexual desire but to reiterate Black women's bodies as available sites of gendered racial difference for American viewers. The illustration unlinks West Indian women's labor from the local urban economy, instead positioning them as quaint, picturesque outsiders with little to contribute to the Canal project. U.S. audiences sought out images such as these as a visual space in which to imagine the reach of America's rule into the boundaries of civilization, marked here by the presence of Black women.

Washing laundry, a seemingly menial task, was essential to the smooth operations of the Canal, from house to hospital to hotel. Yet white women continued to belittle this labor performed by Black women:

Getting our laundry done was another trying problem. On the far bank of the stream, squatted on the rocks, a company of women gathered each day to wash. 'The city laundry,' said one of the men jocularly. Here buttons were knocked off clothing with a lavish hand, but never found or sewed on again. I watched this gabbling bunch of black women at their work and decided that our family wash should never go to the *city laundry*. The clothes were soused in the water, rubbed all over with soap, then placed on a rock, pounded and beaten with a mighty swack-swack.[86]

Rose Van Hardeveld located these river laundries as sites of dirtiness and savagery, sarcastically separating them from white American spaces. But her comment also shows how rivers functioned as social spaces for working West Indian women that white Americans could not penetrate or understand. Black laundresses could work on their own time, among friends, and were free to do as they liked. While their employers attempted to contain their movement and regulate their work inside the American home, they built robust social networks and carved their own public work spaces in areas Americans perceived as the outskirts. In these corners of swirling water and layered clay, West Indian women gathered and talked as they performed this essential service.

At the official Cristobal laundry, prices could range from one cent for washing a collar to five dollars for cleaning and pressing a fancy dress.[87] West Indian women, not beholden to the price schemes of the ICC, could and often did charge higher prices for their work. One American man described haggling prices with a Black laundress as a battle with an adversary: "A week on shipboard with a baby produced considerable soiled clothing and the land-lady recommended a laundress, who, after counting up to sixty-eight pieces, offered to launder them for twenty-five cents 'American money' a piece. I saved her life by leaping quickly in front of my wife, and she finally consented to do the laundering for ten cents gold a piece."[88] The narrator presents him-self as a victim of the laundress's attempt at taking advantage of a young, white American family. But his story also shows that Black laundresses un-derstood the high demand for their work and negotiated for higher prices. This laundress sized up her American clients and asked directly for gold American coin, thus assigning a higher value to her labor and defying the racial discrimination of the roll system.

As the previous chapters have shown, working West Indian women faced intense surveillance of their relationship and intimate practices through lo-cal Canal Zone ordinances and police investigations. They also faced habit-ual judgment from bosses and customers, who felt righteous in pointing out the perceived moral failings of the West Indian women around them. In a suggestive story, a white American woman named Mrs. Phelps urgently needed to get her laundry done and drove to one of the "colored" neighbor-hoods of the Canal Zone in search of her usual laundress, Angelina. When she walked in, Mrs. Phelps "found Angelina's room fairly swarming with progeny. Little chocolate-colored pickaninnies of every age and hue stood in wooly-headed curiosity, looking at their mammy's 'White Lady' come to call. Among the brood, Mrs. Phelps noted with amazement one little white child about two years old . . . evidently a relic of some white man's disregard for the color line." Mrs. Phelps saw the child as evidence of immoral interracial sex. She became taken with the child and demanded that Angelina compli-ment the "pretty baby," both calling attention to the child's difference from the other children and implying that the baby was somehow more deserving of praise for its lighter skin. Angelina responded with little enthusiasm. Eventually, "the stolid indifference of her face changed a trifle and she burst out, 'Yes'm, he's pretty, all right. But tells you for true, Miz Phelps, I ain't never goin' to have no more white babies. They shows the dirt too plain!'"[89]

Mrs. Phelps repeatedly asked Angelina to make sense of the lighter-skinned child for her, her obvious desperation for an answer indicating a sense of alienation and threat when confronted with the physical evidence of someone crossing the color line. She sought affirmation of the value of white skin from her laundress, but Angelina did not answer her interpellation. She instead refuted Mrs. Phelps's assessment of the child's beauty, flipping the implied racial hierarchy of her comment. Angelina retorted that it was whiteness, not Blackness, that is unclean and "shows the dirt." Angelina's response to Mrs. Phelps also functions as reproach to her boss for interrupting her off-work hours and intruding into her private life. Her comment was ultimately no protection against an employer who invaded her home, but it still boldly expressed Angelina's discomfort with Mrs. Phelps's insinuations and made a claim on her own time, labor, and privacy.

Whereas live-in domestic workers shared their daily lives with their bosses, most laundresses maintained a separate home life, traveling to American neighborhoods only to work. The "laundress-lady" relationship depended on carefully constructed boundaries. The American housewife clearly held the economic power, but the stories show that most white women behaved with a certain deference toward West Indian laundresses because the service they provided seemed so grueling, yet so necessary. Because laundresses worked as semi-independent contractors, they had more leeway in relationship to American "ladies" than domestic servants. Rose Van Hardeveld commented on what she perceived as laundresses' arrogance saying, "Washerwomen were asked to clean the kitchen floor after they finished the washing, which seemed to them an outrage."[90] In fact, Van Hardeveld's quote highlights West Indian laundresses' resistance to their bosses' additional expectations and demands. They could and did refuse to do extra work for their customers, along with demanding high prices for their essential labor. Despite living apart from American homes, their spaces could be invaded and criticized by their bosses, as Mrs. Phelps did with Angelina. This they also resisted, sometimes overtly calling out the "dirt" that marked the relationships between white and Black residents of the Canal Zone, structured as they were by segregation and criminalization.

Many women did not work for white Americans at all, instead providing services almost exclusively to Silver Roll laborers. Jane Hall, the woman from the opening of this book, owned three boardinghouses in the town of Culebra. Culebra was teeming with laborers working on one of the most dangerous sites in the Canal, the Culebra Cut, where the mountainous landscape posed a challenge to Canal engineers who wished to join Gatun Lake with the Pacific Ocean. Hall chose a strategic site to set up a boardinghouse, a place where demand for worker housing outweighed supply, ensuring that her business would grow. Like other West Indian women before her, Jane Hall capitalized on the opportunities opened up by the migrant labor regimes of U.S. expansion for her own gain, but she also provided necessary housing for underserved Silver laborers.

Single West Indian workers, forced to live in low-quality housing and eat low-quality food, often sought shelter outside the ICC barracks. In a hearing before the U.S. Senate, the first chief engineer of the Canal, John F. Wallace, admitted that "we were never able to house the Negroes."[91] He further explained the difficulty of running a boardinghouse for West Indian workers: "If we got a man to keep a boarding house, and he boarded our employees, he had to run the risk of collecting their board, you understand, from the men. If they suddenly took a notion to go home, and left the Isthmus, and left that board uncollected, the keeper of the boarding house would lose that money."[92] Due to the high turnover of Silver Roll workers, Wallace explained, running a boardinghouse was not a financially stable enterprise, even for the American government. It was instead West Indian women like Jane Hall who took it on themselves to provide this service, realizing the potential economic benefits.

In 1906 Hall owned two houses and was in the process of building a third. A local contractor described one of the houses as having two floors, topped with zinc roofs, and a veranda in front.[93] For a contract of 12.00 Panamanian silver a month, Hall would rent a room with a bed and a dresser. The construction and repair of her various houses as well as her interactions with various boarders brought her repeatedly to the Canal Zone District courts, usually in pursuit of unpaid debts. Between 1906 and 1907, Hall participated in six cases brought to the Second Judicial Circuit Civil Court at Empire. Three cases deal with Hall's debt to builders contracted to repair and frame her properties, while the rest regard debts tenants owed her. Hall's persistent interactions with the courts show her as a distinct public figure in Culebra, well-known to both West Indian workers and American administrators. The cases evidence how Hall negotiated with the highest institutions of power in the Canal Zone to protect her independent business and earnings. However, this same business depended on the extractive labor regime that forced Silver workers into desperate housing situations and punished them even for minor debts.

On August 6, 1906, Hall hired the contractor Rufus Melhado to begin work on one of her houses.[94] The contract described the structure: an 80 × 30 two-floor building, with seventeen doors and seven windows, independent rooms on the top floor, and partitions on the ground floor. After working on the house for a while, Rufus sued Jane for debt, claiming that she had not paid any of the promised installments. Jane countered that Rufus had not finished the construction and, having left the house unfinished, should not expect payment. The court interviewed witnesses and sent an inspector to the house, who revealed that Melhado had, in fact, left the house "insecure" and not "worth any value." After much deliberation and "heated discussion between the contestants," the municipal court judged in favor of Melhado to the sum of 125.00 silver. Hall immediately asked for an appeal. During the appeal, the court upheld the previous decision in favor of Melhado. However, the damages were assessed at a much lower value, granting Melhado only 25.00 silver plus court fees around $13.00. Though she lost the case, Hall was willing to manipulate the judicial system until she paid a substantially lower sum.

Hall's already sizable holdings in 1906 raise the question of her background before the construction period. The cases contain no biographical information. Jane could have arrived in Panama decades before the Americans, during the French construction. It is plausible that Jane was already a businesswoman in Jamaica or at least traveled with enough money to cover the start-up costs of her boardinghouse. In nineteenth-century Jamaica, "colored" women were the most common providers of hospitality and were often mistresses to white men who funded the establishment of their lodging houses.[95] Taking advantage of the economic situation in the Canal and sensing the need for worker housing, Jane could have traveled to Panama to establish a boardinghouse and perhaps to escape the bonds tying her to a white man in the islands. Jane Hall, like other West Indian laundresses, higglers, and domestic servants of the Canal Zone, provided intimate labor that was essential to sustaining the Canal project. Unlike them, however, she was not tied directly to white American customers and employers; instead, she negotiated her business with other Silver residents through the Canal Zone courts. By suing Silver workers, Hall protected her independent business and amassed personal wealth.

In the case that opened this book, Hall sued her tenant, China Byasta, in March 1907 for debt on his rent.[96] Hall alleged that Byasta had vacated his room without proper notice and without paying the remaining rent. Byasta refuted this account, saying instead that Hall had placed a lock on his room and denied him access to his belongings, even though he had continued to pay rent. Hall called up at least eight witnesses to Byasta's two, including former tenants and contractors who had worked with her, and eventually won the case on appeal. Byasta was forced to pay her $9 U.S. gold and the court costs. Though it is difficult to know the exact details of what happened between Hall and Byasta (none of the witness statements survive in the file), the case nevertheless shows Hall's ruthless determination to receive the rent owed to her. She was willing to sue Byasta even for a relatively small amount and, in the process, leave him with few housing options. While the case shows her savvy navigation of the courts and the roll system, it also shows that Hall's entrepreneurship depended on the desperation and demand of Silver workers.

*　*　*

White women's memoirs chronicle Black West Indian women's diasporic strategies of survival and entrepreneurship against the background of early twentieth-century U.S. imperial expansion. West Indian women bore the burden of social reproduction in the Canal Zone, shouldering the responsibility of providing for the residents of the area, particularly for West Indian men who received inferior food and services. Their presence in the American home in the Zone presented a foil for white women to imagine themselves as pioneers, envisioning the imperial encounter as a domestic interaction between boss and servant. But, for West Indian women, migration and work in the Canal Zone were not at all understood through a narrative of the frontier, of a civilizing project, or of the unruly jungle. While subsidizing the construction effort, West Indian women's labor of social reproduction also allowed them to work semi-independently, save money for themselves, provide for their communities, and cultivate spaces of social and economic autonomy. West Indian women's priorities—financial independence, mobility, self-presentation, their families—shine through even in stories meant to degrade them. But their entrepreneurship was not a simple and heroic counter to American priorities in the Canal Zone. In many cases, as with Jane Hall, women's attempts at financial autonomy affirmed the structures that kept Silver workers dependent and vulnerable.

West Indian women's experiences nevertheless disrupt the romanticized symbols of the loyal and quiescent "mammy." Limited by the constraints of a racially segregated system and subject to limitations from their bosses, West Indian women wore colorful and attention-grabbing outfits while performing hard labor, haggled and raised their prices to meet the persistent demands of their clients, carved out their own workspaces, performed work at their own pace, and left their jobs for other readily available opportunities. Their labor of social reproduction maintained white American homes and by extension the settler colonial project of the Canal Zone, but it also fostered economic practices that sustained West Indian communities in Panama and the diaspora far beyond the concerns of the American administration. As the next chapter will show, these practices extended throughout transatlantic circuits of kinship even after a family member's death on the Canal construction effort.

CHAPTER 5

The Value of Death

Remembering the early years of construction, a West Indian man named Alfred Dottin expressed the overwhelming sense of mortality that pervaded the period: "The working conditions in those days were so horrible it would stagger your imagination. . . . Death was our constant companion. I shall never forget the train loads of dead being carted away daily, as if they were so much lumber."[1] The risk of death indeed enveloped the Canal Zone as tropical diseases flourished in the mosquito-prone environment and dynamite explosions from the excavation of the Culebra Cut dislodged mountains of rock on the workers. These risks disproportionally affected Silver Roll workers, who held the most dangerous jobs on the construction and lived in cramped conditions. By the official count of the ICC, disease and workplace accidents claimed the lives of 5,609 employees.[2] West Indian workers accounted for 80 percent of these deaths.[3] However, taking into consideration the deaths of civilians in the Canal Zone and in the terminal cities of Panama and Colón, the total death toll rises above 25,000.[4] This number is likely still an underestimation; many deceased West Indian persons remained unidentified by the Zone police or died forgotten among explosions and landslides. Some succumbed to malaria or yellow fever outside of an official hospital or simply eluded accounting because they were not contracted employees.

For Canal authorities, the death of a Silver worker was, at most, an inconvenience. For families in the Caribbean who relied on the income and sacrifice of their loved ones working in Panama, the death of a Silver worker could instead mean deep sadness, starvation, poverty, and hardship. Death, however, was not just an ending. For West Indian families, it also meant the beginning of a long process of mourning and struggle with colonial authorities who controlled the flow of goods and information across the Caribbean. When a Silver worker died in the Canal Zone, West Indian relatives, mainly women, sent petitions to British colonial administrators for the saved earnings, cherished belongings, and wages owed that their family member had left behind. The laborious interventions of West Indian women remaining in the islands, who reached out to colonial authorities in an effort to locate their deceased relatives, ensured that some of these effects made it back to families and kin. In sending petitions to their colonial governments, West Indian women activated their economic entitlements as British subjects, as wives (legal or not), and as inheritors, as they tried to collect monies potentially lost with the death of a family breadwinner in the Canal Zone. Their interactions with British colonial and American Canal Zone authorities were nevertheless circumscribed by gendered and racialized understandings of dependency, subjecthood, and financial responsibility that defined whose property was valuable and who was deserving of aid.

When male West Indian workers died during service killed by mistimed blasts, falling rocks, flooded rivers, or disease, their deaths became, at best, a tally in the official record. Many of them went unidentified and uncounted. It is thus only through West Indian women's interventions with imperial authorities that we can see the social and economic repercussions of the many deaths that marked the construction period, how they affected individual families, and how they set off the circulation of money through the islands. This archive of grief and mourning starkly elucidates the negligence of U.S. racial capitalism in Panama and the dynamic West Indian women developed to memorialize their deceased kin. West Indian women's interventions with imperial authorities contested the devaluing of West Indian lives during the Canal construction and reincorporated West Indian men into their extended Caribbean kinship networks, even in death. Despite the overwhelming carnage of the construction, and despite the disregard for Black lives, West Indian women pursued and defined their own ways of mourning.

Women's requests came in the face of a death caused, directly or indirectly, by the Canal construction. To access information and the belongings of their family members, they were forced to contend with the administrative and moral requirements of the Canal's bureaucracy. But women's interventions with the authorities and the money they received also circulated within alternative Caribbean economies defined by family and kinship. West Indian women used the belongings, wages, and compensation owed to their relatives as a way to financially sustain themselves and their kin, and to honor the death of their loved ones. Their requests help us contextualize these deaths not as a number or a loss to the productivity of the Canal project but as a part of loving diasporic Caribbean communities contending with the displacement of migration and the massive loss of life.

The predominance of West Indian women as petitioners for effects is the direct inverse to the prevalence of West Indian men as migrant Canal workers. The Canal Commission contracted twenty thousand male laborers from Barbados alone, an entire 10 percent of the island's total population at the time.[5] It was mainly these male migrant workers who earned and sent back remittances of "Panama money" to their families in the Caribbean and mainly these men who died in the course of construction. West Indian women who stayed in the islands were the primary intermediaries to imperial authorities in the aftermath of these deaths; they were the ones who requested, received, saved, and spent the money left by their family members. The money remaining after a workers' death only circulated by the explicit demand of West Indian women seeking their husbands' or brothers' effects. Whether remittances, compensation, or wages owed upon death, it was West Indian women who managed the money that arrived in the islands as part of transnational household strategies of social reproduction. Women then placed this money in savings banks, bought food and other household items, and used it to care for elders and dependent children.

Finding, receiving, and administering the estates of West Indian men, as small as many properties were, was no easy task. It required women to contact various administrators and confirm the deaths of their relatives (for whom they rarely had direct addresses), collect documentary evidence of their destitution and their legal relationship to the deceased, and show persistence in the face of continued roadblocks. It further involved West Indian women learning how to address themselves to financial administrators, advisers, accountants, and diplomats who controlled the flow of money from the Canal Zone. Even in the face of death, West Indian women performed the labor of social reproduction when they required the state to take the financial and emotional needs of their families into account and claimed their right to the leftover belongings of their kin.[6]

The entanglement of "death and wealth and power" was not new to the Canal Zone—it marked slave colonies like Jamaica throughout the eighteenth century, where the high mortality rate among both enslaved Africans and Europeans deeply shaped social and political relationships. What historian Vincent Brown calls the "mortuary politics" of these groups—their funeral and commemorative practices—served to reaffirm colonial hierarchies of power but also served as sites of resistance and survival for enslaved Africans.[7] As in Jamaica, death defined the early years of the Canal construction, where it disproportionately affected West Indians. Whereas in a slave economy planters were at least nominally responsible for the social reproduction of the labor force, in the imperial free labor economy of the Canal Zone, West Indians mediated U.S. administrators' lack of responsibility in sustaining labor through a process of legal and financial claims-making. West Indians engaged in a process of mortuary *economics*, negotiating an indifferent bureaucracy in order to redefine the value of their relatives in death.[8] In response to the diasporic migration and accompanying death toll of the Canal construction, West Indian women fashioned a new rite of memorialization through their petitions for wages left and owed. These women demanded that the U.S. Canal administration recognize Black men's deaths that might otherwise be forgotten.

The issues relating to effects and compensation were not centrally located in Panama but were instead transnational disputes that required the cooperation of British colonial administrators. In the first four years of construction, when there was no established process for requesting effects, West Indian women sought the intercession of anyone who would help them, including colonial governors and secretaries, emigration agents on the islands, or the British consul in Panama, Claude Mallet. For the most part, they addressed their requests to the British rather than American employers, presented themselves as British subjects in their communications, and saw colonial administrators as their first point of contact. This initial approach through British colonial administrators provided petitioners with a forceful legal authority with which to substantiate their claims to the ICC. After 1908 the U.S. Canal administration established an official procedure for requesting compensation for deaths that occurred during employment, but it continued to require West Indian families to contact U.S. officials through British colonial representatives in Panama. As in their interactions with the Canal Zone administration and its legal courts, West Indian women mobilized their relationship with British colonial powers as one strategy for contending with the overlooked deaths of their loved ones in Panama.

Even before migrants left for Panama, they learned about both economic opportunities and untimely deaths in the Canal Zone from local newspapers and word of mouth. Aware of the potential dangers, West Indian workers nevertheless migrated there and indeed found a society marked by disease, violence, and workplace accidents. In Panama, migrants re-created Afro-Caribbean burial traditions while generating new forms of mourning adapted to the dislocation and harshness of their new lives. Back in the islands, families used transnational diplomatic and kinship networks to learn about the financial afterlives of their deceased relatives. West Indian women wrote pleading, and sometimes critical, letters to British colonial administrators to seek answers and request leftover belongings. This process changed in 1908 when Congress passed the first U.S. federal accident compensation law. The law forced West Indian women to negotiate a hardening of the calculation of the value of a deceased worker's lost potential labor. Nevertheless, women continued to rely on their own established strategies to make financial claims regarding their loved ones and to mourn the loss of West Indian lives.

News of Money, News of Death

Death and money had a close relationship in Panama. As Jamaican poet Claude McKay put it, even though "malaria suckin' out we blood," West Indians flocked to Panama because "poo'ness deh could neber come / And dere'll be cash fe sen' back home."[9] The promise of jobs and money during an economic depression in the islands lured many West Indians to Panama during the Canal construction, where they encountered rampant disease, racism, and workplace accidents that left them maimed or killed. Nevertheless, the dangers and potential death seemed worth it in exchange for "cash fe sen' back home." Recruiters, newspapers, and word of mouth reinforced the relationship between money and danger to West Indians considering work on the Canal.

The Isthmian Canal Commission sent agents William J. Karner and S. E. Brewster to the main ICC recruiting station in Barbados and S. W. Settoon to the French Antilles in search of labor for the construction of the Canal. These agents placed advertisements in local newspapers that disseminated news about job opportunities in Panama promising good food, board, and pay after a medical examination. The consistent requirement of smallpox vaccinations and medical examinations hinted at the threat of disease during a time when malaria and yellow fever were rampant and deadly in the Zone. From the earliest years, these advertisements of financial promise appeared alongside simultaneous reports of danger, infection, and mortality. One November 1905 article in the *Barbados Advocate* reported that sixty-two Barbadians recently returned from Panama said money and employment was plentiful, but that they had seen their deceased fellow laborers "interred almost the same place that the drinking water had to be taken from."[10] Reports on the prevalence of disease in the Canal Zone circulated widely in Caribbean and U.S. newspapers.[11]

Rumor and word of mouth were even more successful in disseminating the notion of Panama as a land of economic prosperity. Everyone knew of somebody who had left the islands in search of work in the Canal. Kinship and friendship networks served an essential role in transmitting information about the project and encouraging others to migrate. Bonham Richardson's oral history informants recounted hearing that, in Panama, "money was like apples on a tree."[12] Eventually, returnees and news sent from workers in Panama prompted the *Weekly Illustrated Paper* to report in 1909 that "the returned men have been practically recruiting agents of the most effective sort."[13]

Word of mouth also weighed the risk of death with the promise of pay. West Indian workers sang both of these popular songs as they were headed to Panama:

Fever and ague all day long
At Panama, at Panama,
Wish you were dead before very long
At Panama, at Panama.[14]

We want more wages, we want it now
And if we don't get it, we going to Panama
Yankees say they want we down there,
We want more wages, we want it now.[15]

On a ship bound for Panama, American journalist Albert Edwards heard a chorus of West Indian voices singing the first song. He noted that the men on board sang it "with great fervor" despite the gloomy theme. In his *Harper's Weekly* article about the journey, he referred to the traveling West Indians as a "cargo of black ivory," characterizing these Black men as valuable commodities to be transported to the Canal. West Indian migrants heading to Panama understood the risks of death and disease there—they knew that the Yankees saw them as no more than expendable labor—but they weighed these concerns against the potential economic gains. Workers chanted the second ditty as they left plantations in Barbados, criticizing the low wages they received for farm work on the island. And as that song expressed, they wanted more wages and they wanted them now. Rather than a disincentive, these songs served as a rallying cry for workers gathered on steamboats departing for Colón. In the public arenas of the Caribbean, these songs created an image of the Canal project that tied death and economic promise together with a discourse of masculine worthiness.[16]

West Indians were right to be wary of Panama. A former white American track master of the Panama Railroad, S. W. Plume, described the mortality in the Canal Zone: "We used to run one train in the morning out of Colón up into Monkey Hill [where Silver employees were buried, later to become Mount Hope Cemetery]. Over to Panama it was the same way—bury, bury, bury, running two, three, four trains a day with dead Jamaican niggers all the time. I never saw anything like it. . . . They die like animals."[17] Plume's quote describes not only the pervasive atmosphere of death in Panama but also the general disregard American managers had for the lives of these Black laborers. While awed by the volume of casualties, Plume nevertheless saw these men as subhuman and devalued their lives and deaths. Plume skirts placing responsibility for these deaths on the American project, instead suggesting that it was part of Black workers' nature to "die like animals." And indeed, these dead men were treated like animals. West Indian Constantine Parkinson remembered how bodies were dug up after an explosion, saying "It was a very awfull sight" but also noting how commonplace death had become to everyone around him. Ultimately, Parkinson suggests, these bodies were treated as disposable because "all the boses want is to get the canal build."[18] For West Indians, the casual deaths of the early construction period instilled a deep trauma. Every single respondent to the Isthmian Historical Society's 1963 competition for "the best true stories of life and work on the Isthmus of Panama during the construction" vividly recalled West Indians' proximity to death. Amos Park wrote, "Those days were horrible days to remember. Those were the times you go to bed at night and the next day you may be a dead man."[19]

The numbers verify the ubiquity of Black deaths during this period. According to the statistics of the Isthmian Canal Commission, which started regular record-keeping in fiscal year 1906–1907, out of the total deaths of employees and civilians in the Canal Zone and the terminal cities of Panama and Colón, Black men made up more than half. More so than the raw numbers, the differing rates of death among white and Black employees show the disproportionate effect of disease and violence on Silver workers; for the years of construction, the rate of death for Black employees was triple that of white employees.

Yet these numbers also obscure the many bodies that went uncounted and the person behind each of these deaths. While the annual reports listed the name of every dead white American employee, they never mentioned deceased Black employees. Many corpses of West Indian men remained unidentified by the Canal Commission. Some, for example, were never located after a dynamite explosion buried them under an avalanche or when men drowned after a cayuco failed to carry them across the swollen river; others could not be identified (such as the "unknown male negro uncovered by Steamshovel no. 201 from the debris of the premature explosion").[20] When

Table 1. Deaths in the cities of Panama and the Canal Zone, including civilians and employees, according to ICC Annual Reports

Fiscal Year	Total deaths of Black and white residents	White Men	White Women	Black Men	Black Women
1906–7	3,670	411	134	2,290	745
1907–8	3,100	479	194	1,625	745
1908–9	2,807	425	177	1,440	711
1909–10	2,735	324	143	1,418	810
1910–11	3,409	366	158	1,837	998
1911–12	3,163	373	144	1,646	965
1912–13	2,944	296	131	1,570	909
1913–14	3,190	271	157	1,641	1,070
TOTAL	25,018	2,945	1,238	13,467	6,953

SOURCE: I gathered the data for this table from the Isthmian Canal Commission Annual Reports for every fiscal year. This table excludes deaths of Chinese and unidentified residents, which were always comparatively very low given their smaller population numbers. These can be found in the original Annual Reports.

they did find a body or in cases of "accidental death," the Canal Zone police would submit a Report of Death describing the deceased and the possible causes of death. For example, a report from 1908 described an unidentified Black man found floating in the Chagres River: "From the appearance of the body it had been in the water several days, its clothes were entirely gone with the exception of an old pair of shoes and socks which were on its feet. The crabs or fish of some kind had torn the flesh from its head, arms, and legs. . . . Identification was impossible as the body had been nearly half devoured."[21] This man, like many Black West Indian men in the Canal Zone, died and was buried in a segregated Silver cemetery without a name, without notifying his kin, and without anyone assuming responsibility. This was the case even with men who were directly employed by the Canal and whose deaths were witnessed. For example, as the men of Gang #264 finished setting up a minefield for a controlled explosion, "a flash of lightning ignited the charges and the whole exploded simultaneously." One Black man died in the resulting explosion. The report notes that he was "evidently one of the men of gang #264," but despite knowing his affiliation, the man could not be identified.[22]

When the police found an unidentified (or unidentifiable) dead body, they took it to the hospital to receive an examination by the coroner. The coroner's jury would then pronounce a judgment on the cause of death, while the police continued an on-the-ground investigation questioning witnesses and surveying the location. These judgments often blamed West Indians for their own deaths. In one train accident, the coroner decided that "the deceased (who was evidently deaf) while walking along the main line P.R.R. was struck and received injuries which caused his death. . . . No blame is attributable to the engineer as several persons distinctly heard the successive blowing of the locomotive's whistle."[23] That other passengers heard the whistle provides evidence, for the ICC, of the engineer's inculpability and the deceased's responsibility for his own safety. The man run over by the train could have indeed been deaf, but the coroner's proof lay not so much in the man's possible hearing disability (which the coroner merely assumed) but in the assessment of the man's response in comparison to the passengers on the train. Similarly, A. T. Cooper in the Dredging Division reported to his supervisor that a Black man had drowned while working with him, but that it was the man's own fault as Black workers "jump off and on before a boat is alongside and all headway lost and have no one to blame but themselves if anything happens."[24] These reports blamed the deceased for their fatalities, sidestepping the larger concerns about workplace unsafety that the Canal's brutal construction had engendered. These deaths were accidents, but they were accidents endemic to a project governed by haste and carelessness for workers' lives.

In one case, the bones of a Black man were found underneath a noose tied to a small tree. It was ruled a suicide. Zone Corporal Charles Palacio decided that, in his opinion, "the deceased came to his death of his own volition and by his own hands, because of the almost childish nature of the contrivance used to end his life and also, because the class of people to which he evidently belonged, judging by his garments, is not often waylaid and disposed of in similar manner."[25] The class of people to which he "evidently belonged," the corporal explained, was that of common Silver laborers. He ascertained the man's race "from a few curls of kinky hair which can be seen attached to the noose." To dismiss possible claims of murder, he assured that Black Silver laborers were rarely "disposed of" in this manner, though he makes no obvious connection to practices of lynching. The corporal judged this a

suicide based solely on assumptions about Black people's primitive practices, with no consideration of either lynching or the psychological and material conditions that might have driven a worker to suicide.

The Police Department occasionally attempted to identify these bodies
by asking the neighbors of surrounding villages about them, but rarely did
Black residents share their knowledge with the police. In one investigation,
the chief lamented that West Indians in the nearby town were "concealing
the knowledge because of the interest in the case shown by the Police."[26] West
Indians correctly assumed that the police worked alongside the Sanitary Department to discipline those who disposed of their dead outside of the commission's norms. Distrustful of these authorities, many West Indians also
gave false names to employers upon their arrival in Panama, making it "impossible in some cases ever to identify the deceased."[27] The ICC was thus not
a reliable source of news about West Indian deaths and did not much bother
to keep track of deaths that it did not need to justify.

Burial in Panama

The period of the late nineteenth and early twentieth centuries marked a
"death revolution" in the United States and Western Europe with the profes-
sionalization of funeral rites and the transition of death from the family home
to the hospital.[28] This shift proved decisive in the Canal Zone, where the administration placed death under the umbrella of public health and disease
containment. Beginning in 1905, the laws of the Canal Zone required a certificate of death signed by the attending physician and overseen by the Board
of Health to acquire a burial permit.[29] These permits cost one dollar for everyone who was not a Canal Zone employee and designated the cemetery, location of the grave, and name of the deceased. The Panama Railroad also
charged for transporting corpses across the Canal Zone. All the Zone cemeteries came under the supervision of the Sanitary Department.[30] The administration's concern with corpses, then, had little to do with the restitution of
family ties or respect for the dead but with sanitation.

In multiple reports, members of the Sanitary Department remarked on
the barriers that distance, cost, and distrust of authorities created for West

Indians seeking to bury their dead through official means.[31] When one of their own died, West Indians in the Canal Zone instead tried to honor their passing while avoiding obtrusive and expensive ICC oversight. They also attempted to re-create some Afro-Caribbean burial traditions. In her memoir of the construction era, a white American woman disdainfully described a West Indian funeral, saying: "The very worst of all was the wailing for the dead that came from the labor camp below us. When one of their number died the friends and kindred of the deceased would gather in the room where the corpse lay. All night long they would drink rum and wail and sing Old English Gospel hymns in the flattest, most unmusical way possible."[32] Later, when a young West Indian boy died, she described "a weird sound" arising from the labor camp: "Five black females, their hair standing out like brush, were making their way toward the station, screaming and wailing, wringing their hands, their bodies weaving from side to side. . . . Their noise was deafening."[33] She found out that these women were not directly related to the deceased boy and condemned their spectacular grief: "I learned that the noise which I thought was caused by deep sorrow was simply a noise to let off emotion which they aroused in themselves at will."[34]

Putting aside her obvious scorn for West Indians, the description echoes many burial practices from the British Caribbean: how mourners walked in a procession; how the community came together to hold a wake; how women acted as central figures in funerals; how wakes were accompanied by dancing and singing, often of Protestant hymns; and how mourners made offerings of food and drink to appease the "duppy," or spirit, of the deceased.[35] Though the observer decried what she perceived as their excessive "hysteria," especially as the child was not their direct family relation, in fact the passage shows how extended kin assembled to mourn the dead in Panama. These women likely provided support for the family of this dead Black child, and grieved for the young child's death as if he were one of their own in a place where close family was hard to come by. Some of these celebrations could be part of traditional Afro-Caribbean "Nine Nights" observances, during which wake attendees mourned until the deceased would be granted safe passage to the afterlife.[36]

Prior to the construction period, Black working-class funerary and spiritual rituals in the postemancipation Caribbean were "pathologized, criminalized, and folklorized" by the press, courts, and traditional church establishment.[37] Laws in 1849 and 1911 in St. Vincent, and 1873 in Jamaica attempted to control how British West Indians organized wakes. In islands like Trinidad, wake organizers and obeahmen were prosecuted for disorderly conduct, disturbing the peace, or fraud.[38] Nevertheless, working-class West Indians throughout the region continued re-creating these rituals, which helped "reconstitute social relationships and notions of belonging to a specific place or community."[39] Family land in particular served as a potent symbol of reaffirmation of the kinship collective during Jamaican wakes.[40] In Panama, West Indians did not own family land passed down through generations and were unlikely to have kinship groups of the sort they had in the islands. In the absence of close family or the long-standing ties formed within island communities, West Indian women in Panama led newly settled migrants in re-creating burial rites from the Caribbean for the people who died far from home.

Evidence of West Indian funerary rites in Panama in the early years of construction lies almost exclusively in sources that similarly "pathologize, criminalize, and folklorize" these practices.[41] Canal authorities privileged concerns about sanitation and frequently castigated folks for improper waste management, including that of corpses. White American women, as in the memoir just mentioned, characterized West Indian mourning rites as animalistic. Nevertheless, West Indians in Panama found ways to honor and bury their dead. Their burial practices drew on Afro-Caribbean rites that centrally featured women and began to draw lines of reciprocity and obligation among a newly formed West Indian community. They also involved new adaptations to the context of Panama in ways that attempted to skirt the anonymized burials of the Canal Commission.

Another death report from the Canal Zone police stated that the corpse's "feet were tied together in the manner used by West Indians in preparing a body for funeral."[42] A related report about the same body also noted that it had been found with a "cream-colored cotton blanket, probably wrapped around the body" and "strips of canvas of a curious pattern." These cloths, which befuddled officials, were perhaps a funeral shroud tied around the deceased. Preparing the body in clothing had been a key part of Afro-Caribbean burials since slavery. Canal police recognized evidence of West

Indian burials in other cadavers they discovered. Regarding a Black male adult body found in a box floating on the Camacho River in 1914, the coroner's jury decided, based "on their familiarity with the class of people living in the vicinity in which the body was found, and its present isolation and consequent absence of sanitary conveniences," that it had been "placed there in execution of methods adopted by friends or relatives of the deceased for his burial."[43] The body was reburied in an unidentified grave in the Empire cemetery, anonymous to the Sanitary Department employees who interred him, but known to the West Indian neighbors who might have arranged this burial and informed his kin. West Indians sometimes made do with watery burials in makeshift coffins, such as the box that enclosed one of these found corpses, marked "C&E Morton Preserved Provisions Manufacturers, London."[44] A number of Black West Indian corpses were found floating in the rivers of the Canal Zone. The coroner's jury read each of these as cases of "accidental drowning," but some might have been bodies put to rest in the water by West Indians looking to avoid the administrative process of burials through the ICC.

Friendly societies also served a role in connecting funeral practices from Panama to the Caribbean. These were volunteer associations founded in the wake of emancipation as tools of economic survival that extended mutual aid to members in case of sickness, old age, or death, particularly with funeral arrangements. The early twentieth century was a period of incredible growth for friendly societies throughout the region. At the beginning of the construction, in 1904, Barbados had 92 Friendly Societies with around 13,933 members. By 1914, the end of construction, this number had more than tripled, to 285 societies with over 42,000 members.[45] While mostly middle-class or upwardly mobile Black men participated in these societies during their early founding, by the twentieth century women dominated some of these organizations, such as the Victoria Royal Union in the Bahamas.[46] These societies continued the work of providing members with financial support after a death even as West Indians migrated in greater numbers. West Indian widows sometimes asked the consul to acquire the death certificate of a relative to present it to their local friendly society to receive their benefits.[47]

As West Indian communities grew more established in Panama, they also began to create their own friendly societies there, which acted on behalf of their members. For example, the Easter Lily Lodge #45, Order of Good Samaritans of Empire, Canal Zone, paid for the funeral and administered the estate of Rachel Bath, a St. Kitts native who died in the Zone with "very valuable jewelry and household furniture" on January 26, 1912.[48] As a West Indian domestic named Daisy explained to her boss, friendly societies served an important financial purpose in the face of the racial discrimination of the Canal Zone:

> We all belongs to a society or lodge of some kind. Colored peoples must do it. Them don't get much money and it very hard to save; but by belonging to a society, we know we be looked after when we sick, and have a funeral when we die. We pay seventy-five cents or a dollar a month to the society and if we get sick, we get three dollars a week to live on till we can go back to work again. When we die, we know we be buried nice. But that isn't all. When even a little baby dies in Panama, there must be papers fixed up and it means all day walk up and down, walk up and down. . . . The society has officers to take care of all that for us.[49]

West Indians could not rely on ICC benefits or sick leave; instead, they re-created the mutual aid societies they had formed in the islands to take care of each other and to mediate with the Canal's bureaucracy. Friendly society members received elaborate funerals. The deceased would be accompanied by a funeral procession in which society members in full regalia served as pallbearers. Members of the Guiding Star Lodge No. 14 (Independent Order of the Fishers of Galilea), for example, would expect to receive a twenty-four-hour notice to attend funerals in formal attire and to bring any musical instruments they could.[50] Elaborate funerals organized by friendly societies or lodges became a common part of West Indian–Panamanian tradition in the years following construction as these organizations grew in number and stability.[51]

Despite the barriers to re-creating the funeral rites they practiced in the islands, West Indians in Panama found ways to commemorate their dead and reaffirm their social ties. Within the sanitary and legal parameters of the Canal Zone, perhaps sending their kin to watery graves seemed like a more honorable burial than the unmarked headstones of the Silver cemeteries. West Indians in Panama restituted spiritual value to their dead through these rituals, connecting them to long-standing cross-Caribbean traditions. Women played central roles in these ceremonies, as singers, dancers, and cooks, and perhaps even as those who prepared bodies for burial.

Requesting the Effects of the Dead

The same ships that delivered mail to the islands also brought the official list of dead compiled by the Canal administration. This list was held at the Emigration Office where relatives could inquire about their family members.[52] In Barbados, a special police force sometimes personally informed relatives of their loved ones' deaths from the Canal Zone rosters. Occasionally, families would receive a dreaded black-bordered envelope in the mail with the somber news.[53] The Official Gazettes also published notices of some deaths as authorities tried to locate relatives on the islands. However, many people did not receive information about the death of their family members from these official sources. As ICC reports document, many of the men who died during this period remained unidentified by the Canal authorities and their families were left in the dark about their loved one's survival.

In the early years of construction, relatives of deceased Canal workers had no obvious avenue through which to request the wages and property of their loved ones. Grieving West Indian women chose to issue requests to British administrators to intercede on their behalf and acquire the effects of their deceased kin. Men sometimes sent these requests, such as Barbadian Joseph N. Miller's letter regarding the belongings of his daughter, Miriam Coulson, who had been murdered by her husband in the Canal Zone.[54] However, the great majority of requests came from West Indian women. Their petitions show how they negotiated an indifferent bureaucracy to learn about their relatives' deaths and to gain access to their remaining property. West Indian women developed the process of requesting effects from U.S. authorities through British colonial intermediaries as an ad hoc strategy of survival, commemoration, mourning, and the recovery of family wealth.

Women sometimes contacted colonial authorities in desperation to inquire about their relatives when they stopped receiving regular correspondence or began to hear rumors. Maud Weeks of Rock Hall Village, Barbados, for example, wrote to the colonial secretary asking for the "favour of seeking up to see if John Ethelbert Weeks is dead for me as I am in a fright to know if he is."[55] The colonial officials of the islands would then write to Claude Mallet, the British consul in Panama, requesting information about the West Indian man in question. Mallet contacted American authorities through various channels, including the ICC hospitals at Ancon and Tabernilla or the specific department for which the deceased worked. He would then relay this information back to the island governments, along with whatever information he could gather about the cause of death and remaining property.

More commonly, friends or kin in Panama would inform people back in the islands of sudden deaths. For example, Margaret Smith of Kingston learned about the death of her husband Frederick in 1906 from another Silver worker named John Smith. John wrote to her about the "great trouble" he went through to acquire the £8.20 in wages still owed to Frederick as he had to visit the inspector of police and the British consul in Panama several times, eventually managing to gather the money and send it along to Margaret at 18 Tulip Lane in Kingston. He ended his sorrowful missive saying "Dear Mrs Smith don't fret too much I know it is great feeling to you toward the loss of a husband you must not give away knowing that we all have to die. We know not where our bones may lay."[56]

John's intimate ties with Frederick spurred him not only to go through the bureaucratic travails of acquiring the dead man's belongings but also to write a candid and emotional letter to his widow. John's letter reinforced the overall feeling of mortality that West Indian men and women grappled with during the construction period. He showed resignation to death as a universal, but his comment that "we know not where our bones may lay" reflected his anxieties about dying while displaced, far from family and homeland, and in the face of an apathetic American bureaucracy. John understood that, were it not for his intervention, Margaret might never have learned of her husband's death, or received his wages. In essence, he feared that Frederick's (and his own) death would pass without remembrance or memorialization, that their bones would lay among those of other unnamed Black workers who gave their lives to the Canal. Faced with the loss of her husband, Margaret at least learned of Frederick's death from a sympathetic friend who brought her emotional and financial succor at a time of great distress. John concluded his letter to Margaret even offering to raise Frederick's child as his own, rounding out this diasporic circuit of kinship and community responsibility.

West Indians like Frederick, John, and Margaret Smith likely learned of the Canal Zone as a space of economic promise and deathly peril from friends and acquaintances, perhaps from other kin who had left to work in Panama or workers from nearby plantations who sang popular songs about the wages to be gained from construction work. Margaret then heard about John's death and regained his property through the intervention of another Silver worker. It was through these extended social networks that West Indian men and women learned and transmitted financial knowledge about the Panama Canal, spurring further migration and connecting the developments in Panama to the economic futures of the islands.

Acquiring the effects of the deceased from the authorities was rarely a simple, linear process. For example, in late 1905 the British Consulate in Panama received a Report of Death sent by the chief of the Timekeeping Division regarding John Mahon, a carpenter in the Engineering Division who had died from pneumonia. This report outlined his effects of $20.00 gold, $6.40 silver, and 1 pound 1 shilling currency, which had been turned over to the British Consul in Panama.[57] His wife, Frances Mahon, was not informed. She did not receive news of John's death until she herself wrote to the governor of the Canal Zone asking about him and received a missive from the Department of Civil Administration with the enclosed Report of Death.[58]

Desperate to receive further information, Frances Mahon also contacted S. E. Brewster, the U.S. emigration agent in Barbados, asking him to intercede on her behalf with the Canal authorities. In a letter to the governor of Barbados, Frances Mahon complained, "I sent to Mr Brewster Government Agent touching the matter and has been so disrespectful to me that I was more than ashame (sic). While grieved for the loss of my husband and then to be snubbed by the person to whom I expected to have got information from was more than painful."[59] Frances Mahon's letter illustrates the different value imperial authorities assigned to her husband's death. While she was deeply grieved, Brewster saw little importance in responding politely or rapidly to her request. Frances's letter negotiated between criticizing Brewster's behavior and continuing to plead for aid as a "humble petitioner . . . in straitened circumstances." She walked a tightrope between subversion and deference, pointing out the faults in the bureaucratic apparatus that would ignore her husband's death while also positioning herself as a destitute and needy subject. John Mahon's property was eventually sent to the governor of Barbados in January 1906, yet Frances did not receive the money until March 31, 1906. In April she wrote again to the colonial secretary, demanding her husband's clothes and tools. There is no evidence that she received them.

For some West Indians, it was actually impossible to receive the few belongings their loved ones had left behind because the Canal authorities perceived them as insignificant. For example, the belongings of Millicent Marshall's son Garfield, who died gruesomely run over by a train, were "destroyed by police as valueless."[60] For Americans, West Indian women's requests seemed onerous, their husband's property a mere trifle, hardly meriting recovery. For families back on the islands, in contrast, gaining information and a few clothes and tools seemed like an urgent way to honor and remember the deceased. For a woman in financial straits like Frances Mahon, these leftover monies could provide much-needed assistance. At the time, $20 in American currency was a substantial sum.[61] Some women received much larger amounts; Mary Gibson requested her husband's owed wages from the British vice-consul to the sum of $293.73.[62]

Once this money returned to the islands, West Indian women sometimes saved it in a local financial institution or invested it in family property. In doing this, they put the money West Indian men had earned with their blood and labor in Panama back into family networks in the islands, such as Mary Ann Gibbs did after her son Wilbert's death. Wilbert Senhouse arrived in Colón from Barbados on the ship *Trent* on September 20, 1905.[63] On December 12, Wilbert wrote his mother, Mary Ann, a deeply affectionate letter. He gave his "Ma" lots of advice on relationships and budgeting, noting the small remittances he had sent her so far. He closed the letter with: "Please tell sister and Jacob and all the children howdee for me, tell them I was sick and went to hospital for a week which caused me not to send any more money for you. . . . I remain your loving son."[64]

On January 10, less than four months after his arrival, this ominous hospital visit turned into Wilbert's death in Miraflores Hospital. Three months after that, Mary Ann Gibbs forwarded this same personal letter to the governor of Barbados as part of her application for her son's effects, and thus, his death and her mourning became part of the archive. Her letter to the governor is businesslike:

> I beg humbly and respectfully to lay before His Excellency the Governor the attached letter and envelope from my son, Wilbert Senhouse, who I have been to understand since his writing has died at Panama. My son left this island at the close of the crop last season for the Isthmus, I don't know whether as an emigrant, probably so, and I am informed by last mail both of his death and of his having money and other belongings at the Panama Hospital. I pray his Excellency's sympathy in making enquiries into the matter with the view of all my son's belongings being handed to me.[65]

The letter's similarity to the many other letters from mothers and wives during these years suggests it was written with the help of a lawyer and/or just followed a relatively standard format. Few of these letters include any evidence of a lawyer's intervention, other than the repetitive nature of the address to the authorities. A series of petitions from Mary Gibson in British Guiana were signed by J. G. Applewhaite, who assured that he had "read and explained the foregoing to Mary Gibson who appeared to understand and approve of the same to which she affixed her mark in my presence."[66] It could be the case that some of these letters were written by legal intermediaries, but women's demands nevertheless shine through. Letters like that of Mary Ann Gibbs's asked the state to acknowledge their grief and respond with information about their relatives. Gibbs rejected the mere bureaucratization of Wilbert's death, where he would become another name among the death rolls.

Senhouse does not appear in the published Mortuary Records of Panama as he died before record-keeping became consistent later in 1906. Gibbs's intervention, then, like that of many other West Indian women, recorded a world external to the one that marked Black people as "animals," as S. W. Plume of the Panama Railroad had callously remarked. The colonial secretary received Gibbs's application and made inquiries to Claude Mallet. Handwritten on the side of his letter, a note explained that Wilbert "died of pneumonia, Miraflores Hospital, no effects, 14.40 due in wages."[67] There is no further explanation of either Wilbert's death or whether this information and his wages were relayed to Gibbs, but since the consul and governor fulfilled many of the other requests, there is a reasonable chance that she did.

Indeed, we can assume that Mary received some money because, a few months after this exchange, on September 23, she opened account #48374 at the Barbados Savings Bank in Bridgetown, where she was listed as living in the same parish and working as a domestic servant.[68] It is no coincidence that Mary Ann Gibbs engaged in all these financial activities around the same time. As a domestic in Barbados, she likely did not make enough money to warrant having a bank account until her son began to send her remittances. William's letter evidenced that he regularly sent her small amounts of around five dollars as remittances, apologizing for making her travel to pick these up at the post office: "I know it will be very hard for you to continually going into town but you must be contented for I cannot do better."[69] The $14.40 in back wages owed to Wilbert, along with any other effects he might have accrued, were likely sent to Mary later that year. Following Mary Ann's deposit of this money in the Savings Bank reiterates the use of these petitions as strategies of diasporic connection and economic survival for West Indian women. Through these requests, women like Mary Ann Gibbs asserted the dignity and worth of their loved ones in the face of a bureaucracy that devalued them while also rerouting owed wages and leftover money back to family and kin who depended on them.

Calculating the Value of Death

With the passing of the Congressional Act of May 30, 1908, families of deceased workers could begin to officially request compensation for deaths that had occurred during employment with the federal government.[70] The bill was the first general accident compensation law in the United States. It only covered employees in hazardous occupations, defined as "arsenals, navy-yards, manufacturing establishments (such as armories, clothing depots, shipyards, proving grounds, powder factories, etc.), to construction of river and harbor work, and to works upon the Isthmian Canal."[71] The law clearly saw the massive labor undertaking of the Canal as warranting unique mention. Indeed, the Bureau of Labor Statistics admitted in 1914 that "nearly one half of the accidents and of the compensation paid refer to employment under the Isthmian Canal Commission, with its 25,000 to 30,000 employees, largely unskilled, and working under conditions involving a high degree of hazard."[72] There were few critics of the bill in Congress and it passed with an overwhelming majority of 48 Yeas to 1 Nay (with 43 abstentions). Supporters cited equivalent legislation in Europe on workmen's compensation passed at the height of the Industrial Revolution and the desire to regularize a process that was seen as a burden on the legal system and produced an unfair distribution of compensation.

The creation of a federal injury and death compensation program also had clear precedent in Civil War soldiers' pensions, which the sociologist Theda Skocpol pinpoints as the beginning of the modern welfare state.[73] Pensions for Civil War veterans consumed more than 40 percent of the federal budget in the 1890s, making it the single largest federal expenditure of its time.[74] The process for workmen's compensation echoed that of war pensions, where soldiers and widows had to submit extensive proof of their service, injury, relationships, and behavior supported by documentation from doctors and notaries. The laws were also similarly color-blind, meaning that they did not explicitly mention race and thus theoretically did not discriminate. Yet African American petitioners were less likely to be awarded pensions than their white counterparts, stemming from the disadvantages they experienced in the application process rather than from the law itself.[75]

This dynamic reasserted itself in unique ways in the case of workmen's compensation awarded to Canal employees a decade and a half later. Though the law was technically color-blind and open to all federal employees regardless of citizenship, West Indians faced distinct limitations before they could even be eligible for application. Along with the difficulty in travel and communication time that disadvantaged those living in the islands, West Indians had to first identify their dead as ICC or PRR employees—a project complicated by the carelessness with which some of these corpses were treated. They also had to provide documentary proof of official marriages for legal wives to make claims on compensation, a relationship that was uncommon in the islands. Finally, they faced the racism and discrimination of the Canal administrators who decided on these matters and who, as with many other West Indian deaths, often sought to displace blame from the commission onto the deceased themselves. Due to these various impediments, West Indian women did not engage with the compensation act in large numbers. Instead, they continued using the same strategies of contacting their colonial representatives to honor their dead and receive their effects.

Compensation was paid in cases of injury or death, except when there had been negligence or misconduct on the part of the employee. Every accident or death that called for compensation first had to be reported by the official superior of the employee in question to the designated claims officer in the chairman's office no later than the second day after the accident using form CA-1, or form CA-3 in case of death. These reports had to be accompanied with certificates issued by ICC physicians. In cases of death, section 4 of the act established that the claimant entitled to compensation had to file an affidavit within ninety days of the death "setting forth their relationship to the deceased and the ground of their claim for compensation," also accompanied by a physician's report.[76] Petitioners had to present affidavits witnessed by local police, a notary public, or a local clergyman who testified to the person's destitution and need for a pension, and assured authorities of a legitimate tie between the parties. Under the general law, claims were approved by the secretary of commerce and labor, but in the Canal Zone, the final decision rested with the chairman, who might personally approve, disallow, or request further investigation of a claim.[77] The burden of compensation fell on the same branch of service where the person had been employed. Claimants for compensation resulting from death received "the same amount, for the remainder of the said year, that said artisan or laborer would be entitled to receive as pay if such employee were alive and continue to be employed."[78]

For West Indian women, the official procedure reiterated the process they had already practiced throughout construction; it required them to contact the ICC through the intervention of the British consul. By late 1908, the British had created a standardized form to communicate requests for effects. If they judged that a petitioner was also eligible for compensation under the act, they would forward the ICC claims form which, along with the above specifications, also required a certificate from the police magistrate before whom the claim was signed and a letter from the British consul.

The bill entitled "a widow, a child or children under sixteen years of age, or a dependent parent" to receive compensation. The first draft of the bill made provisions only for dependent "mothers," which was changed to "parent" before the bill passed, highlighting the ways Congress already saw these relationships of compensation as gendered.[79] The final act in fact "contains no provision . . . for a dependent widower even though by reason of infirmity he might be entirely dependent on his wife's earnings."[80] Dependence, as understood by the act, was not merely financial but a gendered relationship where the primary claimant was always imagined to be a woman or a child. A few parents applied as a couple, but almost every single one of these requests was disallowed for failing to establish dependence since the father was expected to provide for the family. Most women did not officially work for the ICC and thus their families would not have been eligible to make requests under the act in the aftermath of their deaths. Requests for compensation thus came overwhelmingly from women in the islands due to the demographics of ICC workers and the understanding of dependence that structured these claims.

Demonstrating a legitimate relationship could be easily accomplished if a wife or mother had been listed as the beneficiary of the worker in the emigrant registration process, but it proved more difficult when multiple family members sought compensation or when "illegitimate" wives and children requested the continued financial support the migrant had provided. In a letter to Consul Mallet regarding the claim for compensation for Stanley Howell's widow, the acting governor of Jamaica responded that "the Laws of this Island do not recognise such relationship known as 'Common Law Marriages' whereby a man and wife may live together without any previous Ecclesiastical or Civil ceremony."[81] The act of May 30 explicitly stated that it did not provide for "illegitimate wives" or divorced wives "in [their] own right." This was a shift from the prevailing practice regarding the return of effects or wages owed. Though the governor of Jamaica did not recognize common-law marriages in conversation with Canal administrators, in practice British authorities sent effects and owed wages to common-law wives with little oversight. The act did allow that "the amount payable on account of children of the deceased may be paid to such illegitimate or divorced wife as guardian and for the benefit of children of the deceased."[82] Thus, while "illegitimate" partners could not receive compensation directly, they could be recognized as legal guardians of the deceased's children and could make claims to the ICC on those grounds.

According to the records of the Bureau of Labor Statistics, "nearly one half of the fatal accidents" claimed under this federal act (which covered all federal employment in U.S. territory) occurred in the Canal Zone.[83] The highest number of fatalities reported there came during the first year following the act, though less than 40 percent of relatives filed claims on these (Table 2). Canal administrators rationalized the low percentage of requests citing many relatives' remoteness or ignorance of the law when it first went into effect.[84] The number of fatalities was likely even higher in the time preceding statistical recording as the early years of the Canal construction involved some of the most dangerous tasks. The high mortality rate of the early years coincides with the high number of requests for effects considered in the previous section. Eventually, the number of fatal incidents reported and claims filed dropped almost by half in 1912–1913, anticipating the end of construction when fewer workers were needed on the project.

Table 2. Claims approved per number of claims filed and fatal accidents reported

Year	Fatal accidents reported	Number of claims filed (percentage of reported fatal accidents)	Number of claims disallowed (percentage of claims filed)
1908–9	233	93 (39.9%)	29 (31%)
1909–10	231	124 (53.7%)	27 (21%)
1910–11	207	148 (71.5%)	26 (17%)
1911–12	218	131 (60.1%)	32 (24%)
1912–13	117	69 (59%)	13 (18.8%)

SOURCE: U.S. Bureau of Labor Statistics, *Report of Operations*, 40–41.

West Indian women who sent requests for compensation from the Isthmian Canal Commission on behalf of "accidental death" during employment often described grisly deaths in attempts to validate their claims. Millicent Marshall of Bridgetown sent a lengthy letter about her recently deceased son, Garfield, saying that he "was employed by the Americans as a brakesman on the train at Gatun Panama, Canal Zone, the destruction of his body that caused his death was this, the train ran across his back almost dividing his upper body and smashed his left hand in pieces and one of his feet."[85] Millicent's letter not only describes her son's and her own suffering in the most specific terms but it also reiterates that this accident occurred to him during work, making her case for compensation.

Like the letters requesting effects, West Indian petitions for compensation highlight the precarious circumstances of these women, such as that of Clara Jones from Barbados, who obsequiously begged the governor for attention to her appeal: "Your petitioner is in a very poor state and condition and unable to help herself and your humble petitioner will ever acknowledge His Excellency's kindness and gratitude."[86] Similarly, Elma Washington, whose relative was run over by eleven railroad cars, begged the governor to "use your influence" and explained that she was "solely dependent on this man . . . and his death will make a great material difference" in her circumstances.[87] These petitioners used a specific language of humility and abject poverty to sway the cases in their favor, given that proving dependence was such a crucial part of compensation requests. Like some of the women in Chapter 3, these petitioners also appropriated the language of patriarchal deference to speak to white colonial administrators.

Petitioners could be denied their relatives' pensions for myriad reasons, some administrative, like failing to file a claim within ninety days, others more subjective, such as whether the claimant had failed to show sufficient proof of destitution. The Canal Commission did not maintain records of claims decisions separated out by race or nationality nor was every claim accompanied by a corresponding decision in the archive. Thus, it is difficult to ascertain which claims were approved or disallowed. However, cross-examining the petitions with the statistics reveals that most disallowed claims were indeed in response to requests from West Indian women. For example, in fiscal year 1911–1912, of the thirty-two claims for fatal accidents that were disallowed, at least thirteen came from West Indians, as evidenced by letters sent by Frank Ward, the claims officer, to the British authorities specifically denying the application. This does not mean that there were not more but that at least thirteen have specific proof of disallowance.[88] Even these incomplete numbers evidence that at least 40 percent of disallowed claims decisions went to West Indians. Some claims were disallowed because the deceased had not been "in the course of employment," such as that of Richard Matthews's mother in Barbados, who was told her son was "evidently so engrossed with his guitar that he did not hear the train approaching" when he was killed. The claims officer recommended denying her claim.[89] By fiscal year 1912–1913, only thirteen claims were disallowed—five for parents not showing dependence, five for injury not in the course of employment, two for negligence or misconduct, and one for an occupation not covered by the act. At least two of the claims disallowed for failing to show dependence came from West Indian couples (mother and father)—claims which the authorities found unconvincing because of gendered expectations that a husband could still provide for his wife, despite the fact that these West Indian couples provided extensive proof of their destitution and dependence on their now-deceased son.

As Table 2 shows, the majority of claims were approved. Of those that went to West Indian claimants, British administrators often tried to disburse the money properly, sending letters throughout the islands attempting to locate dependents. Sometimes they split compensation, if multiple valid claims had been approved, such as in the estate of James A. Prout, which was divided between his mother, the guardian of his child, and his legal widow.[90] The average amount of compensation received for the death of an ICC employee was around $640.74 at its highest and $410.77 at its lowest, which would be an astounding sum, equivalent to several years of wages for a working-class West Indian woman.[91]

However, this act did not radically change the strategies West Indian women used to contact authorities and request their loved one's property. Petitions for effects and belongings continued to far outnumber official claims for compensation even after 1908. Various structural barriers to access, including the marriage requirement, the sometimes-unofficial nature of West Indian employment on the Canal project, the prevalence of disease (not covered by the act and by far the highest cause of death) and lack of sanitation in West Indian lodging, the difficulty in identifying deceased Black men, and the racist understandings of West Indians' own culpability, limited the opportunities for West Indian families on the island to even apply for compensation. This did not stop women from contacting authorities to make inquiries after their relatives and to blame the Canal project for their deaths, but for the most part they did not make official monetary claims on the ICC.

The act solidified a relationship between death and labor value in the Canal Zone that had previously been informed by the pressures West Indian relatives placed on colonial authorities. West Indians had to present their compensation claims under the legal conditions put forth by the act. Common-law wives and extended relatives had little or no recourse to request these funds. Relatives could still request and receive effects after the act, but only a select few could claim the large payouts stemming from official U.S. compensation. The act disavowed the large-scale effects on public health and labor conditions that the Canal construction had on the region, asserting that it was only liable when an employee died in a manner directly related to employment. By connecting value exclusively to the technical aspects of the Canal construction, the act thus diminished the importance of West Indian workers who did not come under the purview of the ICC and valorized those in death only as a direct expression of their connection to the construction effort.

Despite the increasing bureaucratization and legal hurdles, West Indian women continued to use kinship networks for information, mobilizing languages of feminine humility to make their claims, and affirming both the violence of the Canal project and the value of West Indian lives in their requests. These intimate petitions countered the indifference of authorities and statistical records that claimed Black lives were inconsequential except in their contributions to projects of imperial infrastructure. In West Indian women's letters, the lives of workers who traveled to the Canal mattered as part of an extended and mobile circum-Caribbean network of kinship and care.

*   *   *

West Indian women's interventions highlight how they negotiated the dislocations of migration by caring for their communities in death. In sending these petitions, women asserted a vision of rights and obligation that prioritized the needs of their families and kin in the face of an imperial administration that regarded Black workers as important only to the extent that they provided work for the Canal. By leading funerals in the Canal Zone, by memorializing their deceased relatives, and by collecting and distributing the financial gains these men had painstakingly earned in Panama among their families, women's labor of mourning reproduced the collectivity of West Indian life even after death. The seeds of community that women sowed in these early years continue to bear fruit. The segregated Silver people cemeteries of the Canal Zone lay for decades in gross neglect, with headstones badly worn and graves unidentified. Starting in 2006, the CGM (Corozal, Gatun, Mt. Hope) Cemetery Preservation Foundation, founded by a West Indian Panamanian woman, Mrs. Frances Williams Yearwood, spearheaded a preservation effort for these burial grounds. In 2010 the World Monuments Fund declared these endangered sites and in 2012, after much lobbying, the Panamanian National Assembly passed Law #7 declaring the three cemeteries National Historic Patrimony. Today, the organization continues its efforts by helping families in Panama and the Caribbean locate the unmarked graves of their loved ones and trying to integrate Silver histories into Panamanian educational curricula.

CHAPTER 6

Private Honor and Public Lives in Panama City

On May 22, 1917, Barbadian Rebecca Williams denounced her Barbadian neighbor Louisa Thompson, whom she alleged would get drunk and berate her, saying her genitals "smelled like rotten fish and cat's dung."[1] Rebecca insisted that Louisa was only jealous because they were in direct competition as higglers who both sold candy. The fight had not stopped merely at insults; Louisa had threatened to make their landlord evict Rebecca from the tenement building they shared. Louisa loudly and dramatically insulted Rebecca in a fight over market territory, hoping that rumors and social pressure would result in her eviction. Rebecca did not take this lightly and brought a case of *ultrajes*, or insults, to the local *corregidor*, or municipal judge, to defend her reputation against Louisa.

This kind of case was not unusual in the municipal courts of neighborhoods of Panama City that bordered the Canal Zone, which housed West Indian immigrants and workers living in Panama as an alternative to the discrimination of the U.S. territory. These areas had further expanded as a result of the 1912 depopulation order that had expelled all remaining West Indians living in the Zone. In the years following depopulation, West Indian women far outdid every other category of plaintiff in bringing cases to municipal Panama City courts. More than half of all the cases in the central corregiduría of Calidonia, for example, were insult suits brought by West Indian women against fellow West Indian women. These were variously named *injurias*, *provocaciones*, *ultrajes*, or *calumnias*, which all essentially meant the same thing—slander or a verbal insult to the dignity or honor of another.

The process of depopulation cast West Indians into an in-between space— rejected from living in the Canal Zone while unable to access the substantive benefits of Panamanian citizenship. Though an escape from the rigid segregation of the Zone, West Indian women nevertheless faced unique challenges in moving to Panama, where elite visions of honor butted up against women's vernacular articulations of reputation. Through their municipal court suits, West Indian women claimed reputation in the context of social inequality and political exclusion in Panama. Panamanian understandings of gendered citizenship dictated a particular script of honor that cordoned off the sexual and private from the public sphere—an untenable distinction for West Indian women who lived, worked, and transited continuously through public space.[2] West Indian women rejected these "normative scripts of sexual citizenship" in Panama that cast them as dishonorable.[3] Instead, they interjected their notions of reputation into the Panamanian public sphere, informed by Afro-Caribbean women's countercultural traditions of brash sexuality such as "slackness" in Jamaica and *jamette* culture in Trinidad, both associated with Black urban working-class women.[4] They thus forced the municipal institutions of Panama City to contend with their own versions of reputation.

As in Rebecca Williams and Louisa Thompson's case, West Indian women invariably used the idiom of sexual impropriety to tackle these interpersonal conflicts, whether they were, at heart, of a sexual nature or not.[5] West Indian women often directed these insults toward other women, seemingly reproducing elite characterizations of their behavior as dishonorable. But, as Lara Putnam notes for working-class women in Puerto Limón who engaged in similar patterns of legal participation, these vulgar exchanges were rather "scripts" through which women performed a "street theater" of personal reputation.[6] West Indian women's quarrels and complaints served as strategies of survival and deployments of erotic agency. Through them, West Indian women claimed space and reputation, protected their families, and defended their incomes during a period of liminal belonging in Panamanian territory.

The category of honor has a long-standing history in Latin America, where it defined hierarchical relationships throughout the colonial period, legitimizing landholding, political access, and patriarchal power over subordinates. One's honor depended on birth, lineage, nobility, religion, and racial purity as well as on public reputation and behavior. As elites sought to modernize postindependence Latin American nations in the nineteenth century, they molded these colonial codes of honor to liberal projects of state-making.[7] While committed to developing representative government on the basis of individual equality, liberal codes of law retained social hierarchies and transferred some of the patriarchal authority formerly invested in male heads of household to the state. As in other regions of Latin America, honor in twentieth-century Panama remained informed by patriarchal codes of public standing; colonial Iberian discourses of purity, race, and legitimacy; and norms of female sexual behavior.[8] For Panamanian women, to be honorable meant maintaining sexual propriety, remaining dependents of a patriarch, and practicing public decorum. It further meant to be publicly and visually recognized as honorable, a notion informed by behavior, reputation, dress, class, and race. These normative expectations of honor shaped the bounds of citizenship as it delineated access to political, economic, and legal power for those who were unable to access or display honor.

In the context of the Canal construction, honor and inclusion were further informed by the extension of U.S. influence into Panamanian affairs and its threat to the power of Panamanian elites, which they understood as an attack on their honor and sovereignty.[9] U.S. administrators took charge of hospitals, banks, and police forces in Colón and Panama City. They overhauled city infrastructure, building roads, bridges, and trams. U.S. soldiers traveling across the Zone's borders fueled the growth of red-light districts in these same cities. American politicians interfered directly in Panamanian politics, forcing the resignation of Carlos Mendoza in 1911 and supporting the election of Belisario Porras a year later, the first among many direct interventions. Thus, while many Panamanian elites collaborated with the United States, they simultaneously resented the perceived undermining of their power as both elite patriarchs and representatives of the newly formed state. They resented, as well, the West Indian immigrant population that they deeply associated with the arrival of the United States, seeing it as an unwelcome intrusion into their established national social hierarchy. This left West Indian migrant women with little access to honor in the Panamanian context, marked by their racial difference, their independent work in the public sphere outside of patriarchal structures, and their association with the U.S. project.

The category of honor did not play a central role in Afro-Caribbean societies as it had historically in Latin America. Rather, as anthropologist Peter
Wilson has explained, Caribbean value systems were structured around a
tension between reputation and respectability. In his classic 1973 formulation
of this dynamic, he defined respectability as the bourgeois, Eurocentric values oriented toward church and the home that maintained social hierarchy,
and reputation as the indigenous, Afrocentric counterculture that defied these
values with verbal dexterity, trickery, and mobility.[10] According to Wilson,
while men embody the values of reputation, Afro-Caribbean women sub-
scribe to respectability and are more invested in following Eurocentric
moral codes. Feminist Caribbean theorists have strongly opposed Wilson's
binary, showing that Caribbean women also performed central roles in countercultural resistance through higglering, religious practice, and family
land trusteeship.[11] Moreover, these theorists argue, Wilson's model ignores
how Black women, caught at the margins of power, have historically been
forced to juggle both reputation and respectability.[12]

This is precisely the tightrope that West Indian women walked in Panama, where U.S. and Panamanian authorities defined moral and sanitary personhood and the limits of inclusion. Women's daily conflicts transpired in
the context of the end of construction, the massive depopulation of the Canal Zone, and the subsequent movement of West Indians to Panamanian territory amid growing xenophobia. These material circumstances imposed
distinct imperatives of honor on West Indian women, who had little standing in either Zonian or Panamanian society. West Indian women's quarrels
with each other were central to their struggles for reputation and respectability within an environment where they were constantly suspected of dishonorable labor. The scarcity of honor for Black West Indian women structured
their public claims to reputation.

These women did not self-consciously use the language of rights or citizenship. Indeed, at the time, most West Indian women residing in Panama
would either be ineligible for citizenship, which required ten years of con-
tinuous residence, or had not petitioned for it. These women's insults could
sometimes replicate elite and imperial ideologies of honor and reproduced
discourses of racial, class, and gender exclusion against their own neighbors

who were dealing with situations of domestic violence or precarious labor. But by bringing cases to the municipal judge, these women claimed public space and extracted apologies from their rivals to reassert their reputation and negotiate "niches of autonomy" within their neighborhoods.[13] They also forced nascent Panamanian legal institutions to deal with their quarrels and, at least at the local level, treat them as they would a Panamanian citizen.

The early legal codes of Panama detail how the state defined honor through a separation of public and private spheres, linked to hierarchical racialized and gendered understandings of who was honorable. Understandings of honor arose not only from legal documents but also from the quotidian relationships of urban life in West Indian neighborhoods of Panama City like El Marañon. A combination of U.S. pressures and Panamanian elite interests marked these newly formed West Indian neighborhoods as sites of immorality through urban development projects that built red-light districts in the vicinity of these communities. This placed West Indian residents, particularly women, precariously adjacent to vice, marking them as less honorable by association with the public lives of sex workers. Cast as marginal to the body politic and at the bottom of a hierarchy of honor, West Indian women nevertheless sought the intercession of the Panamanian state to claim reputation by bringing insult cases to their local municipal courts against fellow West Indian women. Through these intimate disputes, West Indian women managed their relationship to urban space in Panama during a complex juncture of heightened nationalism and anti–West Indian sentiment. In their vulgar everyday quarrels, they challenged elite discourses of honor and claimed social standing within their neighborhoods.

Crimes Against Honor in Panama

The most distinct articulation of honor in Panama came through its legal codes, which outlined crimes that caused dishonor (such as insults and provocation), as well as crimes mitigated by a participant's reputation. Throughout the codes, honor was tied to the intrusion of private matters into the public sphere and associated almost exclusively with women's sexual behavior. "Crimes against honor" delineated the problem of private concerns being made public and considered a person's public reputation in assigning punishment. The codes paid particular attention to women's sexual behavior, specifying that offenders were not guilty of wrongdoing in cases of homicide against disloyal wives and outlining lessened penalties for abortion if women confessed to committing these crimes to hide their state and preserve their honor. This articulation of honor as a clear-cut distinction between public and private placed West Indian women, whose lives and labor challenged that separation, at odds with expectations of femininity in Panama.

Throughout the construction decade, the legal codes of Panama (civil, criminal, and penal) were in fact adoptions of the most recent Colombian codes, which had remained in effect after Panama's independence from Colombia. Eighteen days after the proclamation of Panama as an independent republic, on November 21, 1903, the provisional government announced Legislative Decree 19 maintaining the same judicial organization and legislation that had reigned in the department of Panama in decades prior.[14] Panama would not adopt its first republican code of laws until October 1, 1917, three years after the Canal's completion.[15]

The 1890 Colombian Penal Code contained an entire chapter dedicated to "Riñas y Peleas" (Quarrels and Fights), defined as a "singular combat between two or more people, whether they enter into it by mutual consent, or by provocation by one of them, or by some incidental accident."[16] Provocation specifically included that which caused "affront, dishonor, or denigration." Injurias comprised four occasions:

1. "an offense made verbally to the individual's honor, credit, dignity, and that which constitutes their moral propriety,"
2. the "dissemination of purely private or domestic vices,"
3. "Defamation, that is, words that involve opprobrium or contempt told to a person's face,"
4. refusing to give signals of respect to those required by law, and,
5. publicly reproaching another for a committed crime or fault.[17]

Each of these instances involved the private made public, whether words told "to a person's face," a public reproach, or the airing out of "private vices." The fourth occasion considered not giving signals of respect in public a crime against honor, showing the ties between urban space and the culture of honor as well as the importance of the collective acceptance of these codes and signals. The law further specified the patriarchal structures that defined these insults; it was never considered injuria if it was committed by parents/fathers (*padres*), teachers, tutors, bosses, and superiors against their subordinates.

Honor was taken seriously throughout the 1890 Penal Code, which stipulated the dignity and enlightenment of the offender and their obligations toward society as attenuating circumstances for punishment. Honor, or dignity, was thus a relational category, dependent on the opinion of others and on public standing vis-à-vis society. The parallel between dignity and enlightenment hints at the class markers of honor in Panama; to be educated and cultured (accessible only to a privileged few elites) meant to be honorable. A person's honor could have serious effects on criminal outcomes. The crime of abortion, for example, normally carried a one- to three-year sentence for a woman found to have committed a successful one. But, the code added, "If she were an honorable woman and of good reputation" and if her only motivation was to "conceal her fragility," the period of imprisonment would be considerably shorter, only five to ten months.[18] The code does not explain how to identify an honorable woman (it would be up to the judges), but the discourses that so easily linked West Indian women to sex work and public lives characterized them as less honorable than other women in Panama. Black West Indian women were rarely afforded the privilege of fragility.

The first official Panamanian Penal Code separate from its Colombian antecedent was not elaborated until 1916, under a commission appointed by President Porras.[19] The code was officially adopted in October 1917. Though most of the cases in this chapter would have been heard under the earlier Penal Code, the new legal statutes of 1917 give a sense of the ideas about honor that circulated in Panama at the time, promoted by the same elites who ruled Panama and developed its urban neighborhoods. The 1917 code further solidified notions of honor, cataloging injurias and calumnias under the banner of "Crimes against Honor."[20] Injuria gained a new moral angle in the code, which defined a grave offense as "the ascription of a vice or moral failing, the consequences of which could considerably harm the reputation, credit, or interest of the victim."[21] The gravity of these insults depended on the "condition, dignity, and circumstances of the offended and the offender."[22]

The code retained its concern about the public nature of these crimes, exacerbating the punishment depending on how widespread the insults had been disseminated. Notably, the only other mentions of honor in the 1917 Penal Code were in the crimes of infanticide and abortion, where the penalty lessened if a woman committed these crimes to hide her "deshonra."[23] An honorable woman did not engage in premarital or extramarital sex and, importantly, hid evidence of any sexual behavior from the public eye.

The criminal justice system, consisting of circuit and municipal courts and a federal Supreme Court, oversaw crimes against honor as outlined in the Penal Code. But Panama residents could also bring complaints to their local corregidor, a public functionary who answered to the district Alcalde or mayor. The alcaldes ruled over large districts, organized into smaller corregimientos or municipalities, each of which had its own police force and municipal judge. For example, the District of Panama, which encompassed Panama City, comprised four corregimientos: San Felipe, El Chorrillo, Santa Ana, and Calidonia.[24] The corregidor had jurisdiction over an array of minor crimes outlined in the administrative and police codes, such as petty theft, small-time fraud, minor insults, and some assaults. The corregidor was not an elected position and had few other legislative counterweights—they answered only to the alcalde, not to the judicial branch.[25] They had close ties to the local police and served as an immediate arbiter of minor crimes investigated by the force, though they also heard complaints brought by community members of the district.

Under Article 163 of the Administrative Code of 1916, "the goods, rights, and actions of foreigners will be protected by the same judges, tribunals, or administrative authorities that protect those of nationals," meaning that West Indian immigrants had access to the same legislative institutions as Panamanian citizens, though they faced the barriers of language, money, and familiarity with local institutions.[26] Nevertheless, any resident within district boundaries could technically make claims to the local corregidor. District residents who sought to pursue certain claims, such as insult, could choose to submit these to the corregidor directly for a quick ruling and lessened penalties. Corregidores were, at least ideally, embedded in their communities and ostensibly understood local conflicts with a certain empathy that federal or district courts might have lacked. The corregidor system thus permitted district residents to, at times, forgo direct police intervention in their disputes and to proceed through a complaint more efficiently than in the traditional judicial system of Panama.

Understanding the legal definitions of honor and the administration of justice in Panama further contextualizes West Indian women's insult cases as an alternative script to dominant national discourses. West Indian women, who lived in crowded tenements and worked as domestic servants and market hawkers, had little chance of securing honor, as per the legal codes of Panama, by living their lives in private. Instead, they practiced their own codes of respect and reputation and negotiated publicly within their local Panamanian legal system to instrumentalize their definitions. For West Indian women, reputation was built on the loud and public defense of their behavior among their immediate community, not in hiding private matters from the public eye to maintain their honor.

Honor and Urban Space in Panama City

While honor was legally codified, it also depended on relational observations of status and reputation in public spaces. West Indian women's public lives— their work in others' homes and in street markets, their independent migration, their common-law marriages—made them morally suspect in the eyes of Canal Zone and Panamanian administrators. Moreover, as West Indian women settled in Panama, they found certain conditions that further cemented their exclusion as second-class subjects and distanced them from honorable behavior. In Panamanian territory, West Indians were forced to live in tenement housing built adjacent to red-light districts, regulated under municipal laws that limited public displays of private (i.e., intimate or sexual) behavior. Though Panamanian attempts at controlling morality were not directed solely against West Indian women, the regulation of these multiracial red-light areas contributed to the creation of normative, quotidian understandings of honor and respectability in Panama's public spaces that directly affected the Black West Indian women who resided in these neighborhoods.

The Panamanian state excluded West Indians in several ways during the early years of increased migration into the national territory. It did not provide free plots of land for West Indians displaced from the Canal Zone as it did for Panamanian citizens and European immigrants.[27] It enforced segregation on railroad cars between Panamanians and West Indians.[28] It built barriers to naturalization and withheld the benefits of substantive citizenship from those who were able to naturalize.[29] Panama's structural discrimination against West Indians took a particularly gendered expression when seen at the level of urban neighborhoods in Panama City, where a combination of U.S. influence, Panamanian regulation, and elite real estate investment solidified the discursive and geographic association of West Indian neighborhoods with immorality.

West Indian settlement in Panama City was concentrated in the neighborhoods of El Marañon, Guachapali, and Chorrillo.[30] El Marañon, now the site of the West Indian Museum of Panama, and Guachapali immediately next to it, had seen West Indian settlement since the period of the railroad in the 1850s, with the construction of wooden boardinghouses that sheltered workers who could not otherwise afford lodging in Panama.[31] As the Canal construction began, West Indian migrants continued to move into these neighborhoods adjacent to the Zone, creating a massive influx of new tenants and new construction of tenement housing. Both neighborhoods were incorporated into the *corregiduria* of Calidonia. Chorrillo is located on the southwest side of the city, on the opposite end of the Casco Antiguo (the old city) from Calidonia. Chorrillo became a predominantly West Indian neighborhood during the construction decade and remains so to this day, still scarred from heavy bombing during the 1989 U.S. invasion of Panama.

These areas were across the border from the Canal Zone. Residents could easily board the Panama Railroad to take them to their jobs at various stopping points on the line. This proximity attracted Canal employees and served as a selling point for Panamanian landowners capitalizing on the real estate boom that followed construction and depopulation. These landowners advertised Chorrillo as a neighborhood that would inevitably benefit from the economic development promised by the Canal's completion, such as a 1914 *Star and Herald* ad that declared: "The Canal completed and in operation will make Balboa, Ancon and Panama the most active part of the Isthmus, with CHORRILLO as the center of this activity. The future of the Chorrillo District is, therefore, assured. No part of Panama was ever built up as quickly as was Chorrillo."[32]

These celebratory ads obscured how this development process forced West Indians to desperately seek housing in Panama and allowed Panamanian elites to profit from their demand. The Joint Land Commission, a binational legal body created to decide on all claims of compensation for property expropriated by the United States in the Canal Zone, expelled West Indians from the Zone and denied most of their land claims. Meanwhile, they approved the claims of Alberto B. de Obarrio, who posted the 1914 ad to sell lots from his existing holdings in Chorrillo. In 1919 Obarrio received compensation and compound interest on his expropriated Canal Zone property to the value of $16,027. This property, named "Los Pocitos," abutted Panama City and included both a quarry and land "as adaptable for building purposes as the adjoining District of Chorrillo."[33] Thus, the Joint Land Commission granted elite Panamanian men like Obarrio large sums after assessing their land's value as potential real estate, while leaving West Indians with few housing options and little, if any, compensation.[34] This dynamic financially fed the construction of neighborhoods like Chorrillo as impoverished West Indian enclaves.

The cheapest room in Panama City in 1905 cost around $6 Panamanian silver a month but usually ran much higher, from around $12 to $20. This would rent you a room in a two- or three-story wooden tenement building with a zinc roof, built around a central courtyard. The ground floor was sometimes occupied by a local business, such as a saloon or a Chinese-owned grocery and convenience store. Each floor had a wide veranda running across its length. The balconies held charcoal stoves as apartments were cramped and an indoor kitchen created too much of a fire hazard. The nicer buildings had a shared sink and latrine for each floor. Otherwise, the entire building shared one facility in the courtyard for everything from washing up to cleaning a chicken. As British traveler Winifred James commented, "In these houses scores of families live together, and on the verandahs and balconies everything happens."[35] Cramped quarters and shared facilities made everyday life a public affair, particularly for the women who used these common areas as both living and work spaces to provide domestic service, cook, wash or iron laundry they had taken in from their clients, and supervise children.

To improve ventilation, the rooms were sometimes separated by walls that did not reach the ceiling. A West Indian woman complained to the alcalde that her room was separated from her neighbor's merely by a wall panel and that her neighbors' three chickens kept her up at night.[36] Jamaican journalist Henry de Lisser commented on a West Indian neighborhood in the city of Colón: "You wonder how human beings can have consented to live amidst such frightful surroundings." He described the stagnant water, buzzing flies, and rotting animal matter that surrounded the tenements, all filled to their utmost capacity.[37] This crowdedness was by design. Boardinghouses across Panama City were built and owned by Panamanian elites and American investors, who built this "rigorously commercial" form of architecture guided by the primary criteria of obtaining "the maximum number of individual rooms for workers and temporary tenants . . . without any consideration for human life."[38]

West Indian neighborhoods, which grew exponentially in the years after the Zone's depopulation, also became associated with the sex trade as part of new urban planning efforts by Panamanian political and economic elites. Prostitution was illegal in the Canal Zone but allowed and regulated in Panamanian territory. The sex trade was concentrated in the red-light districts of Panama City and Colón, known respectively as the Navajo and Boca Grande. These areas lay adjacent to the central districts of both cities, within easy access for guests and arrivals from across the border of the Zone who sought entertainment in Panama. As the *Colón Starlet* reported in 1906, tenement buildings often had saloons on the ground floor that were constantly busy from the sale of liquors to the tenants of the same buildings.[39] These mixed-use living and commercial establishments sometimes served as sites of sexual labor, blurring the line as to what constituted a red-light district or business.

Alcaldías oversaw the licensing of local brothels, registering sex workers, and mandating medical exams. The alcalde served as an administrative official, judicial authority, and commander of the district police. Panamanian law promulgated and enforced by these alcaldes regulated prostitution in ways that deeply marked urban space. For example, Decree 18 of 1912 in

Panama City stipulated that the entrance of a brothel must have "resistant wood shutters which will have fixed curtains and will be at least ¾ the size of the door," while Colon's Municipal Decree 48 of 1912 forbade prostitutes from visiting public places in indecent dress, "walking in the interiors of Parks," or riding in "open coaches or automobiles."[40] Municipal regulations thus had rather more concern with public spectacle than with health or sanitation. Most of these laws sought to silence and segregate erotic labor from the public sphere, even stipulating the length of curtains that would hide the activities inside a brothel.

These regulations were meant to reduce the visibility and movement of sex workers in response to complaints from area residents, such as American Walter Stephens who in 1916 described how prostitutes had started working in buildings facing the railroad line, where they sat "in the open doorways with their legs cocked up and their skirts sometimes above their knees showing their naked skin above the full display of neat purple stockings with red garters and pretty white bow ties a strong contrast to their depraved looking faces."[41] He was particularly offended by "a fat black damsel with no shirt on but a short pink petticoat split open wide in the front" who, against sanitary guidelines, had dumped a bucket of dirty water off her front porch. Stephens's complaint focused on the prevalence of sex workers in the area that connected the Canal Zone to Panama as an issue of sanitation and morality, though his eager description of their stockings perhaps belies a more erotic interest. It was precisely women's status in this in-between area, where people of different classes and races came together, that propelled him to write this complaint, using the figure of an unsanitary Black woman (decidedly meant to signify a West Indian woman) to stoke the concerns of authorities.

As Stephens's complaint shows, these municipal regulations did not exist separately from U.S. opinion and influence. American officials constantly interceded on local decisions regarding red-light districts, such as barring leases for vice businesses on Panama Railroad property and persecuting those suspected of "white-slave trafficking" under the Mann Act. For example, in 1911 the government of the Canal Zone complained to the Panamanian government of three "houses of prostitution" on Panama City's J Street. These "resorts" were "operated so openly . . . without any restraint whatsoever" that they were "decidedly objectionable" to the Ancon residents who used this road to transit from the Canal Zone to Panama.[42] Panama's secretary of foreign affairs, Federico Boyd, assured the government of the Canal Zone that, on their recommendation, the alcalde would close these establishments.[43]

While influenced by U.S. interests, these legal stipulations were also local elite remakings of Panamanian national law. In 1913 President Porras sought to further solidify Panamanian national sovereignty by appointing a commission to write the first legal codes of Panama. Led by Carlos Mendoza and including men such as Harmodio Arias, Ricardo Alfaro, and Angel Ugarte, the commission represented the same urban oligarchy that owned property throughout the emergent West Indian neighborhoods of central Panama City. These elites, a veritable who's who of the wealthy republican *hombres públicos* of Panama, brought their own notions of morality to their reenvisioning of the Panamanian nation. As historian Jeffrey Parker shows, this elite perceived themselves as protectors of the Panamanian nation from the incursion of American imperialism, in particular the sexual appetites of U.S. soldiers. Foreign prostitutes, though immoral and in need of strict regulation, were seen as a necessary buffer for the protection of respectable Panamanian women.[44] It was thus the same cadre of elite men who simultaneously promoted the project of Panamanian nation-building through a discourse of morality, established a set of legal codes that privileged honor for respectable women, and profited from tenement housing and red-light businesses in West Indian neighborhoods.

Panamanian elites explicitly shaped urban space in relation to sex work by backing the creation of red-light districts. The notorious Cocoa Grove was founded in 1911 by Panamanian authorities who conceived it as a periphery of the urban core, where they could displace unwanted prostitution. As a 1916 plan of the area shows, however, the entertainment district was only a periphery from the perspective of these same elites.[45] In fact, it was located in the middle of Chorrillo, a newly formed neighborhood populated by West Indian transplants from the Canal Zone, bordered by Calle B in the north, Calle Mateo Iturralde in the south, and abutting the cemetery on its western flank.

Cocoa Grove held many cabarets and joints (particularly "Negro Joints") but also some "Bed Houses" and a few Chinese shops and restaurants (or "Chop Suey Joints"), meaning people of many different nationalities made their lives and businesses in the area.[46] The records further show that, despite criticizing its presence as a red-light district, the majority of property owners in the area were the same elite Panamanian families, many under the association of the Panama Real Estate Company. This included the famous Arias family, to which Harmodio and Arnulfo, two notoriously xenophobic Panamanian presidents of the 1930s and 1940s belonged. It also included other political elites such as Augusto S. Boyd, whose father, Federico, presided over the Municipal Council, served as acting president for a short period and, coincidentally, was tapped by U.S. authorities as Panama's representative on the Joint Land Commission. Boyd was one of the very judges whose decisions expropriated land from West Indians in the Zone and forced their resettlement to Panama where they would then be forced to pay rent on property owned by his family.[47] Thus, while regulating and criticizing prostitution, these elite Panamanians also profited from the expansion of the sex trade during the construction years.

West Indian residents of Panama did not always appreciate the construction of entertainment districts in their vicinity. A group of disgruntled Silver employees living in Guachapali sent a letter to the head of the ICC civil administration expressing their fear that "what we would consider a calamity, may be realized—that is, the fact of either compelling us to live alongside of women of ill repute, to the evident detriment of ourselves and our families, who although humble, should not be scorned or else compel us to give up our work."[48] This letter, signed by members and leaders of the Baptist and Christian Mission Churches—all men, all Canal employees—drew a line between respectable and humble West Indian families and the sex workers who lived alongside them. The letter reflected the very particular viewpoint of churchgoing, married, and relatively well-employed West Indians who understood this proximity as an "evident detriment" to themselves. The writers used their labor as leverage, threatening to withdraw from work unless the Zone administration responded to their complaint. Though no such specific strike happened, issues of respectability in relation to nearby red-light districts continued to structure West Indian understandings of their own positions in Panamanian society.

For some working-class West Indian women, red-light districts like Cocoa Grove could instead provide an escape from the stricter expectations of marriage and served as a way to create financial independence. For example, in an assault case between Martinican Ercilia Clair and her partner, Jamaican laborer Thomas Price, Ercilia declared to the corregidor that she had left Thomas to become a prostitute in Cocoa Grove. The case started on January 12, 1914, when Thomas hit Ercilia on the head after a fight over some money in his room on Calle 25 Este.[49] Thomas and Ercilia had lived as husband and wife for seven months but, according to her testimony, she left him for Cocoa Grove because of "a scandal for which she went to the police" and because they had "no money with which go out."[50]

As a site of entertainment and a place to enjoy activities deemed illegal in the Canal Zone such as prostitution and gambling, Cocoa Grove already existed as an interstitial zone, where hostilities and tensions among residents and colonizers bubbled constantly under the surface.[51] Brothels like La Boheme and the Tuxedo, Chinese lottery shops, and saloons butted up against each other in a ten-block area. Here, workers, prostitutes, bartenders, waitresses, and entertainers, hailing from many places including the West Indies, Panama, France, and the United States, engaged in many forms of salacious entertainment.[52] Areas like Cocoa Grove "provided an escape from the more regimented, respectable, and segregated world of the Zone" for American soldiers, marines, and Canal employees.[53] As policeman Harry Franck explained, "Panama and Colon serve as a sort of safety valve" for Canal Zone employees to let off steam.[54] It played a similar but complex role for West Indian women, who could go there as audiences seeking entertainment but also as workers who themselves provided the entertainment. Ercilia herself saw sex work in Cocoa Grove as an avenue for securing her own finances. But the enmeshing of Cocoa Grove with West Indian neighborhoods meant it could never serve as an uncomplicated escape for West Indian women, who already traversed and worked in adjoining spaces and whose lives could not necessarily be separated from the red-light district. Ercilia, for example, did not choose to visit Cocoa Grove purely for temporary entertainment like American soldiers but rather to leave an abusive relationship in which she remained entangled. She would have made some money but was likely still subject to financial insecurity and violent assault from customers and bosses. Cocoa Grove could mean a continuation of abuse, poverty, and police surveillance as much as it could mean entertainment or opportunity.

Living in one of Panama's West Indian neighborhoods also meant being subject to police surveillance and violence. As an anonymous West Indian "Sympathizer" wrote to the *Star and Herald* in 1914 about Chorrillo: "Thus far we are left alone in a strange land to strangers. Had it not been for the Americans we would have been massacred by Panamanian police many times in this district. One day during this past month Policeman No. 412 (hat number) handcuffed a West Indian to his horse and galloped up Twenty-Third Street, cuffing the prisoner on the head and face while the horse was going."[55] The letter shows not only the shocking cruelty with which local police treated West Indians but also the despair some West Indians felt at living in a strange land where they had few sources of support. The police further enforced prostitution regulations in these neighborhoods and embroiled themselves in the intimate lives of its residents. Ercilia and Thomas's case, for example, came in front of the corregidor because agent no. 130 of the Panama police happened to walk by, see her wound, and arrest them. Ercilia had been in trouble before, arrested for *escándalo*, and worried that this would be a new arrest under that charge, insisting that they had made no escándalo during their fight. She saw police intervention not as protection from domestic abuse but as a potentially incriminating factor that would result in further trouble with the law.

After depopulation, West Indians moved to Panamanian territory where they concentrated in urban districts adjacent to the Canal Zone such as El Marañon and Chorrillo. Though some of these neighborhoods had seen West Indian settlement since the mid-nineteenth century, the influx of migrants spurred a real estate boom that drove the rapid construction of ramshackle tenement buildings to house the new arrivals. These buildings were owned by a small group of elite Panamanians who both profited off this urban development and actively shaped it through their influence in national and local politics. These neighborhoods also became the planned sites of new red-light districts meant to regulate the increased demand and supply of sex work and entertainment in Panama as a result of the Canal construction. The criminalization of sex work in the Canal Zone and its concomitant legalization in Panamanian territory, the construction boom that fueled the growth of West Indian tenement housing alongside red-light districts, the continued concern with sanitation and public respectability that structured Panamanian legislation, and the everyday policing of West Indian life in these growing neighborhoods all deeply shaped West Indian life in Panama. Together, these developments contributed to making morality, honor, and respectability central concerns for West Indians trying to establish themselves in this strange new land.

Defending Reputation in Panama City

Though pressures from American and Panamanian authorities crucially shaped the establishment of West Indian neighborhoods in Panama, these communities also came into being through the everyday encounters of residents like Rebecca Williams and Louisa Thompson. The case files of municipal corregidores provide an on-the-ground view of how West Indian women understood their relationship to their neighbors in terms of reputation. These cases show a distinct predominance of working-class West Indian women as plaintiffs in insult suits with other West Indian women. Rebecca and Louisa's case illustrates the themes that marked all these women's conflicts: a concern with sex work and sexual impropriety, the use of public rudeness to defend personal reputations, and an ongoing battle over belonging and territory in newly formed neighborhoods. West Indian women for whom Panamanian versions of honor were inaccessible relied not on veiling the private from the public for social standing but rather on the capacity to loudly fight back against attacks on their reputation.

As much as the cases attest to West Indian women's loud and public claims for recognition, they also testify to their extreme vulnerability. These women resided in crowded tenement housing at constant risk of eviction, they faced abuse from their partners, they eked out a living in peripheral economies, and they faced persistent suspicion of prostitution from American authorities in ways that marked their everyday lives. It is precisely in these arenas where they were most vulnerable that West Indian women turned on each other. In their frequent references to sex work, partner abuse, and eviction during their quarrels, we can see West Indian women's own awareness of their vulnerability to legal, physical, and discursive violence in Panama.

These strategies did not spring up spontaneously in Panama. In late nineteenth- and early twentieth-century Barbados, women outnumbered men in prisons, accused mostly of petty crime such as "disorderly conduct, using abusive language, and so on to assaulting and beating."[56] In 1901–1902, these crimes accounted for 55.18 percent of the female prison population.[57] This speaks not only to the discipline and surveillance women faced but to their navigation of their role as public figures in streets and marketplaces through the strategies of what officialdom called disorderly conduct and abusive language. In Trinidad, the young, unmarried, Creole, and working-class female population was also frequently charged with indecent behavior, disorderly conduct, and obscene language and developed the oppositional jamette culture that scandalized elite Victorian values and served at the forefront of social protest.[58] In an 1869 protest against the Contagious Disease Ordinance that required voluntary medical examinations of suspected prostitutes, jamettes, "without political power, unorganized and mostly illiterate . . . used the only tools available to them, shouting and screaming their way to their weekly examination, flagrantly demonstrating their resentment in ways that attracted attention to them as a group. Ironically, such behaviour only reinforced the negative stereotypes that 'decent' society already applied to them."[59]

In Panama, working-class West Indian women turned again to these strategies, the "only tools available to them." They appropriated and creolized official discourses of sanitation and prostitution to claim their reputation and protect their nascent neighborhoods. West Indian women asserted themselves rudely and publicly through their fights, challenging the binary of public/private that structured notions of honor in Panama. Though they sometimes reiterated stereotypes about Black women's immorality, they also forced the new legal institutions of Panama to contend with and recognize their claims to reputation.

My discussion of these cases draws from the corregiduría of Calidonia, which included the West Indian enclaves of El Marañon and Guachapali. I focus on the year immediately following the end of construction, 1914, along with a handful of cases from the years 1915 through 1917. I focus in on this period for two reasons. First, the new Panamanian Penal Code went into effect in 1917 and changed the legal environment. Second, my focus is on the initial transition of West Indians to Panama in the years after depopulation, before the establishment of more distinct community organizations. Unfortunately, the case files for these early years are woefully incomplete, thus complicating attempts at long-term assessment. For the year 1914, for example, the municipality of Calidonia holds only 46 cases, despite the fact that the last extant file is Docket #120 for a case heard in early November (implying the existence of at least 74 cases unaccounted for).

Nevertheless, these cases show some distinct patterns worth looking at more closely.[60] Within those 46 cases, West Indian women served as plaintiffs in 16, far outdoing every other category of plaintiff. In comparison, West Indian and Panamanian men, respectively, brought nine and eight suits, while Panamanian women only brought three (two of these by the same woman). Women of nationalities other than West Indian very rarely brought cases to the corregidor, even in other municipalities, such as nearby multi-ethnic Santa Ana. The remaining cases show a smattering of other nationalities including Colombian, Italian, and American. Out of the 16 cases West Indian women brought to the corregidor in 1914, half (8) were insult suits brought against other West Indian women, sometimes paired with scandal or assault. These general patterns held for other proximate years. For May–December 1917 (the other months not included among the files), West Indian women served as plaintiffs in 20 out of 31 cases, an entire two-thirds of all the cases the corregidor heard for half that year. Fourteen of those (45 percent of total cases) were for insults.

If a fight escalated, both participants could face up to twelve days in prison, but even for small disputes, participants were often required to provide a *fianza de paz*, a legal promise to observe peaceful behavior. These bonds were usually set at fifty silver pesos and required women to have a guarantor. This was the most common outcome for insult cases; in almost half the cases between West Indian women, both were required to present fianzas de paz, especially when both participants brought witnesses that supported their narrative. Thus, the value of these cases did not usually lie in punishing your opponent but in the public airing of grievances. In front of the judge and a slew of witnesses, a woman could retell her version of events and defend herself against allegations. Though the corregidor never made anyone recant or apologize for libel, the women nevertheless saw the local court as a place to set the record straight. More rarely, one of the participants was found guilty and given a short prison sentence. In 1914 only two of the injuria cases resulted in prison sentences. In Irene Geddes's complaint of ultrajes by Delfina (possibly Delphine) Todman, Irene brought three witnesses to Delfina's zero. Delfina was given ten days of commutable arrest.[61]

In one case of slander, Jamaican Claris Bennett accused Barbadian Ambrosina Prescott of insulting her publicly.[62] Claris and Ambrosina lived in the same tenement. In Claris's statement, she declared that on August 19, 1914, Ambrosina started insulting her obscenely as she was returning from work. Ambrosina went to Claris's room to investigate whether "[Claris's] husband had hit [her] the night before," but Claris "[didn't] want anything to do with her," and told Ambrosina to mind her own business.[63] Since that day, Ambrosina had spread rumors about Claris's marital situation around the neighborhood. When Claris asked her to stop, Ambrosina responded that Claris was "no more than a dirty whore, that [her] parts were all rotten, and that [she] should go back to Cocoa Grove again as a whore."[64] Two other witnesses, Jamaican laborer Stafford Powell and Jamaican washerwoman Rosa Williams, reiterated Claris's statement, adding even more colorful language to Ambrosina's insults. Rosa, for example, added that Ambrosina had asked Claris "how many men used her that she got sick and had to go to the hospital to cure themselves," implying that Claris was spreading venereal disease.[65] Since the women lived under the same roof, in a home shared with other families, their insults and quarrels were likely public knowledge in the neighborhood. Claris and Ambrosina's dispute arose precisely from their closeness. Their lives were deeply intertwined with each other and with their neighbors, all working-class West Indians. The great majority of these cases took place in parts of the neighborhoods and tenements West Indian immigrants inhabited that were in earshot of other residents, in the areas of the "informal economy of working women," the patios for laundry and cooking that doubled as domestic and social gathering spaces.[66]

In her declaration, Ambrosina denied most of Claris's statement, saying she had done nothing at all on August 19. She then turned the accusation around and blamed Claris for slander herself, saying she had called Ambrosina a whore and told her she needed to "pack her trunk and move to Cocoa Grove."[67] As in Ercilia Clair's assault case, Cocoa Grove arose as both a real and symbolic space on which the women placed immorality, aberrant sexuality or behavior, and dirtiness rhetorically. Ambrosina and Claris, in trying to negotiate the domestic abuse Claris faced, continually referred to Cocoa Grove, displacing the real violence of the home onto their own bodies and into that symbolic space. The continual invocation of Cocoa Grove speaks to the women's awareness of this contradiction as they condemned sexual practices under the roof of their communal home and rhetorically expelled them to the dangerously close red-light district.

Notably, their fight had started with Ambrosina's attempt to investigate whether Claris was experiencing abuse from her husband. The insults that followed regarding sex work and Cocoa Grove were the language of their fight but not its object. Rather, Claris brought the case to the corregidor to defend her reputation from accusations that her husband mistreated her and that she was doing nothing in return. Ambrosina had spread these rumors around the neighborhood and it was this that escalated the situation. Ultimately, Claris and Ambrosina were both asked to present fianzas de paz, which Claris did, but Ambrosina chose instead to move out of the house and away from the neighborhood. The state punished both women for slander, but Claris won the standoff between them. If the fight was not ultimately about the insults but about Ambrosina's rumors, Claris's case successfully put an end to them. In forcing Ambrosina to leave, Claris also reinforced her own reputation among her neighbors. They would likely think twice before spreading rumors about Claris in the future if it meant having to leave their home.

As in Claris and Ambrosina's case, the conduct of West Indian women's husbands was often a subject of dispute. Jamaican Sarah Bryan brought a case against Louisa Spencer for insulting her husband, who was imprisoned in the Canal Zone for theft, with the suggestion that she might be disloyal.[68] Jamaican Irene Geddes brought one against Delfina Todman for insults, after Delfina had come to her house several times in the night to speak to Irene's husband alone.[69] Irene described their enmity as stemming from her "depriving my husband from ever going to her house, to avoid having any discord with the aforementioned woman," after which Delfina had started insulting Irene. For these women, reputation meant asserting their loyalty and primacy in their marriages, whether these were official or not. Irene was less concerned about Delfina's insults. Rather, she used the Panamanian municipal courts to threaten Delfina so as to stop her interfering with her marriage.

Husbands sometimes got involved in West Indian women's affairs to defend their reputation. For example, Jamaican tailor Salomón (likely Solomon) Hylton denounced John Redman for insults after both their wives had been in the courts fighting less than a month before.[70] Salomón alleged that neither Redman nor his wife had stopped bothering him and his wife, accusing them of *brujería* (witchcraft) and scandal. Salomón essentially reiterated his wife's complaints, bringing extra pressure on their attackers and continuing to defend his wife's reputation. Isaac Cooper brought a case against another man, James Gittens, for spreading rumors that his wife had betrayed him and slept with Gittens.[71] The testimonies reveal that the accused man might have in fact raped Cooper's wife. However, the case is not centered on the sexual abuse but on the woman's reputation, which Cooper sought to defend. In this case, the West Indian woman in question had little say over her representation or her bodily safety. This vulnerability to sexual assault was likely present for many West Indian women who could not directly defend themselves on this matter. Instead, they loudly defended their reputation from other women's attacks.

West Indian women's disputes often manifested as threats to force people to move out of their homes. Claris told Ambrosina to go to Cocoa Grove. In Jamaican Julia Evans's short complaint against Charles and Rosa Patterson, she said they had accused her of being a prostitute and a *bruja* and they "won't be happy until they make me move out of the house and indeed have indisposed me to the landlord."[72] She eventually withdrew the complaint from the courts, perhaps after forcing her neighbors to desist with their threats. In the case between Barbadian domestic workers Bertha Alleyne and Beatriz Taylor, Bertha said "[as I] was washing my face in the faucet, she [Beatriz] approached me and said that I'm a sow for washing my face there and that she was going to tell the owner of the house so he would kick me out of there and force me to move."[73] These cases were not just verbal fights about reputation but had real consequences on the living conditions and makeup of West Indian neighborhoods. The threats were invariably tied to accusations of unsanitary or aberrant sexual practices. Other plaintiffs did not make these same threats. Only in cases involving West Indian women did participants threaten each other with eviction, belying West Indian women's perception of the interrelation between women's sexual behavior and notions of community respectability as well as women's policing of their neighborhoods through other women's behavior.

The case between Bertha Alleyne and Beatriz Taylor extended beyond an everyday domestic dispute. Though it ostensibly began as a simple row over name-calling, Beatriz's insults toward Bertha soon grew more vicious. In front of their neighbors, as Bertha left for the early morning market, Beatriz yelled at her "that my [Bertha's] mother always kills my children and that I personally take them to the cemetery and that I've buried so many children that I'm myself a cemetery."[74] This accusation could mean a few things but likely implied that Bertha's mother had assisted her in obtaining several abortions. Panamanian law specified different punishments for honorable and dishonorable women who obtained abortions, dependent on their "buena fama anterior," presumably to be established by witnesses. These legal conditions established that individual circumstances (i.e., a woman's reputation) superseded the severity of the crime. Yet Beatriz did not legally accuse Bertha of abortion or infanticide, but of insults. Once again, the fight was over reputation.

For West Indian women, rumors of abortion and infanticide attached to their reputation in particular ways that were informed by racist colonial tropes. Across the British Caribbean, claims of Black women's supposed hypersexuality and their attendant lack of maternal instinct had circulated as early as the sixteenth century and persisted throughout the period of abolition.[75] These assumptions continued to inform approaches to public health in the late nineteenth and early twentieth centuries, when colonial states across the Caribbean invested in material and infant welfare initiatives to increase population growth and ensure the reproduction of a healthy workforce. These elite actors perceived poor Black West Indian women's behavior as the locus of the problem—they were uncivilized, immoral, and unable to follow sanitary protocols—rather than blaming poverty, racism, or lack of public health access.[76] They crafted regulations and programs that propagated a vision of respectable behavior predicated on uplifting the race and reinscribing Victorian ideologies of maternal caregiving in an effort to train Black women to be good mothers.[77] Though they did not substantially change working-class West Indians' practices, these state-sponsored programs certainly permeated public consciousness in the region as to the interrelation of motherhood, respectability, sexuality, and sanitation. These same ideas would have informed West Indian women's fights in Panama, where sanitation had gained such distinct prominence. As a way to call Bertha's honor into question and insult her, Beatriz associated her with long-standing discourses of bad motherhood and infanticide that had shaped the experiences of Black working-class women with public health in the region for decades.

The matter of Beatriz Taylor's name—she was perhaps called Beatrice but was recorded under a Hispanicized spelling—reminds us that West Indian women's use of the municipal courts also meant engaging with a system of male, Panamanian, and predominantly Spanish-speaking interpreters, lawyers, and guarantors. The municipal court of Calidonia provided an interpreter for most cases involving British West Indians. In at least two cases, when the usual interpreter was not present, the court capacitated an ad hoc interpreter.[78] Only the interpreters' Spanish translations of the claims remain, evident in the many transliterated and misspelled Anglo names. It is unclear what other matters these interpreters might have misunderstood or how West Indian plaintiffs might have been disadvantaged by this system or used it for their own benefit. Nevertheless, it is telling that West Indian women persisted in using these courts despite the language barriers to mutual understanding. They saw the new legal institutions of Panama as a place where they could exert some power over their circumstances. West Indian women engaged with Panamanian state institutions from their first years of settlement in the territory, making claims to be heard and respected even as foreign nationals.

Rarely did plaintiffs call on the services of a lawyer for cases in municipal court, which were often resolved by quick bench decisions, unless the case escalated. In the case between Beatriz Taylor and Bertha Alleyne, both of these Barbadian domestic workers did contract local lawyers. Bertha, the plaintiff, hired notorious Panamanian lawyer Pedro de Ycaza while Beatriz hired Howard Guinier (a Jamaican-born but naturalized Panamanian lawyer).[79] Ycaza and Guinier fought the case on administrative errors, but eventually both women were given fifteen days of commutable arrest and a severe warning. Ycaza was a well-known figure around the neighborhood and one of the rare Panamanian men to himself bring an insult case against another Panamanian man who had questioned his impartiality as a lawyer.[80] That Bertha hired Pedro de Ycaza to represent her speaks to her familiarity with the Panamanian court system and the patriarchal social relationships that structured it. These few cases do not show that lawyers made a significant difference on outcomes, but they do show the women's investment in contesting these accusations. Hiring a lawyer meant spending more time and money on the case. Associating with a respectable middle-class Panamanian man like Ycaza was a public display of confidence and of proximity to honor.

Witnesses provided the most crucial component in building a case. In most cases, eyewitness statements provided the only proof of the events, and contradictory or absent witnesses could easily cause a judge to dismiss a complaint entirely. For example, in Bertha Alleyne and Beatriz Taylor's altercation, the testimony of Jamaican laundress Annie Brown led the judge to conclude that both women had been equally at fault.[81] In Martinican Maria Miguel's case of "force and violence" (in fact, an attempted rape) against Barboly Pollis, the lack of eyewitnesses led to no resolution.[82] West Indian women called on the power of their close social relationships among neighbors to provide witness to their accusations. These witnesses were most often other working-class West Indian women who shared living or work spaces with the plaintiffs. They came from various islands—primarily Barbados and Jamaica but also Grenada, British Guyana, and Martinique—attesting to the diverse cross-island alliances women formed in these spaces. In cases between West Indian women, non–West Indian witnesses were rare except for the occasional Panamanian laundress or servant, who likely worked alongside the women involved. For example, Virginia Bridges defended herself against Veroni Bernard's accusation of insult by presenting four character witnesses—three were working-class Jamaican women, one was a Panamanian ironer from the state of David (thus herself an immigrant to Panama City from a distant province).[83] Whereas plaintiffs of other ethnicities called on a variety of witnesses—Italian Atillio Pecorini called on a Jamaican groom, two Italian laborers, one Colombian and one Italian domestic servant, and one

Colombian mechanic; West Indians more commonly relied on other West Indian witnesses, not necessarily but often from the same island.[84]

The witness statements testify to the closeness of tenement living and to the ways West Indian women also supported and looked out for each other. In Barbadian Rebecca Jordan's case against Adolphus Spencer for injury, she brought two other Barbadian women as eyewitnesses.[85] One of these women lived next door and, after hearing Rebecca scream in her home, rushed over to help her and found Rebecca bleeding on the floor and Adolphus threatening her with a gun. The other woman was familiar with Rebecca and Adolphus's history and had come to Rebecca's house to babysit her two children the day that she witnessed the assault. Both women had close relationships with Rebecca and supported her statement. Thus, the cases reveal not only discord among West Indian neighbors but also a tight-knit community bound by obligation.

*   *   *

The prevalence of West Indian women as plaintiffs in the municipal cases of Calidonia shows how West Indian women's concerns shaped the urban life of their communities in Panama, who heard their fights in common patios, participated as legal witnesses, and sometimes faced the threat of eviction after attacking the wrong woman. It shows the constant pressure women faced to defend their reputation among their West Indian peers through loud and colorful insults as a strategy of survival as they faced housing vulnerability, legal exclusion, and suspicion of immorality. But it also shows how West Indian women's fights challenged the dominant frameworks of honor that structured respectable femininity in Panama. In those early years of settlement, West Indian women could not and would not be bound by the binaries of public/private and honor/dishonor that placed them at the bottom. Instead, they asserted their own understandings of reputation; what mattered was your standing among your West Indian neighbors and this was worth fighting for by any means necessary, even if it meant evicting your neighbor. West Indian women settled in Panama without the access or protection of citizenship; they were forced to deal with legal definitions of honor that excluded them and limited options for affordable housing that placed them in proximity to red-light districts. In the face of these exclusions, they negotiated a form of belonging by forcing local Panamanian institutions to hear their complaints and concerns, using municipal courts as an arena to present their side in this broad battleground over morality. These battles over morality and respectability would continue to define West Indian immigrant women's experiences even after the Canal's completion as they firmly settled in Panama or left to find opportunity in New York or Cuba.

CHAPTER 7

A Female Vanguard

The Canal officially opened on August 15, 1914, to little fanfare, eclipsed by the news of impending war in Europe. For West Indian men and women, the inauguration must have entailed a mix of pride and concern as the end of construction also signaled the end of secure employment. Some decided to stay and make their lives in Panama; some returned to their home islands with the money they had saved. Many left to seek further opportunity in places like Santiago de Cuba and New York City. As they followed different paths in the aftermath of construction, West Indian immigrants found themselves in a world of hardening national borders and rising xenophobia, exemplified by the U.S. National Origins Act of 1924 but echoed across the Americas. Black West Indian immigrants' encounter with the rise of race-based immigration policy meant navigating increasingly violent systems, but it also generated a flowering of creative cultural and political responses to this exclusion—the literary and musical outpourings of the Harlem Renaissance, the Black internationalist imaginings of the Garveyite movement, the radical demands of Black communists and labor organizers.[1]

Only recently have historians begun to understand the work that West Indian women did to generate and undergird these practices of diaspora.[2] West Indian women's experiences of circum-Caribbean migration in the early twentieth century, not exclusively but primarily to Panama, supplied the financial wealth, flexible labor, patterns of kinship, and strategies of social reproduction that sustained West Indian migration in the interwar period. Their domestic labor provided a consistent sector for wages that was in demand across receiving sites of migration. Their work cooking, hosting, and taking care of children and the networks of obligation they had built among their kin and nonlegal partners supported the various practices of organization and sociability that helped West Indian communities thrive. Women's work as household financial managers generated the ship passage and "show money" that immigration authorities demanded for travel, eventually helping to build familial wealth in the form of real estate and fostering upward mobility among West Indian immigrants.[3]

West Indian women had learned something from the previous migrations where they faced imperial administrations that actively rejected them, triply oppressed by their gender, race, and class.[4] In Panama, they developed a pragmatic dynamic to help navigate the exclusions of U.S. empire while securing their survival and that of their families. The period following the construction sharpened Black immigrants' exclusion globally. They relied on women's strategies of social reproduction to navigate the vicissitudes of U.S. imperial governance and xenophobic nationalism in Latin America and the Caribbean. Throughout the interwar period, West Indian women continued defying parameters of migration established by governments and corporations, fighting for their dignity and autonomy in the workplace, navigating gendered discourses of respectability, and fostering intimate and financial networks among their kin.

The period following World War I marked an increasingly restrictive era in immigration policy accompanied by the development of new ideas about citizenship, belonging, integration, and race. Though the United States had restricted certain types of immigration before the 1920s, notably with the Page Act and the Chinese Exclusion Act, the 1924 Johnson-Reed or National Origins Immigration Act marked the first comprehensive national immigration law.[5] It placed numerical limits on entry based on a hierarchy of racial and national difference that privileged those of Western European stock while limiting immigration from Africa, Asia, and Eastern Europe under restrictive quotas. The act produced a racialized image of a white and Western European nation, following from the assumption that only these kinds of immigrants could easily integrate.[6] It also marked the rise of new restrictive technologies such as the Border Patrol.[7] The act did not technically ban Black West Indian immigrants but it did not allocate any quotas specifically to island colonies, placing them instead under the umbrella of the country to which they were dependent and forcing West Indians to fight for visas alongside British citizens and other British colonial subjects. In practice, this law essentially cut off the flow of immigration from the islands that had until then been relatively unobstructed; the number of Black immigrants dropped precipitously from 12,000 in the first six months of 1924 to under 800 in 1925.[8]

Though not explicitly discriminatory against West Indians, these laws regulated entry under very specific understandings of kinship; only legal spouses and children of U.S. citizens could enter as nonquota immigrants. This restriction particularly affected working-class West Indian immigrants, who often did not legally marry and relied on extended kinship networks for support. Thus, as historian Lara Putnam explains, "the very patterns of non-legalized, flexible family practice that had facilitated and been intensified by international labor migration now undermined migrants' ability to claim rights to entry and return" after 1924.[9] These laws also had the effect of privileging immigrants who followed normative models of the respectable, middle-class, conventionally sexualized family.[10] It simplified paths to migration for those who were legally married, had sufficient financial resources, and sought to bring their legitimate children. These factors ensured that the lives of middle-class West Indian immigrants would be more well-documented than, say, a single, poor, Black West Indian woman who made her living through higglering or sex work. Indeed, most of the women featured in this last chapter were mothers, legally married, and part of the respectable or striving middle class.

Restrictive immigration legislation was not limited to the United States. The profits created by the export boom of the early twentieth century bankrolled the rise of oligarchical elite regimes across South and Central America, including in Panama, that sought to modernize and civilize their nations while also protecting the "native" labor market from competition by migrant workers and foreign capital.[11] These new regimes were deeply concerned with the predominance of nonwhite populations in their racially mixed societies. Informed by global notions of scientific racism, they sought to "whiten" their nations through subsidized programs of European immigration and to subsume native Black and indigenous populations under a mestizo identity.[12] They violently persecuted Black cultural and religious practices and political organizing, and placed restrictions on mobility and citizenship for non-white immigrants.[13] Panama's Law 13 of 1926 outlawed the immigration of non-Spanish-speaking Black and Asian immigrants, regardless of country of origin.[14] Laws following in 1938 and the infamous 1941 constitution reaffirmed Panama's commitment to immigration exclusion and investment in growing technologies of border control, such as the Servicio de Policia Preventiva.[15] National governments across Latin America also passed laws urging U.S. employers to privilege "native" workers. In 1930s Costa Rica, the author of a local editorial expressed concerns about the effects of the continued migration of West Indians, asking "What do we want Costa Rica to be: White or Black?"[16] These discourses of "xenophobic nationalism" extended throughout Latin America and the Caribbean, further restricting the conditions of citizenship for Black immigrants and their native-born children.[17]

In the postwar period, West Indians found themselves caught in a global immigration regime of anti-Black exclusion and amid the violent repressions of increasingly nativist national governments. They responded by creating protective subcultures, enacting diasporic ties, and making demands on employers and nation-states.[18] Thrown further into the margins, these communities drew on strategies that Black women—already triply marginalized—had used during the Canal construction. Black women served as a vanguard of the early twentieth-century Caribbean diaspora, physically and materially facilitating migration. Their roles as social, financial, and affective links among Caribbean kin—sending and receiving remittances, initiating family migration, housing relatives, managing land, organizing childcare and education, cooking for social events—uncover the everyday workings of diaspora.

Radicalism and Community-Building in Panama

Leaving Panama was by far the prevailing choice for West Indian migrants following construction. The Canal Commission repatriated thirteen thousand West Indians by 1921 and many more left of their own volition.[19] But some chose to stay; they had built homes and businesses in Panama, joined local churches and organizations, and raised Panama-born children. In 1920, 9,425 British West Indian men and 8,278 British West Indian women resided in Panama City—a fraction of those who had migrated through, but nevertheless a substantial community that made up almost 20 percent of the entire Panamanian population (this is without accounting for the second generation already born in Panama which would bring the proportion much higher).[20] By 1930 West Indians and their descendants in Panama numbered over thirty thousand.[21]

The 1904 Panamanian constitution established jus soli citizenship, regardless of the parent's nationality. It allowed naturalization for those who had resided in the country for over ten years, stated their wish to become citizens, and could "profess a science, art, or industry" or prove the possession of a certain unspecified amount of real estate or financial capital.[22] Panamanian citizenship was thus technically within reach for West Indians during the decade of construction, but they rarely sought to formalize this relationship, remaining as foreign nationals. Though ostensibly subject to the same rights and protections as Panamanian citizens, except for voting and holding public office, in practice West Indians faced housing and labor discrimination in Panama as well as a growing elite consensus that West Indians could not be assimilated into the mestizo nation. The same year of the Johnson-Reed Act, for example, saw the publication of Olmedo Alfaro's *El peligro antillano en la América Latina: La defensa de la raza* in Panama, a eugenicist tract against "the Antilleans who infest our main cities" and "whose presence is detrimental for Panama, for its racial stock, and for its good name abroad."[23] Panamanian laws of the 1920s began to reflect this growing xenophobia. Law 13 of 1926 prohibited immigration of "Chinese, Japanese, Syrians, Turks, Indo-orientals, Indo-Aryans, Dravidians, and blacks from the Antilles and Guyana whose original language was not Spanish."[24] This law disproportionately affected West Indian immigrants, who far outnumbered the other listed groups in migration to Panama. The Legislative Act of October 19, 1928, then proceeded to strip birthright citizenship from those born in Panama to foreign parents until they came of age and claimed it, meaning children born to West Indian parents held conditional citizenship until they turned twenty-one.[25]

West Indians' difficult position in Panama was exacerbated by the Canal administration's rollback of Silver employee wages and benefits following construction. They cut the number of Silver employees from 38,000 in 1913 to 9,000 in 1921 and demoted almost every remaining Silver employee, lowering the standard wage.[26] Through an executive order, President Woodrow Wilson canceled all rent on Canal property but only for Gold Roll employees, forcing the remaining Silver residents to continue paying exorbitant rents or move to Panama, where rent was sometimes even higher. West Indians who moved to Panamanian territory retained ties to the Zone, where they worked, socialized, or sent their kids to school. The Canal Zone maintained its system of segregation, which forced West Indians into struggles with the administration over inadequate Silver clubhouses and schools.

This era of rising xenophobia also saw the consolidation of a West Indian Panamanian community through churches, recreational facilities and social clubs, lodges and friendly societies, the Black press, labor unions, and Black nationalist organizations like the United Negro Improvement Association (UNIA). In 1919, for example, the *Workman* listed at least thirty-two friendly societies and this number kept growing throughout the 1920s and 1930s.[27] In 1928 Sydney Young started the *Panama Tribune*, which became the longest-running West Indian newspaper in Panama.[28] The West Indian community made social and cultural hubs out of Silver clubhouses in the Zone and unsegregated venues in Panama, like the Teatro Variedades and Teatro América.[29]

These local institutions helped West Indians survive in Panama and cultivate networks across migrants from different islands. As they did in Cuba, Costa Rica, and Harlem, they served as antidote and protest to the racist exclusion in Panama and the Canal Zone.[30] Out of all of these, the UNIA's Black nationalist and anticolonial politics proved by far the most popular. Founded in 1918, it would eventually grow to have thirty-nine branches in Panama, including its base at Colon's Liberty Hall, some with memberships of over one thousand. Garvey himself visited in 1921 to promote the Black Star Line, as did Henrietta Vinton Davis in 1919 and Amy Ashwood Garvey in 1929.

As historian Carla Burnett has shown, the grievances of West Indians organizing in Panama throughout the 1919–1920 strikes were expressed primarily through the language of Garveyite racial uplift and articulated as anxieties about sexuality and manliness.[31] During a Labor Day March in 1919 against the Silver Rates board, for example, West Indian Canal workers held up placards reading "Must our girls be sacrificed on the altar of vice? No!"[32] The *Workman* entreated West Indians to call "the Negro house" to order and exhibit the "real qualities of manhood."[33] This discourse held up the nuclear family, consecrated by church marriage, as the ideal basis for the advancement of the race. It decried the negative moral effects of reduced Silver wages on normative family structures, arguing that "theft, prostitution, and other dreadful vices are highly encouraged when labor is half paid and the necessities of life denied to honest toil."[34] Low wages were "sending our best girls into the lowest depths of degradation and prostitution."[35] Garveyites condemned the prevalence of prostitution and promoted a virile Black nationalism. Editorials castigated women for their lack of morality, noting that "no commercial or political strength can fill for a people that moral and social status which its women fail to create."[36]

Concerns about sexuality and morality did not arise sui generis from the minds of male labor organizers and Garveyites. As the insult cases of the previous chapter showed, working-class West Indian women had for some time intervened with the Panamanian state to assert their own versions of sexual citizenship. West Indian women had begun articulating complex local responses to racial and gender discrimination since their earliest years in Panama; their suits before the municipal judges were a political utterance of their belonging. They confronted Panamanian definitions of honor and instead upheld their own practices of respect and reputation. Women's earlier interactions with Panamanian municipal institutions over the terms of honor show an alternative understanding of respectability that also prevailed within the West Indian community.

West Indian women in Panama, like many of those who left, cultivated Afro-diasporic kinship networks, developed critiques of local xenophobia, engaged with Black nationalist politics, and championed early Black feminist causes. Like much of the interwar Black press, the *Workman* and the *Panama Tribune* mostly relegated women's issues to their own small column. The *Tribune's* "Of Interest to Women" section, which started in 1928, was run by Amy Denniston, who had migrated from Jamaica to Panama as a young child. She joined a small, but important, cadre of Black internationalist women like Amy Jacques Garvey and Maymie de Mena who used the women's sections of the global Black press to debate their role in racial uplift.[37] In the pages of the *Tribune*, Denniston negotiated between her advocacy for the West Indian community in Panama through a rhetoric of respectability, and her critique of the exclusion of Black women from these imaginings of racial progress.[38] Linda Smart Chubb, born in Panama to Jamaican parents, also briefly wrote a column for the *Workman* in 1926 tackling issues of respectability and Black womanhood.[39] She advocated for the expansion of educational opportunities for West Indians, served as a secretary for the British West Indian Welfare Committee, and was elected deputy mayor of Colón in 1948. Leonor Jump, born in Panama to a St. Lucian mother, became the first woman principal of the La Boca Normal Training School in the Canal Zone. West Indian women like these avidly joined civic organizations and engaged with the Black press. As historian Kaysha Corinealdi argues, it was these women's personal and professional experience with diaspora and Black internationalism that provided the groundwork for their eventual leadership roles in the West Indian Panamanian community.[40] These women fostered forms of "vernacular citizenship" in the shadow of U.S. empire and Panamanian xenophobia.[41]

The Afterlives of "Panama Money"

As the SS *Nerissa* pulled up to Ellis Island in 1923, Adriana Viola Clement saw "New York rise shining from the sea."[42] Just arrived from Barbados, Adriana marveled at the "white people like peas! And not one of them speaking the King's English." She presented her papers and fifty dollars of "show money" to the authorities and moved in with her brother in a house in the Brooklyn neighborhood of Bedford-Stuyvesant. She worked part-time as a domestic servant, trying to make ends meet alongside fellow Bajan and eventual husband Sam Burke. They had a daughter in 1929, Paule Marshall. Paule would go on to write the famed novel *Brown Girl, Brownstones* (1959) and win some of the most prestigious national awards for fiction writing.

Adriana Viola Clement's story resonates with that of the 36,480 Caribbean immigrants who lived in New York City by 1920. Her daughter's memoir clues us in to a crucial dynamic that made this migration possible—Adriana's passage and the "show money" required by U.S. authorities "had come from a single source: Panama Money."[43] At the time, the cost of a ticket could be as high as sixty-five dollars.[44] The remittances sent by Adriana's brother Joseph from Panama had funded the family's purchase of "canepieces," or plots of sugarcane, in Barbados that were rented out and sold to fund a relative's passage. This real estate operation was managed exclusively by the matriarch of the family, Alberta Jane Clement. Alberta, who Paule Marshall called the "Chancellor of the Exchequer" of the family, was the recipient of Joseph's remittances and the architect of the canepiece endeavor that funded Adriana's migration to Brooklyn.

Due to the demographics of Panama migration, it was often West Indian women who received, saved, and invested Panama money sent by male laborers employed on the Canal. Stories like that of Adriana Viola Clement show how these remittances fueled later migrations and depended on diasporic household financial strategies managed by West Indian women. Though scholars have considered the effects of Panama money on the islands, they have paid less attention to the gendered relationships that structured the circulation of this money.[45] Alberta Clement's canepiece scheme exemplifies the transnational circulation of Panama money among West Indian kinship networks, showing the collaborative management of remittances as part of larger household strategies that centrally involved women as financial agents.

Money arrived in the islands through various routes. Postal remittances, sent through an official system, tallied high returns for the years of construction, with a fivefold increase between 1906 and 1907 in Barbados.[46] The Canal Zone governor Charles Magoon wrote that in the one-month period after the establishment of a transmission system, money orders to the West Indies added up to $7,242.72 (approx. £1,487) and that "of nine thousand foreign letters registered in the Canal Zone from January 1st to June 30th [1906], over ninety per cent were addressed to West Indian points."[47]

Returnees also brought money back personally and had to report the amounts to the harbormaster, while others sent money in envelopes in the care of friends or kin traveling back to the islands. These return migrants often under-declared the amount of money they brought back. A columnist in the *Barbados Agricultural Reporter* wrote: "We are of the opinion that the amount of money brought back to the island by emigrants who returned from

Panama during the five years (1906–1910) was greater than the £20,000 a year which they are said to have declared to the Harbour Master on their arrival. People of the emigrant class are not given to taking persons of the official class into their confidence."[48] West Indian mothers, sisters, and wives in the islands served as the primary recipients of Panama money. Some families used this money to build independent businesses, like corner stores or small village shops. Others used it for survival, depending on remittances for food and sustenance. Still others used it to buy fashionable consumer items from Broad and Swan Streets in Bridgetown, hoping to show off their wealth to their neighbors. The Savings Bank of Barbados, an institution meant to serve the working class of the island, saw an increase in the rate of banking activity and new account openings during the construction years, where more than half of depositors were women.[49] Like Alberta Jane Clement, quite a few West Indians also reinvested this money in land.

No known survey exists that shows the acreage or location of lands purchased during this period as most were bought by informal means. Nevertheless, contemporary commentators in Barbados consistently spoke about the rise in Black landownership. Henry Lofty, a merchant and political representative for the urban parishes of Bridgetown and St. Michael, noted in 1929 that "people sent back money from Panama with which to buy land and put houses on them; and since then, other persons have bought places of two or three acres here and there."[50] Chattel houses bought and expanded with Panama money still dot the landscape of Barbados, upgraded with striking red paint, shingles, or an extra story meant to showcase the newfound wealth of the returnee and their family.[51]

The expansion in landownership was due to the combination of the increased money flow from Panama and the effects of the long sugar industry depression on the island, which had forced many plantation owners into bankruptcy and foreclosure. Land speculators bought and subdivided depreciated plantations from the Court of Chancery and sold these parcels, often informally, to Barbadians with Panama money. Woodville Marshall argues that the rise in working-class Barbadian landownership during this period created a radical shift in urbanization.[52] From nineteen villages in the pre-emancipation period, Barbados had 359 villages by 1946.[53] Two hundred of these alone—what Marshall refers to as "remittance villages"—were developed in the period following the Canal construction, appropriated from approximately nine thousand acres of plantation land.[54]

The work of speculators created a sharp inflation in land prices. Whereas in 1917 an acre could be purchased for £20, by 1925 prices upwards of £100 became increasingly average.[55] White land speculators made massive profits of 50 to 200 percent over the purchase price from sales of small plots of land to Barbadians.[56] Yet, while speculators certainly shaped this process and profited from exploitative, discriminatory sales, it was the newly acquired purchasing power of Barbadians with Panama money that truly set off these massive changes. As Earl Greaves remembered about his parents, "Papa and Mama sweat to get that land from Panama. Panama sweat and Mama sweat and come to Barbados to buy the land."[57]

The 1911 Barbados census explicitly comments on the phenomenon of female land buyers: "That land should have been purchased by so many women of the labouring class is not surprising as it is known that emigrants to Panama have not been forgetful of those left behind, and have remitted money, sufficient in many cases, to enable them to pay the necessary deposits and obtain possession of small holdings."[58] The census reiterates the understanding that remittances circulated as part of family household strategies that depended on working-class Black women, who were the ones to receive remittances, make deposits, and obtain possession of land. The number of small landholdings in Barbados rose from 934 in 1840 to 18,000 in 1930.[59] These numbers hide the family networks associated with each individually listed owner; landholdings were not attached to individuals but rather served as "family ground" that funded circuits of responsibility and kinship. As with the Clements, one family member would travel to Panama and send money to buy land, which then funded another family member to travel to the United States and earn further money to support the family. Thus, landownership and property sales could serve as a mechanism for migration for families in islands like Nevis, Barbados, and Jamaica.[60]

Property ownership also became a goal on arrival to the United States for women like Adriana Clement or Ruth Walrond. Ruth, a native Barbadian, moved to British Guiana with her husband and had her first son in 1898. A few years later, her husband deserted them. She then moved to the growing port city of Colón. For Ruth, Panama provided the possibility of starting anew and becoming financially independent. Though conditions were difficult, especially for a single Black mother, Ruth established herself in Panama, where her son Eric Walrond received an education and became a journalist, a job that led to his eventual migration to New York. She uprooted her life once again at the age of forty-three and arrived at Ellis Island with four children on September 16, 1919, on the ship *Zacapa*. She is listed in the 1940 U.S. Census as the owner of a brownstone at 357 Herkimer Street in the increasingly Black and Caribbean neighborhood of Bedford-Stuyvesant in Brooklyn, where she resided with her family and a young lodger. As in the islands, owning a home in New York City could mean freedom and future stability for the children of Caribbean immigrants. Paule Marshall explained, "It seems to me that those Barbadian women accepted these ill-paying, low status jobs with an astonishing lack of visible resentment. For them they were simply a means to an end: the end being the down payment on a brownstone house."[61] This was not an achievable goal for every West Indian woman, some of whom migrated with few resources and struggled to make ends meet. But for women like Adriana Viola Clements and Ruth Walrond, homeownership in the United States materialized by mobilizing the diasporic strategies of financial circulation among family and kin practiced during the Canal construction.

West Indian Women in Radical Harlem

Miriam was born in Spanishtown, Jamaica, around 1895, one of three daughters. Her mother, for reasons we can only guess, decided to leave her husband and take her three daughters to Panama during the early years of construction (around 1904). Miriam grew up in Panama while her mother supported the family by selling baked goods. It was in Panama that she met her future husband, Arthur Bancroft Clark, and they married when she was sixteen. Arthur was born in Costa Rica to Jamaican parents and later moved to Panama. He had a good-paying job as superintendent for the United Fruit Company. He did not make as much money as white employees but he was comfortable enough that he preferred to stay in Panama rather than try his luck elsewhere. Miriam and Arthur loved each other; later she would say he was always the love of her life. But for Arthur, love did not mean "literal fidelity" and Miriam could not stand for that.[62] The marriage was in trouble.

In Panama, they had two children—Kenneth, born in 1914, and Beulah, three years later. Kenneth came into the world a month before the Canal was completed. Opportunities began to dwindle in Panama for West Indian migrants after the Canal's opening and Miriam sought an escape. Though the children received some bilingual schooling in Panama, Miriam "felt strongly that opportunity for educational and economic advancement was better in the United States than it ever could be in Panama or any of the West Indian islands" and wanted to take her two children away.[63] She repeated her mother's strategy, leaving her husband behind and traveling with Beulah first to Havana, then entering the United States through Tampa on the ship *Mascotte* on June 18, 1918, and finally settling in Harlem. Kenneth would join them soon after.

By 1920, 36,480 immigrants from Cuba and the West Indies had settled in New York City. By 1930, this number had almost doubled to 61,295.[64] Black women outnumbered men in this migratory stream and, by 1920, New York had become by far the main destination for female Caribbean immigrants.[65] Many of these Caribbean men and women, like their southern migrant counterparts, were unmarried (or, like Miriam, unaccompanied). Their migration to Panama—decentralized, of their own accord, often led by family ties, and divorced from employer demand—turned out to be a trial run for their move to Harlem.

Harlem in the 1920s was the place to be. W. E. B. DuBois, Madame C. J. Walker, James Weldon Johnson, Arturo Schomburg, Claude McKay, and Amy Ashwood Garvey were among the many African American and Afro-Caribbean immigrants who called it home during these years of radical creative and political output.[66] Harlem was the site of a cultural and political renaissance that reimagined transnational Black identities and solidarities, fueled by migrations from the South and from the Caribbean islands. Though hard to account for using census data, qualitative evidence points to the importance of West Indian women in supporting family migration and settlement in Harlem. It was through their mothers, sisters, and aunts that well-known male West Indian writers, radicals, and orators such as Eric Walrond, Hubert Harrison, Richard B. Moore, W. A. Domingo, and Cyril Briggs made their way to New York City.[67] These women variously provided encouragement, passage, housing, and sustenance—practices that in a very literal sense ensured these men's survival and success.

In Harlem, Miriam made a living as a seamstress, trying to support her children's education through piecework.[68] Eventually, she got a job in the Garment District, where she likely worked in one of the lower-paying jobs as a finisher, rather than the more lucrative positions of cutter or operator, which were dominated by white immigrant women.[69] In 1920 only 3.7 percent of female garment workers were Black women. This nevertheless marked a significant increase, from 190 Black women in 1910 to 2,450 by 1920.[70] This was due, in part, to the influx of West Indian female migrants to the city, many of whom claimed "dressmaker" as their occupation according to census records.[71]

Due to their exclusion from other occupational choices, most Black women in New York, immigrant and native, worked in domestic service.[72] In 1920 over 60 percent of Black women employed in the United States worked in domestic service, a number that continued to increase as the Great Migration brought more Black women into northern cities and away from agricultural labor in the South.[73] A few found work as live-in maids, which subjected them to everyday abuse and perpetual demand from their bosses. Others had to stand on street corners in the Bronx or Brooklyn every morning, waiting for employers to contract them as day labor in what Ella Baker called the "Bronx Slave Market."[74] They worked long hours in white folks' homes, scrubbing floors on bended knee, subject to the whims of their bosses over this informal work. As in Panama, some Black domestic workers preferred daywork or "living out," because at least "on daywork, you got a job to do, you do it, and that's it. No running around doing a lot of things."[75] They continued using tactics of everyday resistance: slowing down, refusing to do work, and switching employers. Unlike in the Canal Zone, Black women in New York had to deal with competition from white immigrant women for domestic service jobs, which likely blunted some of their attempts at labor autonomy. While the lack of opportunity and the conditions of domestic work limited Black women's wages, their concentration in this field also allowed them an advantage in creating networks of sponsorship and responsibility among other Black working women.[76]

An unknown number of African American and Afro-Caribbean women also worked in the informal economy of New York City as numbers runners, hustlers, and sex workers. LaShawn Harris argues that their participation in these activities, though hard to track, provided "financial stability and a sense of labor autonomy" as well as pleasure for many Black working-class women precluded from joining the formal labor force.[77] Black women used wages from garment work, domestic service, and the informal economy to support their families, to pay for their children's education, to secure housing, and for their personal amusement. Some of this money also traveled back to the islands as remittances. After the Canal's completion, the United States quickly overtook Panama as the primary source of remittances through money orders in Barbados.[78]

Like many residents of the area, Miriam was an "ardent follower" of Marcus Garvey and would take the children to Liberty Hall on 138th Street to see him speak, attracted by his message of racial uplift.[79] Garvey, like Miriam, had spent his formative years in Central America, sharpening his vision on his observations of the racial prejudice West Indians faced in Costa Rica and Panama. By the time Miriam was in Harlem, Garvey had founded the United Negro Improvement Association (UNIA), which had a substantial following from Afro-Caribbean and African American residents of Harlem as well as beyond the United States in Cuba, Panama, and Costa Rica, where his newspaper, the *Negro World*, circulated. Perhaps their shared background of Central American migration made Garvey's message particularly appealing to Miriam. As a garment worker, she also became enthusiastically involved with the organizing efforts of the International Ladies' Garment Workers' Union (ILGWU). In 1929, however, only 2 percent of the ILGWU's membership consisted of Black women.[80] Eventually, Miriam became disillusioned with the union's activism, seeing that those who fought for labor rights could often be the same people who perpetrated racial injustice.

This story, though unique in its specifics, was not particular to Miriam. The pan-Africanist labor leader Maida Springer Kemp's mother, Adina, was born in Panama to Jamaican parents and had sold food during the construction. She migrated to New York City in 1917 on the SS *Alianza* and "immediately joined" the UNIA upon her arrival.[81] She marched with the movement and always brought Maida along. Though she would never be remembered as a leader in the UNIA, women like her did the daily work of bringing people together under its umbrella, inviting immigrants from all over the Caribbean to congregate at her house: "My mother's a marvelous cook and a joyous woman, so there was always a coterie of people and there was singing and there was talking, and beyond that, a realization of a role we had to play in this society."[82] Black women leaders in the global Black nationalist struggle like Mittie Maude Lena Gordon, Amy Ashwood Garvey, and Maymie De Mena had their pragmatic counterparts in women like Maida Kemp's mother, who performed the everyday work of activism on a smaller scale among her own neighbors.[83] Later, Maida herself worked in a garment factory and, like Miriam Clark, joined the ILGWU. She formed part of the strike committee during the 1933 walkout and served in various important leadership roles in the union, creating ties between the labor movement in the United States and Africa. Kemp has received awards for her service from the NAACP, NOW, and the Coalition of Labor Union Women. She credits her radical practice to her early education from her mother and the political influences of 1920s Harlem.

The connection between Panama migration and later labor activism is no mere coincidence but a consistent theme in the lives of New York's West Indian immigrants, who often vocalized the influence this earlier migration had on their perceptions of racial discrimination and labor exploitation. Winston James credits previous experiences of regional migration with placing Afro-Caribbean people "in the vanguard of radical political movements" in the early twentieth-century United States.[84] This connection perhaps seems obvious among male West Indian immigrants who recorded their lives and attitudes during this time. But, as Miriam Clark and Maida Kemp's stories show, these connections also held true for Black migrant women in particularly gendered ways. Historians have recovered the crucial leadership of women like Amy Ashwood Garvey (who spent most of her early life in Panama), Amy Jacques Garvey, and Claudia Jones, who articulated a diasporic vision of Black nationalism and triple oppression, and countered global white supremacy.[85] Their stories converge with the daily activism of regular working-class West Indian women, whose historic strategies of labor resistance and mutual responsibility informed their migration to Panama and their engagement in the U.S. labor and Black nationalist movements.

Kenneth Clark, Miriam's son, would go on to study psychology at Howard and Columbia Universities. Alongside his wife, Mamie Clark, the first Black female PhD in Columbia's psychology program, they researched the effects of racial prejudice on young children through their famous "doll test." Their research would become part of the evidence that helped overturn the "separate but equal" doctrine in *Brown v. Board of Education*. As with Eric Walrond and Paule Marshall's female ancestors, the story of Miriam Clark's life has traditionally been subservient to the biography of her more famous offspring. Yet, in all these cases, it was Black West Indian women who initiated, organized, and financed the migrations of their families, who made a way out of no way to buy homes and pay for their children's education, and who walked the streets in protest and held cookouts at their homes to support Black activism.

From Colón to Cuba

Maradell Atwell Greene was born in the village of Cow Pen, Canal Zone, to two Barbadian parents: Joseph Nathaniel Atwell and Ethel Louise Chandler. Her father worked on the Canal and plied his trade as a shoemaker on the side. Her mother had worked as a dressmaker in Barbados, where her sewing was in demand for weddings and important occasions. Customers could not always pay for her services in cash and this emboldened her to go to Panama in 1908, "because in Barbados you never used to make money."[86] Ethel and Joseph met in Panama and had Maradell around 1911. They lived in the Canal Zone during the early years, but the end of construction found the family living in the Panama City neighborhood of Chorrillo, along with many other West Indians displaced by the depopulation order that revoked the leases of residents in towns like Cow Pen.[87]

A few years after the end of construction, when Maradell was six, her father migrated to Cuba. Prospects in Panama had dried up and many Bajans around him had already left to pursue work in the sugar mills. Although he did not wish for them to follow, Louise traveled to Baraguá a few years later with Maradell in tow, accompanied by two other friends. They could hop on a steamer run by the United Fruit Company, which traveled from Panama to Cuba.[88] In the aftermath of construction, many West Indians sought further economic opportunities in U.S. imperial ventures throughout the Caribbean. Some traveled across Panama to the province of Bocas del Toro, to Honduras, or to Limón, Costa Rica, to join other West Indians working on banana plantations owned by the United Fruit Company.[89] Between 1912 and 1919, United Fruit recruited more than five thousand men to work on banana plantations in Central America. But more than half of Anglo-Caribbean migrants between 1916 and 1920 went to Cuba, enticed by the economic opportunities of the "Dance of the Millions," the sugar boom. In the aftermath of World War I and with the decline of beet sugar, Cuban sugar prices rose, fueling the rapid growth and speculation of the sugar industry driven by U.S. investment. West Indian immigrants supplied the labor that helped Cuba produce one-fifth of the world's sugar by 1920.[90]

Between 1916 and 1920, the years immediately following the Canal's completion, Cuba "received more than half of the total Anglo-Caribbean migration of the first three decades of the century (75,871 out of 142,275)," showing a distinct pattern of migration driven by the lure of U.S. investment.[91] While most West Indians went to Cuba directly from the islands, others had already done stints in Costa Rica, British Honduras, and especially in Panama. At least 6,708 British Caribbean migrants traveled to Cuba from ports in Central America. Some of those recorded as "Central Americans" would have also been of West Indian descent, the second generation that had been born on Panamanian soil of West Indian parents, like Maradell herself.

When they arrived, these immigrants found work on or around plantations, living in company towns and working for the *centrales,* or sugar mill complexes. Santiago de Cuba, on the southeastern tip of the island, was the leading port of entry, but many from Panama entered through the south-central Ciego de Avila region and worked at the Baraguá sugar mill, which held a comparatively high number of Panama migrants. The mill complex was built in 1915 by a group of Pittsburgh inventors but was acquired by the Punta Alegre Sugar Company, a Delaware-based corporation, in 1922.[92] In 1925 Baraguá had the highest output of any U.S. corporate sugar mill in Cuba (98,406 tons).[93] There, West Indians coming from Panama would have found a familiar landscape—a racially segregated company town dominated by a concern for productivity. Migrants grouped themselves by islands of origin, regardless of having passed through Panama in the interim. Barbadians lived in Bajan Town; Jamaicans lived in Jamaica Town. Six Grenadian immigrants founded Grenadian Hall as a social gathering place. This was not the only local institution. The town had four churches—the Salvation Army, the Christian Mission, the Anglican Church, and the Seventh-Day Adventist Church—as well as numerous civic organizations, social clubs, and beneficent societies.[94]

Though the centrales only hired men, West Indian women nevertheless migrated to Cuba. As with the Panama venture, they were drawn by diverse motivations—dwindling economic opportunities, the excitement bred by word of mouth, or, like Maradell, following the trails set by their families and spouses. Whatever their reasons, they migrated beyond the oversight of American sugar companies and despite their wishes. As R. B. Wood, the manager of the Chaparral Sugar Company, told British authorities, "Women arrived here of their own free will and . . . paid their own passage, staying on the estate against the desires of the management."[95] Women migrants were never as numerous as men—in 1919, for example, 77.6 percent of Jamaican people in Cuba were men while 22.4 percent were women—but nevertheless maintained a consistent presence.

Upon their arrival, West Indian women encountered some of the same issues they had faced in Panama. Both British colonial officials and local Jamaican commentators worried about the dangerous "moral environment" Cuba presented for Black women and the potential that they would end up as "practically slaves" in "houses of ill-fame."[96] U.S.-owned sugar companies, desperate to retain workers, often turned a blind eye to practices, like gambling and prostitution, that would have been banned outright in the Canal Zone. The nascent Cuban republic, on the other hand, became quite involved in persecuting prostitution. After vigorous debate, President Menocal abolished regulated prostitution in Cuba on October 23, 1913, with Decree 964.[97] In 1925 the government passed sweeping anti-trafficking laws in order to combat "white slave traffic" that gave wide berth to authorities to detain or deport any individual "likely to become a public burden."[98] Individuals without proof of employment (a common situation for migrant women) risked detention. Though few people were stopped for prostitution in the ports, the Cuban state enacted these laws against Black Caribbean migrants in the

sugar-growing regions, even employing undercover police to root out sex trafficking.

Some evidence of sex trafficking networks between Cuba and Haiti exists. However, as historian Matthew Casey points out, Afro-Caribbean
women's experiences of sex, consent, labor, and commodification complicate
the elite state narrative of "sex trafficking" as a useful analytical framework.
These laws sought to criminalize Black migrant strategies and rested on assumptions of Black women's aberrant sexuality. The attempts of the Cuban
state to contain sex trafficking thus only give us a skewed glimpse at Black
women's experiences while nevertheless suggesting at the sexual exploitation
many vulnerable Black migrant women could have faced.[99]

Most women worked in similar industries as they had in Panama, as domestic servants, laundresses, and dressmakers. In 1921, of 2,805 Jamaican
women who entered Cuba, 1,687 were categorized as seamstresses and dressmakers and 681 as domestics.[100] These two remained the top occupations for
migrant women to Cuba. Some also spent long days in domestic work for
their own households. More likely, women combined a number of these occupations. Maradell used to "mind a little girl" on "t'other side of the mill,"
across the railroad tracks where the Americans lived.[101] After her mother died,
Celia Campbell Jones remembers she "wash plenty of dirty clothes" to support her two younger brothers.[102] Ms. Wilkinson worked for the hotel and
"would go every Monday night and collect the sheets."[103] Despite the relatively
low wages and the need to support their families, these women always put
some money away to post remittances to their families back home. Though
hard to determine, remittances from Cuba to Jamaica during the boom period are estimated to have been around £100,000 to £150,000 per year.[104] Maradell remembered that "my mother used to always send money" to her
grandfather and aunt in Barbados.[105]

They kept transnational chains of connection with the British West Indies in other ways. They frequented Anglican churches. They celebrated Carnival and sang songs like "Sly Mongoose" and "Millie Gone to Brazil." They
danced the Maypole. On Sundays, West Indians from across the provinces
gathered to play cricket. Large tables laden with homemade food cooked by
women accompanied the games. One guest of these cricket outings wrote to
Delcina Marshall's mother saying "he still had the taste of her gravy on his

tongue."[106] They joined friendly societies and social clubs, such as the Grenadian Club, Imperial Club, and Unity Club. Women formed their own organizations, such as the Club de Mujeres Antillanas Británicas, and Estrella de Londres #1 in Camaguey, founded in 1942.[107] As the name of the last club evinces, many of these social activities reinforced migrants' connections to the British empire. For historian Jorge Giovannetti-Torres, their identification and organizational practices around their British connection served as a survival strategy that protected them from a growing anti-Black xenophobia in Cuba and hailed British colonial officials for diplomatic support.[108]

Many of the immigrants were literate and devoted themselves to providing a good education for their children. At first, the local Spanish-speaking Cuban school was the only institution available, but West Indian parents were reluctant to send their children there. Some continued sending kids back to the British islands for their education, where they would be cared for temporarily by other women. Eventually, the Salvation Army and the Christian Mission started keeping small schools, but consistent and organized English-language schooling would only come to Baraguá after 1920 with the arrival of William Preston Stoute from Panama. In Panama, Stoute had worked for a decade as a Canal Zone schoolteacher, but he eventually became involved in the cause of "Negro unity and progress." As he told Marcus Garvey in a letter, "Here in the Isthmus I am doing my bit with my tongue and my pen, especially in the interests of Labor."[109] In 1920 Stoute led the United Brotherhood of Maintenance of Way and Railway Shop Employees in its massive 1920 strike, joined by 80 percent of Silver employees. Canal Zone authorities eventually jailed and deported him, after which he went to Baraguá.[110]

Garvey's movement developed extensive support among West Indian migrants and Afro-Cubans on the island, where there were more than fifty divisions of the UNIA.[111] As in New York, the UNIA served as an institution for Black people to imagine a diasporic unity in the service of progress for the race and Black political and economic self-determination, particularly in host countries where they faced intense discrimination. However, its articulation of Black nationalism also promoted a politics of respectability that castigated wayward women and nonnormative sexuality while upholding participants as *negros finos*, of a higher class than common laborers or Haitian migrants.[112]

Unlike the West Indian women in Panama who often spoke of their choice to pursue common-law arrangements, many West Indian women in Cuba instead referenced their church marriages. The data shows that, for a particular class of West Indians in Cuba, legal marriage did become desirable.[113] Civil marriages in Cuba also show high rates of endogamy during this period.[114] As Delcina Esperanza Marshall remembered, West Indians "intermarried in order to carry on customs and names."[115] However, this data merely points to the desire of a certain subset of West Indians to strengthen community ties with others from the same island. The data does not indicate an overall increase in legal marriage among West Indians. Consensual common-law relationships and cohabitation remained the norm among West Indians in Cuba, despite the archival silence in both the marriage data and the oral histories about these practices.[116]

The gap between West Indian women's memories and their actual practices of marriage in Cuba exemplifies the larger context of the oral histories on which much of the work on this migration relies. These were conducted in the 1990s and, as anthropologist Andrea Queeley notes, are not a factual re-creation of their migration but rather represent how West Indian Cubans understood themselves in the context of the severe economic crisis that marked the Cuban Special Period. In these interviews, West Indian Cubans articulated a certain "Anglo-Caribbeanness" through a discourse of respectability and connection to British traditions.[117] These oral histories served as a moment of "subject-making practice . . . in the context of emergent economic and social disadvantage" for Black residents of Cuba still considered outsiders and suffering from severely restricted economic opportunity.[118] Though West Indians employed respectability as a framework to understand their past, the reality for Black women in early twentieth-century Cuba— where they were subject to investigations of sex trafficking, often lived precarious economic existences, and might have taken on sex work—was likely more complicated. As it did in Panama, respectability became a complex strategy through which Black migrant women negotiated their second-class status in Cuba.

The experience of West Indian women in Cuba reinforces two critical continuities in the history of early twentieth-century Caribbean migration. The first is the expansion of American imperial power throughout the region and its continued impact on West Indian lives. Many West Indians who had passed through Panama made their way next to Cuba, following the trail of American investment. If anything, their experience in Panama had familiarized them with American administrators, labor practices, and segregation policies. West Indian women, whom American companies rarely employed, also found themselves in the currents of U.S. empire, though their migration rebuffed administrators' attempts at keeping them away. The oral histories point to a second continuity; as in Panama, gendered discourses about marriage, religion, and respectability profoundly shaped migrants' lives. While the Cuban state used ideas about female vulnerability and sex trafficking to police West Indians, these migrants sought to define and practice their own version of respectability while navigating the discrimination they faced. Their cultivation of an Anglo-Caribbean culture defied anti-Black discourses in Cuba that sought to criminalize migrant Black women, diminish the labor of West Indian immigrants, and excise Blackness from notions of Cuban nationhood.

It is primarily through West Indian women that the memory of this migration remains alive. Women dominate the gathered oral histories about Baraguá and populate the social events captured by Gloria Rolando in her documentary *My Footsteps in Baraguá*.[119] Until her death in 2009, one of these women, Celia Campbell Jones, served as the unofficial matriarch of Baraguá, the oldest Barbadian still living in the town. These West Indian women vigorously engaged in the same political and migratory trends as West Indian men—they sought more autonomy in their labor, they joined the UNIA, and they petitioned the British for protection. The West Indian women who enrolled their children in British-style schools, went to church and married, and cooked food for Sunday afternoon cricket matches did so in the face of discriminatory Cuban laws and American administrators who saw them as potential deviants. Their sense of Anglo-Caribbeanness developed from a practical response rooted in their everyday practices and gendered marginalization.

*   *   *

The construction era created a series of contingencies—the influx of money into the region, the gendered division of labor that yoked West Indian men to the Canal, the high demand for Black women's entrepreneurial and domestic work—that placed women ambiguously parallel to the Canal endeavor and the growth of American imperial power. From this position, where they were simultaneously in demand and excluded, West Indian women enacted distinct strategies of social reproduction—they appealed to the paternalistic sentiment of imperial administrators, used methods of everyday resistance to gain autonomy in their workplace, positioned themselves as British subjects to petition for legal rights, managed the financial effects of their loved ones, and publicly defended their reputations. Given the lack of opportunity available in the islands, West Indian women used the openings that the Canal construction era provided to establish West Indian communities in Panama and cement financial and labor practices that would sustain the decades of West Indian migration that followed. Whether in Barbados, New York, or Cuba, women facilitated the massive West Indian migrations of the early twentieth century through these same strategies—their financial management of family resources and remittances, caretaking of children and kin, provision of the more practical aspects of survival and sustenance, and maintenance of diasporic social networks. Though the stories are unique to each individual, their strategies reverberate in the experiences of the many West Indian women who similarly guided family migration during this period.

CONCLUSION

The West Indian Museum of Panama stands at a busy intersection on Justo Arosemena Avenue in the neighborhood of El Marañon in Panama City. It is housed in the former Christian Mission Church, built by Barbadian workers in 1910, on land ceded by the U.S.-owned Panama Railroad Company. The museum is located near the gleaming new Cinco de Mayo subway station, inaugurated in 2014 as part of one of the biggest public works projects in Panama in recent years. It was built by an international consortium of French, Brazilian, and Spanish corporations at a cost of around $1.6 million. The museum is maintained and staffed by the volunteer organization SAMAAP, or Society of Friends of the Afro-Antillean Museum of Panama, whose members hail from the local West Indian Panamanian community. On my several visits there, tours have all been led by West Indian women. They tell the story of the rise of the neighborhood interspersed with details of women's daily lives during the construction era, displaying items such as hair irons, quilts sewn by women's clubs, and full-scale re-creations of the veranda kitchens where women cooked. The daily work of Black women, this museum suggests, sustained West Indian communities in Panama. The descendants of these women preserve and honor their contributions to Panama's history not only in the museum but also in their multiple forms of activism throughout Panama and the diaspora.[1] This book builds on the museum's commemoration of Black women's work as an archival provocation to refute the silences and hierarchies of knowledge enshrined by U.S. and Panamanian narratives about the Canal construction.

In many ways, the story told in this book is straightforward: West Indian women migrated to Panama and provided the essential labor of social reproduction that buttressed the construction of the Canal and subsequent Caribbean migrations. Any West Indian could tell you that. In the islands and among the West Indian communities in Panama and elsewhere, people hold distinct historical memories of the construction period, even after the Canal recently celebrated its centennial. They remember their great-uncles who came back to the islands missing a leg from an explosion gone awry, much as they remember their great-grandmothers who made that first move from St. Lucia to Panama to Brooklyn.

Afro-Panamanian scholars such as Jenise Miller and Maya Doig-Acuña continue to reckon with the imperial histories of anti-Blackness that shaped their families.[2] They capture the continued migrations and movements of their West Indian Panamanian families throughout the 1960s and 1970s as they celebrated at the now-defunct Kelso Dining Room on Crown Heights' Franklin Avenue or gathered at Scherer Park in Los Angeles before gentrification and rising rents displaced them. Their stories center kinship and women's emotional and reproductive labor as the central threads that bind their families together across generations marked by slavery, colonialism, violence, migration, and labor. These relationships, for Doig-Acuña, are "the most American of stories. And also the Blackest of stories. The most Caribbean of stories. That is, American anti-Blackness has always been a hemispheric project, and so too have expressions of Black survival and regeneration."[3] This book highlights the hemispheric "expressions of Black survival" that West Indian women developed in early twentieth-century Panama, in the context of growing U.S. imperial power.

The centrality of women to how West Indians remember the construction era stands in stark contrast to state and academic narratives about the period in both the United States and Panama which, at best, see women as ancillary to the major story. As I have shown, however, West Indian survival and the work of construction relied heavily on women's labor of food provision, laundry service, domestic work, and household management. When ICC commissaries and industrial laundries could barely keep up with the demand, West Indian women provided. When American housewives could not deal with the challenges of housekeeping in humid Panama, West Indian women did it. When the commission fed Silver workers food fit only for pigs and denied them entry to cafeterias, it was West Indian women who nourished them. When the ICC depopulated the Zone's Silver towns, it was West Indian women who maintained homes in Panamanian territory and found ways to assert their belonging in a new land.

U.S. administrators understood the importance of West Indian women's labor quite well. They admitted that Silver laborers "won't work anyplace without their women."[4] They acknowledged that Silver workers lived better lives outside of ICC facilities because "as a rule the women are good cooks and their food both in quality and quantity is much better."[5] West Indian women's domestic and care labor subsidized America's empire by sustaining the workforce that built the Panama Canal.[6] But West Indian women proved uneasy imperial subjects; they traveled using their own migratory routes and worked outside ICC authority. U.S. administrators only condoned West Indian women's presence and labor when it contributed to the productivity of the construction effort and remained under their regulation. When West Indian women stepped outside of the imperial economic and moral order— when they migrated alone, worked independently, provided sensuousness and entertainment across racial barriers, or simply loved and lived in ways unfamiliar to U.S. residents—they faced swift repression in the form of confinement, deportation, unemployment, eviction, silencing, and denigration. It is this dynamic that is most clearly evidenced by the archives of U.S. imperial involvement in Panama. If not ignoring them altogether, U.S. sources record West Indian women as either primitive and comical servants or as agents of vice and immorality.

However incomplete these sources might be, to take them at their word is to assume that West Indian women were simply static extensions of their representation in the imperial archive. But these sources also evidence how West Indian women maneuvered the uneasy margins of imperial authority, using practices drawn from a long history of Afro-Caribbean adaptations after emancipation. Like recently freed women who refused legal and church marriage despite pressure from British colonial authorities, West Indian women in the Canal Zone pursued and defended their illegal common-law relationships. Like the laundresses who traveled between Colón and Kingston in the 1880s, West Indian women during the construction period eluded government oversight to ply their domestic and commercial trades to tourists, travelers, and Zonians. Like the West Indians who continued to mourn their dead despite the criminalization of obeah in the islands, women re-created Caribbean mortuary traditions in Panama and requested the left-over belongings and wages of deceased relatives to be passed down through kin. West Indian women's lives were deeply determined by the violence of U.S. empire, but they used diasporic strategies of labor mobility, double-edged alliances, and claims-making to wring out security and material benefits for themselves and their families.

West Indian women were indispensable to the expansion of U.S. capital throughout the Caribbean, but they also functioned as economic actors beyond frameworks that privileged imperial productivity and profit. West Indian women's mostly invisible care work certainly sustained and reproduced the labor power that the project required. The policing and surveillance of Black women shaped the gendered categories that constituted the conditions of possibility for the Canal's construction and the profits it created for the United States.[7] But West Indian women also disturbed, refused, and skirted the structures of racial capitalism in the Canal Zone. They drove up prices of goods and services to capitalize on the high demand for their labor by white Americans and evaded the roll system by forcing customers to pay them in gold coin. They ignored the disparagement of their labor by their bosses and continued to work flexible, independent jobs outside of the ICC's surveillance. They saved, managed, and circulated "Panama money" to provide for their families, finance migrations, purchase former plantation land on the islands, and buy homes that served as central gathering places for Caribbean arrivals to New York City.

The Canal construction brought unprecedented amounts of money to the region alongside new forms of labor discipline and imperial governance. These changes posed unique challenges for West Indian women, who faced multiple, overlapping marginalizations and received little in the way of support from national or imperial institutions in Panama and the Canal Zone. Panama thus served as a testing ground for West Indian women's freedom practices in the early twentieth century, where they learned to navigate the violence, limitation, and opportunities of U.S. imperial racial capitalism. As construction ended and global borders hardened, Caribbean migrants relied on the work of West Indian women to further their networks of migration and survive increasingly xenophobic and anti-Black environments. West

Indian women managed the household finances that paid for ship tickets, show money, and property. They cooked and hosted gatherings where West Indians discussed Garveyism, labor organizing, and other political ideas and reinforced their sense of community. They worked in white American homes in New York City, Panama, and Cuba, saving money to support their families and send for their relatives in the islands.

In prioritizing themselves and their kin, West Indian women worked counter to imperial logics. In the face of violent criminalization, their pragmatism and survival strategies nourished Afro-Caribbean communities and troubled the logics of racial capitalism that circulated throughout Central America, the Caribbean, and the United States. The history of the Panama Canal shows how the spread of racial capitalism depended on the displacement and exploitation of Black men and women but it also reveals a parallel history of Black West Indian women's diasporic countercultural projects of survival and community-making.

NOTES

Introduction

1. *Jane Hall v. China Byasta* (CZ 2nd Cir. 1907), Case 89, Record Group 21: Records of District Courts of the United States, Canal Zone Second Judicial Circuit Civil Court (Empire, Gorgona, Ancon), Civil Case Files, 1904–1914, National Archives and Records Administration, Washington, DC.

2. Michael L. Conniff, *Black Labor on a White Canal: Panama, 1904–1981* (Pittsburgh, PA: University of Pittsburgh Press, 1985); Julie Greene, *The Canal Builders: Making America's Empire at the Panama Canal* (New York: Penguin Press, 2009); Lancelot Lewis, *The West Indian in Panama: Black Labor in Panama, 1850–1914* (Washington, DC: University Press of America, 1980); Velma Newton, *The Silver Men: West Indian Labour Migration to Panama, 1850–1914*, rev. ed. (1985; Kingston: Ian Randle, 2004); Bonham Richardson, *Panama Money in Barbados, 1900–1920* (Knoxville: University of Tennessee Press, 1985); Olive Senior, *Dying to Better Themselves: West Indians and the Building of the Panama Canal* (Kingston: University of the West Indies Press, 2014).

3. "Silver women" is also a direct reference to the most important work on West Indian male labor migration to Panama, Velma Newton's 1985 *Silver Men*. Only three previous works have addressed West Indian women's role in Panama at any length: Julie Greene devotes a chapter in the *Canal Builders* to women in the Canal Zone, with a short section specifically on West Indian women; Eyra Marcela Reyes Rivas's book, *El trabajo de las mujeres en la historia de la construcción del canal de Panama, 1881–1914* (Panama: Universidad de Panamá, Instituto de la Mujer, 2000), deals with women in general, including American, Panamanian, and West Indian women, from the French construction period to the end of the American construction; and Olive Senior discusses West Indian women throughout *Dying to Better Themselves*.

4. For classic works on Black women's labor of social reproduction during enslavement, see Hilary Beckles, *Natural Rebels: A Social History of Enslaved Black Women in Barbados* (New Brunswick, NJ: Rutgers University Press, 1989); Stephanie Camp, *Closer to Freedom: Enslaved Women and Everyday Resistance in the Plantation South* (Chapel Hill: University of North Carolina Press, 2004); David Barry Gaspar and Darlene Clark Hine, eds., *More Than Chattel: Black Women and Slavery in the Americas* (Bloomington: Indiana University Press, 1996); Deborah Gray White, *Ar'n't I a Woman? Female Slaves in the Plantation South* (New

York: W. W. Norton, 1985); and Jacqueline Jones, *Labor of Love, Labor of Sorrow: Black Women, Work, and the Family from Slavery to the Present* (New York: Basic Books, 1985).

5. Newton, *Silver Men*.

6. For more of my thinking on the regulatory mechanisms of the canal economy and women's role alongside it, see Timothy Mitchell, "Fixing the Economy," *Cultural Studies* 12, no. 1 (1998): 82–101.

7. Special Correspondent of the Herald, "A Scandal on the Isthmus of Panama," *New York Herald*, November 25, 1905, Folder: Press clippings on Panama, Box 39, Poultney Bigelow Papers, 1855–1954, Manuscript and Archives Division, New York Public Library.

8. The ICC built very little Silver married housing and stopped building it altogether after 1907. West Indians also had to be legally married to access this housing, which many were not.

9. Mitchell, "Fixing the Economy."

10. Paul Kramer, "The Military-Sexual Complex: Prostitution, Disease and the Boundaries of Empire During the Philippine-American War," *Asia Pacific Journal* 9, issue 30, no. 2 (July 2011): 1–35.

11. On capillary and arterial power, see Frederick Cooper, "Conflict and Connection: Rethinking Colonial African History," *American Historical Review* 99, no. 5 (December 1994): 1516–1545.

12. This argument draws on the work of the anthropologist Charles Carnegie on "strategic flexibility," though Carnegie neither considers the gendered articulations of these practices nor the context of U.S. empire or early Caribbean migration. Charles Carnegie, *Postnationalism Prefigured: Caribbean Borderlands* (New Brunswick, NJ: Rutgers University Press, 2002).

13. My argument is deeply informed by recent groundbreaking works in African Diaspora history that center Black women and complicate notions of agency. I am indebted to Keisha Blain, *Set the World on Fire: Black Nationalist Women and the Global Struggle for Freedom* (Philadelphia: University of Pennsylvania Press, 2018); LaShawn Harris, *Sex Workers, Psychics, and Numbers-Runners: Black Women in New York City's Underground Economy* (Champaign: University of Illinois Press, 2017); Saidiya Hartman, *Wayward Lives, Beautiful Experiments: Intimate Histories of Riotous Black Girls, Troublesome Women, and Queer Radicals* (New York: W. W. Norton, 2019); Sarah Hayley, *No Mercy Here: Gender, Punishment, and the Making of Jim Crow Modernity* (Chapel Hill: University of North Carolina Press, 2016); Tera Hunter, *Bound in Wedlock: Slave and Free Black Marriage in the Nineteenth-Century* (Cambridge, MA: Harvard University Press, 2019); Jessica Marie Johnson, *Wicked Flesh: Black Women, Intimacy, and Freedom in the Atlantic World* (Philadelphia: University of Pennsylvania Press, 2020); and Shauna Sweeney, "Market Marronage: Fugitive Women and the Internal Marketing System in Jamaica, 1781–1834," *William and Mary Quarterly* 76, no. 2 (April 2019): 197–222.

14. Walter Johnson, "On Agency," *Journal of Social History* 37, no. 1 (Autumn 2003): 113–124. Shalini Puri, "Beyond Resistance: Notes Toward a New Caribbean Cultural Studies," in *Small Axe* 14 (September 2003): 23–38.

15. Neferti Tadiar, "Decolonization, Race, and Remaindered Life Under Empire," *Qui Parle* 23, no. 2 (Spring/Summer 2015): 149.

16. Along with some of the works cited above, other works in the history of gender, intimacy, and capitalism have influenced my approach to "Silver women," notably Alexandra J. Finley, *An Intimate Economy: Enslaved Women, Work, and America's Domestic Slave Trade* (Chapel Hill: University of North Carolina Press, 2020); Julie Hardwick, Sarah M. S. Pearsall, and Karin Wulf, "Introduction: Centering Families in Atlantic Histories," *William and Mary Quarterly* 70 (April 2013): 205–224; Ellen Hartigan-O'Connor, "Gender's Value in the History of Capitalism," *Journal of the Early Republic* 36, no. 4 (Winter 2016): 613–635; Ellen Hartigan-O'Connor, *The Ties That Buy: Women and Commerce in Revolutionary America* (Philadelphia: University of Pennsylvania Press, 2009); Susannah Shaw Romney, *New Netherland Connections: Intimate Networks and Atlantic Ties in Seventeenth-Century America* (Chapel Hill: University of North Carolina Press, 2014); Shauna Sweeney, "Black Women in Slavery and Freedom: Gendering the History of Racial Capitalism," *American Quarterly* 72, no. 1 (March 2020): 277–289; and Sophie White, "'A Baser Commerce': Retailing, Class, and Gender in French Colonial New Orleans," *William and Mary Quarterly* 63 (July 2006): 517–550.

17. Works on empire, gender, and intimacy that have informed this approach include Anne McClintock, *Imperial Leather: Race, Gender, and Sexuality in the Colonial Contest* (New York: Routledge, 1995); Ann Laura Stoler, ed., *Haunted by Empire: Geographies of Intimacy in North American History* (Durham, NC: Duke University Press, 2006); Ann Laura Stoler, *Carnal Knowledge and Imperial Power: Race and the Intimate in Colonial Rule* (Berkeley: University of California Press, 2002); and Laura Wexler, *Tender Violence: Domestic Visions in an Age of U.S. Imperialism* (Chapel Hill: University of North Carolina Press, 2000).

18. Matthew Casey, *Empire's Guestworkers: Haitian Migrants in Cuba During the Age of US Occupation* (Cambridge: Cambridge University Press, 2017); Glenn Chambers, *Race, Nation, and West Indian Immigration to Honduras, 1890–1940* (Baton Rouge: Louisiana State University Press, 2010); Ronald Harpelle, *The West Indians of Costa Rica: Race, Class and the Integration of an Ethnic Minority* (London: McGill-Queen's University Press, 2001); Jorge L. Giovannetti-Torres, "The Elusive Organization of 'Identity': Race, Religion, and Empire Among Caribbean Migrants in Cuba," *Small Axe* 10, no. 1 (February 2006): 1–27; Jorge L. Giovannetti-Torres, *Black British Migrants in Cuba: Race, Labor, and Empire in the Twentieth-Century Caribbean, 1898–1948* (Cambridge: Cambridge University Press, 2018); Annette Insa-nally, Mark Clifford, and Sean Sheriff, eds., *Regional Footprints: The Travels and Travails of Early Caribbean Migrants* (Kingston: University of the West Indies Press, 2006); Winston James, *Holding Aloft the Banner of Ethiopia: Caribbean Radicalism in Early Twentieth-Century America* (New York: Verso, 1998); Lara Putnam, *Radical Moves: Caribbean Migrants and the Politics of Race in the Jazz Age* (Chapel Hill: University of North Carolina Press, 2013); Violet Showers Johnson, *The Other Black Bostonians: West Indians in Boston, 1900–1950* (Bloomington: Indiana University Press, 2006). A few exceptions that significantly address women include Asia Leeds, "Representations of Race, Entanglements of Power: Whiteness, Garveyism, and Redemptive Geographies in Costa Rica, 1921–1950" (PhD diss., University of California at Berkeley, 2010); Lara Putnam, *The Company They Kept: Migrants and the Politics of Gender in Caribbean Costa Rica, 1870–1960* (Chapel Hill: University of North Carolina Press,

2002); and Irma Watkins-Owens, *Blood Relations: Caribbean Immigrants and the Harlem Community, 1900–1930* (Bloomington: Indiana University Press, 1996).

19. Michelle Stephens, *Black Empire: The Masculine Global Imaginary of Caribbean Intellectuals in the United States, 1914–1962* (Durham, NC: Duke University Press, 2005).

20. Ibid. Both McKay and Garvey had stints in Panama during the period. See also Lara Putnam, "Borderlands and Border-Crossers: Migrants and Boundaries in the Greater Caribbean, 1840–1940," *Small Axe* 18, no. 1 (March 2014): 7–21.

21. Julie Greene, "Builders of Empire: Rewriting the Labor and Working-Class History of Anglo-American Global Power," *LABOR: Studies in Working-Class History of the Americas* 13 (December 2016): 1–10.

22. Other recent works that inform my reading of the dynamic between labor migration and U.S. empire include Casey, *Empire's Guestworkers*; Giovannetti-Torres, *Black British Migrants in Cuba*; Ismael Garcia-Colón, *Colonial Migrants at the Heart of Empire: Puerto Rican Workers on U.S. Farms* (Berkeley: University of California Press, 2020); Jana Lipman, *Guantánamo: A Working-Class History Between Empire and Revolution* (Berkeley: University of California Press, 2009); Veronica Martinez-Matsuda, *Migrant Citizenship: Race, Rights, and Reform in the U.S. Farm Labor Camp Program* (Philadelphia: University of Pennsylvania Press, 2020); Ana Raquel Minian, *Undocumented Lives: The Untold Story of Mexican Migration* (Cambridge, MA: Harvard University Press 2020); and Ana Elizabeth Rosas, *Abrazando el Espíritu: Bracero Families Confront the U.S.-Mexico Border* (Berkeley: University of California Press, 2014).

23. J. Johnson, *Wicked Flesh*, 1.

24. Aims McGuiness, *Path of Empire: Panama and the California Gold Rush* (Ithaca, NY: Cornell University Press, 2008).

25. For more on this regional dynamic, see Putnam, "Borderlands and Border-Crossers."

26. Senior, *Dying to Better Themselves*, 63.

27. For an extended study of the French recruitment efforts in Jamaica, see chapter 4 of Elizabeth McLean Petras, *Jamaican Labor Migration: White Capital and Black Labor, 1850–1930* (Boulder, CO: Westview Press, 1988); and chapter 3 of Senior, *Dying to Better Themselves*. To my knowledge, there is no book-length treatment of the French construction period or of West Indian life in Panama during that time.

28. Senior, *Dying to Better Themselves*, 66.

29. *Star and Herald*, Panama, June 2, 1884.

30. Senior, *Dying to Better Themselves*, 75.

31. Tracy Robinson, *Fifty Years at Panama, 1861–1911*, 2nd ed. (New York: Trow Press, 1907), 143.

32. Rhonda Frederick, *"Colón Man a Come": Mythographies of Panamá Canal Migration* (Lanham, MD: Lexington Books, 2005).

33. William Crawford Gorgas, *Sanitation in Panama* (New York: D. Appleton, 1915), 157.

34. Michael Conniff has a thorough account of the United States' involvement in Panama's "second independence" in *Panama and the United States: The Forced Alliance* (Athens:

University of Georgia Press, 1992); Walter LaFeber, *The Panama Canal: The Crisis in Historical Perspective* (Oxford: Oxford University Press, 1978).

35. I say "legal" birth because Panama had a complex nineteenth-century relationship to nationhood. See Alfredo Castillero Calvo, ed., *Historia General de Panama*, vol. 2 (Panama: Comité Nacional del Centenario de la República de Panamá, 2004); Alfredo Figueroa Navarro, *Dominio y sociedad en el Panamá Colombiano, 1821–1903* (Panama: Impresora Panamá, 1978); McGuiness, *Path of Empire*; Ricaurte Soler, *Formas ideológicas de la nación panameña: Panamá y el problema nacional hispanoamericano* (San José, Costa Rica: Editorial Universitaria Centroamericana, 1977); Peter Szok, *La última gaviota: Liberalism and Nostalgia in Early Twentieth Century Panama* (Westport, CT: Greenwood Press, 2001).

36. Oliver J. Dinius and Angela Vergara, eds., *Company Towns in the Americas: Landscape, Power, and Working-Class Communities* (Athens: University of Georgia Press, 2011).

37. On Panama as a "black contact zone," see Winston James, "Harlem's Difference," in *Race Capital?: Harlem as Setting and Symbol*, ed. Andrew Fearnley and Daniel Matlin, 111–142 (New York: Columbia University Press, 2019); Mary Louise Pratt, "Arts of the Contact Zone," *Profession* (1991): 33–40.

38. Newton, *Silver Men*, 55–60.

39. Ibid.

40. Ibid.

41. Noel Maurer and Carlos Yu, *The Big Ditch: How America Took, Built, Ran, and Ultimately Gave Away the Panama Canal* (Princeton, NJ: Princeton University Press, 2010), 132.

42. Senior, *Dying to Better Themselves*, 127.

43. Isthmian Canal Commission, *Annual Report of the Governor of the Panama Canal for the Fiscal Year Ended June 30, 1938* (Washington, DC: Government Printing Office, 1938), 72.

44. See Julie Greene's discussion in *Canal Builders*, 62–69.

45. On Spanish workers, see Julie Greene, "Spaniards on the Silver Roll: Labor Troubles and Liminality in the Panama Canal Zone, 1904–1914," *International Labor and Working-Class History* 66 (October 2004): 78–98.

46. Greene, *Canal Builders*, 127.

47. On "native" towns in the Zone, see Marixa Lasso, *Erased: The Untold Story of the Panama Canal* (Cambridge, MA: Harvard University Press, 2019).

48. In Panama, see Carla Guerrón Montero, "Racial Democracy and Nationalism in Panama," *Ethnology* 45, no. 2 (Summer 2006): 209–228; Marixa Lasso, "Race and Ethnicity in the Formation of Panamanian National Identity: Panamanian Discrimination Against Chinese and West Indians in the Thirties," *Revista Panameña de Política* 4 (2007): 61–92. In other Latin American contexts, see Nancy Applebaum, Anne S. Macpherson, and Karin Alejandra Rosenblatt, *Race and Nation in Modern Latin America* (Chapel Hill: University of North Carolina Press, 2003); Jeffrey L. Gould, *To Die in This Way: Nicaraguan Indians and the Myth of Mestizaje* (Durham, NC: Duke University Press, 1998); and Marixa Lasso, *Myths of Harmony: Race and Republicanism During the Age of Revolution, Colombia 1795–1831* (Pittsburgh, PA: University of Pittsburgh Press, 2007). On the myth of mestiçagem, whiteness, and racial democracy in Brazil, see also Marshall Eakin, *Becoming Brazilians: Race and National Iden-*

tity in Twentieth-Century Brazil (Cambridge: Cambridge University Press, 2017); and Barbara Weinstein, *The Color of Modernity: São Paulo and the Making of Race and Nation in Brazil* (Durham, NC: Duke University Press, 2015).

49. For more on the West Indian Panamanian community after construction and the discrimination they faced, see Kaysha Corinealdi, "Redefining Home: West Indian Panamanians and the Transnational Politics of Race, Citizenship, and Diaspora" (PhD diss., Yale University, UMI Dissertations Publishing, 2011); Kaysha Corinealdi, "Envisioning Multiple Citizenships: West Indian Panamanians and Creating Community in the Canal Zone Neocolony," *Global South* 6, no. 2 (Fall 2012): 86–106; Conniff, *Black Labor on a White Canal*; Khemani Gibson, "The Black Cosmopolitans: The West Indian Immigrant Community in Panama, 1914–1961" (PhD diss., New York University, 2020); Lewis, *West Indian in Panama*; Trevor O'Reggio, *Between Alienation and Citizenship: The Evolution of Black West Indian Society in Panama, 1914–1964* (Lanham, MD: University Press of America, 2006); George Westerman, "Historical Notes on West Indians on the Isthmus of Panama," *Phylon* 22, no. 4 (1961): 340–350; and Robin Elizabeth Zenger, *West Indians in Panama: Diversity and Activism, 1910s–1940s* (PhD diss., University of Arizona, 2015).

50. Conniff, *Black Labor on a White Canal*; Michael Donoghue, *Borderland on the Isthmus: Race, Culture, and the Struggle for the Canal Zone* (Durham, NC: Duke University Press, 2014).

51. Marixa Lasso, *Erased*. For a thorough account of the legal battles that followed depopulation, see Allison Powers Useche's forthcoming book, *Settlement Colonialism: Managing Empire in the United States, 1868–1965* (Oxford: Oxford University Press).

52. For more on elite Panamanian exclusionary notions of nationhood, see Szok, *La última gaviota*.

53. Thomas Richards, *The Imperial Archive: Knowledge and the Fantasy of Empire* (London: Verso, 1993).

54. See my further discussion of this archival work in Joan Flores-Villalobos, "Freak Letters: Tracing Gender, Race, and Diaspora in the Panama Canal Archive," *Small Axe* 23, no. 2 (July 2019): 34–56. This is informed by recent critical works on Black feminist archival practice, such as Saidiya Hartman, "Venus in Two Acts," *Small Axe* 12, no. 2 (June 2008): 1–14; Laura Helton, Justin Leroy, Max A. Mishler, Samantha Seeley, and Shauna Sweeney, eds., "The Question of Recovery: Slavery, Freedom, and the Archive," special issue, *Social Text* 33, no. 4 (2015): 1–18, as well as other articles in the special issue; Marisa Fuentes, *Dispossessed Lives: Enslaved Women, Violence, and the Archive* (Philadelphia: University of Pennsylvania Press, 2016); Jessica Marie Johnson, *Wicked Flesh*; Mireille Miller-Young, *A Taste for Brown Sugar: Black Women in Pornography* (Durham, NC: Duke University Press, 2014); Michel-Rolph Trouillot, *Silencing the Past: Power and the Production of History* (Boston: Beacon Press, 1997); and Sasha Turner, "The Nameless and the Forgotten: Maternal Grief, Sacred Protection, and the Archive of Slavery," *Slavery and Abolition* 38 (2017): 232–250. See also Adria L. Imada, *Aloha America: Hula Circuits Through the U.S. Empire* (Durham, NC: Duke University Press, 2012); and Durba Mitra, *Indian Sex Life and the Colonial Origins of Modern Social Thought* (Princeton, NJ: Princeton University Press, 2020).

55. Hartman, *Wayward Lives, Beautiful Experiments*.

56. Ann Laura Stoler, *Along the Archival Grain: Epistemic Anxieties and Colonial Common Sense* (Princeton, NJ: Princeton University Press, 2010).

57. In this methodology, I am deeply inspired by the work of Lara Putnam, *Radical Moves*.

58. Natalia Molina, *How Race Is Made in America: Immigration, Citizenship, and the Historical Power of Racial Scripts* (Berkeley: University of California Press, 2014). In Panama, see Renée Alexander Craft, *When the Devil Knocks: The Congo Tradition and the Politics of Blackness in Twentieth-Century Panama* (Columbus: Ohio State University Press, 2016).

59. For more on West Indian Panamanian community making after the Canal construction, see the forthcoming work of Kaysha Corinealdi, *Panama in Black: Afro-Caribbean World Making in the Twentieth Century* (Durham, NC: Duke University Press, 2022).

Chapter 1

1. The story below is narrativized from an oral history of Griffin's daughter, Adica Moore, conducted in 2020 by Frances Williams-Yearwood of the organization Pan-Caribbean Sankofa. Mrs. Moore remembers her mother's name as Emily Amelia Griffin (née Lewis), though the U.S. Canal Zone census records her as either Emily (1920 Census) or Amelia (1930 Census). I chose the full name as used by her daughter. Some of the material here, on Griffin's possible emotions, is clearly speculation. The facts of her life—her husband's employment on the Canal, her arrival in 1910, her daughter's death, her life in La Boca—are documented in Mrs. Moore's oral history and in U.S. Census documents. "An Interview with Adica Moore," George A. Smathers Libraries Digital Collections, University of Florida, July 17, 2020, https://ufdc.ufl.edu/AA00081353/00001; United States Census, 1930, *FamilySearch*, https://familysearch.org/ark:/61903/1:1:XCVB-N7D, sheet 25B, line 77, family 439, NARA microfilm publication T626 (Washington DC: National Archives and Records Administration, 2002).

2. "Interview with Adica Moore."

3. Herbert George de Lisser, *Susan Proudleigh* (London: Methuen, 1915), Digital Library of the Caribbean (DLOC), accessed September 30, 2019, https://dloc.com/UF00081174/00001.

4. I owe an important intellectual debt for this argument to Jessica Marie Johnson, *Wicked Flesh: Black Women, Intimacy, and Freedom in the Atlantic World* (Philadelphia: University of Pennsylvania Press, 2020), who discusses Black women's strategies of intimacy and kinship in the very different context of the eighteenth-century French Atlantic.

5. Hilary Beckles, *Great House Rules: Landless Emancipation and Workers' Protest in Barbados 1838–1938* (Kingston: Ian Randle, 2004); O. Nigel Bolland, "Systems of Domination After Slavery: The Control of Land and Labor in the British West Indies After 1838," *Comparative Studies in Society and History* 23, no. 4 (October 1981): 591–619; Richard Frucht, "From Slavery to Unfreedom in the Plantation Society of St. Kitts, W.I.," *Annals of the New York Academy of Science* 292, no. 1 (June 1977): 379–388; Thomas Holt, *The Problem of Freedom: Race, Labor, and Politics in Jamaica and Britain, 1832–1938* (Baltimore: Johns Hopkins University Press, 1992); Melanie Newton, "'New Ideas of Correctness': Gender, Amelioration,

and Emancipation in Barbados, 1810s–1850s," *Slavery and Abolition* 21, no. 3 (2000): 94–124; Velma Newton, *The Silver Men: West Indian Labour Migration to Panama, 1850–1914*, rev. ed. (1985; Kingston: Ian Randle, 2004), 26, Table 1: "Prices of Sugar Exports from Jamaica to the United Kingdom, 1846, 1914," 9.

6. Bridget Brereton, "Family Strategies, Gender, and the Shift to Wage Labor in the British Caribbean," in *The Colonial Caribbean in Transition: Essays on Postemancipation Social and Cultural History*, ed. Bridget Brereton and Kevin A. Yelvington, 143–161 (Gainesville: University Press of Florida, 1999); Brian L. Moore and Michele A. Johnson, *Neither Led nor Driven: Contesting British Cultural Imperialism in Jamaica, 1865–1920* (Kingston: University of the West Indies Press, 2004); M. Newton, "'New Ideas of Correctness.'"

7. Hilary Beckles and Verene Shepherd, eds., *Caribbean Freedom: Society and Economy from Emancipation to the Present* (Kingston: Ian Randle, 1994); Brereton, "Family Strategies"; Frederick Cooper, Thomas Holt, and Rebecca Scott, *Beyond Slavery: Explorations of Race, Labor, and Citizenship in Postemancipation Societies* (Chapel Hill: University of North Carolina Press, 2000); Holt, *Problem of Freedom*; Natasha Lightfoot, *Troubling Freedom: Antigua and the Aftermath of British Emancipation* (Durham, NC: Duke University Press, 2015).

8. Anne Eller, "Skirts Rolled Up: The Gendered Terrain of Politics in Nineteenth-Century Port-au-Prince," *Small Axe* 25, no. 1 (March 2021): 61–83; Gad Heuman, *The Killing Time: The Morant Bay Rebellion in Jamaica* (Knoxville: University of Tennessee Press, 1995); Pamela Scully and Diana Paton, eds., *Gender and Slave Emancipation in the Atlantic World* (Durham, NC: Duke University Press, 2005); Matthew J. Smith, *Liberty, Fraternity, and Exile: Haiti and Jamaica After Emancipation* (Chapel Hill: University of North Carolina Press, 2014).

9. Patrick Bryan, *The Jamaican People, 1880–1902: Race, Class and Social Control*, rev. ed. (1991; Kingston: University of the West Indies Press, 2000), 2. For more on beet-sugar production, see Bernadette Jeanne Pérez, "Before the Sun Rises: Contesting Power and Cultivating Nations in the Colorado Beet Fields" (PhD diss., University of Minnesota, 2017).

10. Beckles, *Great House Rules*; Bolland, "Systems of Domination After Slavery"; Melanie Newton, *The Children of Africa in the Colonies: Free People of Color in Barbados in the Age of Emancipation* (Baton Rouge: Louisiana State University Press, 2008).

11. Brereton, "Family Strategies," 150.

12. Trevor O'Reggio. *Between Alienation and Citizenship: The Evolution of Black West Indian Society in Panama, 1914–1964* (Lanham, MD: University Press of America, 2006), 36.

13. V. Newton, *Silver Men*, 9.

14. Lara Putnam traces this changing imperial dynamic in "Borderlands and Border-Crossers: Migrants and Boundaries in the Greater Caribbean, 1840–1940," *Small Axe* 18, no. 1 (March 2014): 7–21.

15. Many scholars have pointed to a Caribbean "migratory culture" or "migratory tradition" in the nineteenth and twentieth centuries: see Mary Chamberlain, *Narratives of Exile and Return* (1997; repr., London: Routledge, 2017); Mary Chamberlain, ed., *Caribbean Migration: Globalised Identities* (London: Routledge, 1998); Bonham Richardson, *Caribbean Mi-*

grants: Environment and Human Survival on St. Kitts and Nevis (Knoxville: University of Tennessee Press, 1983); and Elizabeth Thomas-Hope, "The Establishment of a Migration Tradition: British West Indian Movements to the Hispanic Caribbean in the Century After Emancipation," in *Caribbean Social Relations*, ed. C. G. Clarke, 66–81 (Liverpool: Center for Latin American Studies, University of Liverpool, 1978).

16. Lorna Elaine Simmonds, "The Afro-Jamaican and the Internal Marketing System: Kingston, 1780–1834," in *Jamaica in Slavery and Freedom: History, Heritage, and Culture*, ed. Kathleen A. Monteith and Glen L. Richards, 274–290 (Kingston: University of the West Indies Press, 2001); Sheryllynne Haggerty, "'Miss Fan can tun her han!' Female Traders in Eighteenth-Century British-American Atlantic Port Cities," *Atlantic Studies* 6, no. 1 (2009): 29–42.

17. Bryan Edwards, *The History, Civil and Commercial, of the British West Indies*, vol. 2 (London: T. Miller, 1819), 162.

18. Lightfoot, *Troubling Freedom*.

19. Shauna Sweeney, "Market Marronage: Fugitive Women and the Internal Marketing System in Jamaica, 1781–1834," *William and Mary Quarterly* 76, no. 2 (April 2019): 197–222.

20. See Sweeney, "Market Marronage"; and Rashauna Johnson, *Slavery's Metropolis: Unfree Labor in New Orleans During the Age of Revolutions* (New York: Cambridge University Press, 2016).

21. Bryan, *Jamaican People*, 12.

22. Sidney W. Mintz, *Caribbean Transformations* (Chicago: Adline, 1974). Most historians of the period agree that women pioneered a withdrawal from plantation labor in the Caribbean, particularly on islands like Jamaica that had developed provision grounds/ marketing systems. However, as Brereton points out, in islands like Barbados and St. Kitts, women remained as the primary plantation labor force in the first few decades after emancipation.

23. Keith Hart, "The Sexual Division of Labor," in *Women and the Sexual Division of Labor in the Caribbean*, ed. Keith Hart, 9–28 (Kingston: Consortium Graduate School of Social Sciences, Canoe Press University of the West Indies, 1996); Winnifred R. Brown-Glaude, *Higglers in Kingston: Women's Informal Work in Jamaica* (Nashville, TN: Vanderbilt University Press, 2011).

24. Olive Senior, *Working Miracles: Women's Lives in the English-Speaking Caribbean* (London: James Currey, 1991), 107. See Rashauna Johnson, *Slavery's Metropolis*; and Shauna Sweeney, "Market Marronage."

25. Anyaa Anim-Addo, "Reading Postemancipation In/Security: Negotiations of Everyday Freedom," *Small Axe* 22, no. 3 (November 2018): 106.

26. Charles Kingsley, *At Last: A Christmas in the West Indies* (New York: Harper and Brothers, 1871), 46.

27. Mary Seacole, *Wonderful Adventures of Mrs. Seacole in Many Lands* (London: James Blackwood Paternoster Row, 1857), 9, https://www.gutenberg.org/cache/epub/23031/pg23031 -images.html.

28. Raphael Daello, *Caribbean Literature and the Public Sphere: From the Plantation to the Postcolonial* (Charlottesville: University of Virginia Press, 2011), 45.

29. Ibid., 59–65.

30. Woodville K. Marshall, "The Post-Slavery Labour Problem Revisited," in *Slavery, Freedom, and Gender: The Dynamics of Caribbean Society*, ed. Brian L. Moore, B. W. Higman, Carl Campbell, and Patrick Bryan, 115–132 (Kingston: University of the West Indies Press, 2001).

31. *Annual Report for 1894, Colonial Reports No. 140, Barbados*, C.7847-1 (London: HMSO, 1895), 11.

32. *Annual Report for 1898, Colonial Reports No. 262, Barbados*, C.9046-30 (London: HMSO, 1899), 29.

33. Chamberlain, *Narratives of Exile and Return*, 24; Putnam, "Borderlands and Border-Crossers."

34. Henry James Clarke, *Census of the Colony of Trinidad, 1891* (Port of Spain: Government Printing Office, 1892), iii.

35. G. W. Roberts, "Emigration from Barbados," *Social and Economic Studies* 4, no. 3 (September 1995): 245–288.

36. Putnam, "Borderlands and Border-Crossers."

37. Elizabeth Thomas-Hope, *Caribbean Migration*, rev. ed. (1992; Kingston: University of the West Indies Press, 2002), 5, though also covered by scholars such as Mary Chamberlain, Charles V. Carnegie, Sidney Mintz, and Bonham Richardson.

38. Putnam, "Borderlands and Border-Crossers," 11.

39. Thomas-Hope, *Caribbean Migration*, 4.

40. *Annual Report for 1901–02, Colonial Reports No. 368, Barbados*, Cd. 788-38 (London: HMSO, 1902), 56.

41. *Star and Herald* (Panama, Panama), 37, no. 7561, November 17, 1885, 1, World Newspaper Archive, https://infoweb-newsbank-com.libproxy1.usc.edu/apps/readex/doc?p=WHNPX &docref=image/v2%3A12B280DE2A6C9498%40WHNPX-12CC4CFE29490BC8%40240 9863-12CC4CFE3135B3B8%400.

42. Putnam, "Borderlands and Border-Crossers."

43. *Kingston Daily Gleaner*, December 24, 1902, quoted in Bryan, *Jamaican People*, 100.

44. Moore and Johnson, *Neither Led nor Driven*.

45. Nancie L. Solien, "Household and Family in the Caribbean: Some Definitions and Concepts," *Social and Economic Studies* 9, no. 1 (March 1960): 101–106.

46. Karen Fog Olwig, "The Struggle for Respectability: Methodism and Afro-Caribbean Culture on 19th Century Nevis," *Nieuwe West-Indische Gids / New West Indian Guide* 64, no. 3/4 (1990): 93–114; Cecilia Green, "'A Civil Inconvenience'? The Vexed Question of Slave Marriage in the British West Indies, *Law and History Review* 25, no. 1 (Spring 2007): 1–59; Lightfoot, *Troubling Freedom*; M. Newton, "'New Ideas of Correctness.'"

47. Norbert Ortmayr, "Church, Marriage, and Legitimacy in the British West Indies (Nineteenth and Twentieth Centuries)," *History of the Family* 2, no. 2 (1997): 141–170.

48. Moore and Johnson, *Neither Led nor Driven*, 104.

49. Ibid., 96.

50. Brereton, "Family Strategies"; Camillia Cowling, *Conceiving Freedom: Women of Color, Gender, and the Abolition of Slavery in Havana and Rio de Janeiro* (Chapel Hill: University of North Carolina Press, 2013); Thavolia Glymph, *Out of the House of Bondage: The Transformation of the Plantation Household* (New York: Cambridge University Press, 2008); Sandra Lauderdale Graham, *House and Street: The Domestic World of Servants and Masters in Nineteenth-Century Rio de Janeiro* (Austin: University of Texas Press, 1992); M. Newton, "'New Ideas of Correctness'"; Mimi Sheller, *Citizenship from Below: Erotic Agency and Caribbean Freedom* (Durham, NC: Duke University Press, 2012); Scully and Paton, *Gender and Slave Emancipation*.

51. Natasha Lightfoot, "Sinful Conexions: Christianity, Social Surveillance, and Black Women's Bodies in Distress," in *Troubling Freedom*, 142–166.

52. A. Caldecott, *The Church in the West Indies* (London: Society for Promoting Christian Knowledge, 1898), 108.

53. *Trinidad Royal Gazette*, no. 45, April 29, 1891, quoted in Bridget Brereton, *Race Relations in Colonial Trinidad, 1870–1900* (Cambridge: Cambridge University Press, 1980), 120.

54. Stephen Sutton to General Secretaries, July 8, 1868, MMS Box 200 (microfiche 2418), quoted in Moore and Johnson, *Neither Led nor Driven*, 98.

55. H. G. de Lisser, *Twentieth Century Jamaica* (Kingston: Jamaica Times, 1913), 96.

56. Bryan, *Jamaican People*, 107.

57. Moore and Johnson, *Neither Led nor Driven*, 113.

58. Ordinance 11 of 1863: "An Ordinance to Amend the Law with Regard to the Solemnization and Registration of Marriages," in G. L. Garcia, *Laws of Trinidad, Ordinances of the Council of Government from No. 5 of 1853 to No. 13 of 1866* (London: Waterlow and Sons, 1883).

59. Moore and Johnson, *Neither Led nor Driven*, 122; Persis Charles, "The Name of the Father: Women, Paternity, and British Rule in Nineteenth-Century Jamaica," *International Labor and Working-Class History* 41 (Spring 1992): 4–22.

60. Ortmayr, "Church, Marriage, and Legitimacy in the British West Indies."

61. Myriam Cottias, "Gender and Republican Citizenship in the French West Indies, 1848–1945," *Slavery and Abolition* 26, no. 2 (2005): 233–245.

62. Ortmayr, Table 6: Proportions of Persons Aged 15 Years and Over Who Had Ever Been Married, British West Indies, 1891–1943 (Women), in "Church, Marriage, and Legitimacy in the British West Indies," 155.

63. Moore and Johnson, *Neither Led nor Driven*, 98.

64. Christine Barrow, Table 2: Marriage Rates, Barbados 1891–1993, in "'Living in Sin': Church and Common-Law Union in Barbados," *Journal of Caribbean History* 29, no. 2 (December 1995): 58.

65. *Sixty-Eighth Annual Report of the Registrar General of Births, Deaths, and Marriages in England and Wales* (London: Darling and Sons, 1905), lv.

66. The marriage rates in 1860 were 3.3 in St. Lucia, and 4.1 for Grenada. Ortmayr, "Church, Marriage, and Legitimacy in the British West Indies." See also Juanita de Barros, *Reproducing the Caribbean: Sex, Gender, and Population Politics After Slavery* (Chapel Hill: University of North Carolina Press, 2014).

67. Moore and Johnson, *Neither Led nor Driven*, 98–99.

68. Ortmayr, "Church, Marriage, and Legitimacy in the British West Indies."

69. Moore and Johnson, *Neither Led nor Driven*, 99.

70. Moore and Johnson, *Neither Led nor Driven*, 113 and 372n33.

71. Bryan, *Jamaican People*, 102.

72. Federal Acts of the Leeward Islands, 1948. See an extended discussion of this in Mindie Lazarus-Black, "Bastardy, Gender Hierarchy, and the State: The Politics of Family Law Reform in Antigua and Barbuda," *Law and Society Review* 26, no. 4 (1992): 863–900.

73. Ibid. In nineteenth-century Puerto Rico, as in Jamaica, domestic violence (or cruelty) was a major cause cited in women's divorce petitions. Unlike the cases Findlay describes, however, the majority of divorces in Jamaica were brought and granted on the grounds of adultery. One of the key differences between these two cases is that, since 1879, divorces in Jamaica were granted by state courts, while in Puerto Rico they were overseen by ecclesiastical courts until after the arrival of the United States. See chapter 4 of Eileen Findlay, *Imposing Decency: The Politics of Sexuality and Race in Puerto Rico, 1870–1920* (Durham, NC: Duke University Press, 2000).

74. Moore and Johnson, *Neither Led nor Driven*, 99.

75. V. Newton, *Silver Men*, 7.

76. Six days a week, ten-hour workdays, ten cents an hour. Michael L. Conniff, Table 2: Sample Contracts for West Indian Laborers, 1904–1908, in *Black Labor on a White Canal: Panama, 1904–1981* (Pittsburgh, PA: University of Pittsburgh Press, 1985), 28.

77. *Weekly Illustrated Paper* (Bridgetown, Barbados), August 3, 1907, quoted in Bonham Richardson, *Panama Money in Barbados, 1900–1920* (Knoxville: University of Tennessee Press, 1985), 125.

78. Chamberlain, *Narratives of Exile and Return*, 27.

79. See Putnam, "Borderlands and Border-Crossers," for a discussion of this.

80. *Annual Report for 1904–05, Colonial Reports No. 466, Barbados*, Cd. 2684-12 (London: HMSO, 1905).

81. Ibid., 20.

82. U.S. Senate, Isthmian Canal, *Message from the President of the United States (Transmitting Certain Papers to Accompany His Message of January 8, 1906)*, 59th Congress, 1st Session, Doc. No. 127, Part 2 (Washington, DC: Government Printing Office, 1906), 965.

83. Louise Cramer, "Songs," *California Folklore Quarterly* 5, no. 3 (July 1946): 253.

84. Olive Senior, *Dying to Better Themselves: West Indians and the Building of the Panama Canal* (Kingston: University of the West Indies Press, 2014), 25.

85. Rhonda Frederick, *"Colón Man a Come": Mythographies of Panamá Canal Migration* (Lanham, MD: Lexington Books, 2005), xi.

86. De Lisser, *Susan Proudleigh*.

87. Leah Rosenberg, *Nationalism and the Formation of Caribbean Literature* (New York: Palgrave Macmillan, 2007); Leah Rosenberg, "Refashioning Caribbean Literary Pedagogy in the Digital Age," *Caribbean Quarterly* 62, nos. 3–4 (2016): 422–444.

88. "Emigration from Barbados," July 25, 1911, reference no. CO 28/276/59, folio 405, Records of the Colonial Office, Barbados, Despatches from Leslie Probyn, Governor of Barbados, National Archives, Kew, Richmond, UK (hereafter cited as CO: Barbados, Kew).

89. Letter from Leslie Probyn to Lewis Harcourt (Secretary of State for the Colonies), July 25, 1911, CO 28/276/59, folio 407, CO: Barbados, Kew.

90. Willis John Abbott, *Panama and the Canal: The Story of Its Achievement, Its Problems, and Its Prospects* (New York: Dodd, Mead, 1914), 22.

91. Conniff, *Black Labor on a White Canal*, 27.

92. Entry of Mrs. Mary Couloote, Isthmian Historical Society Competition for the Best True Stories of life and work on the Isthmus of Panama during the construction of the Panama Canal (Panama: Isthmian Historical Society, 1963), DLOC, accessed December 6, 2020, http://ufdc.ufl.edu/AA00016037/00001, all spelling in original.

93. V. Newton, *Silver Men*.

94. Isthmian Canal Commission, Quartermaster's Department, *Census of the Canal Zone, February 1, 1912* (Mount Hope, Canal Zone: I.C.C. Press, 1912), 16. The rest of the population is made up of smaller numbers of other immigrant groups.

95. Conniff, *Black Labor on a White Canal*, 29.

96. Thank you to Lara Putnam for this suggestion.

97. Dirección General del Censo, *Censo demográfico de la Provincia de Panama, 1920* (Panamá: Imprenta Nacional, 1922), 94.

98. U.S. Senate, Isthmian Canal, *Message from the President*, 958.

99. Ibid.

100. Ibid., 969.

101. Ibid., 980. Also, see the affidavit of Ida Raymond, 952.

102. Entry of Alfred Mitchell, Isthmian Historical Society Competition, DLOC, accessed December 6, 2020, https://dloc.com/AA00016037/00080.

103. Rose Van Hardeveld, *Make the Dirt Fly!* (Hollywood, CA: Pan Press, 1956).

104. Stephen Frenkel, "Geographical Representations of the "Other": The Landscape of the Panama Canal Zone," *Journal of Historical Geography* 28, no. 1 (January 2002): 85–99; Julie Greene, "The Women's Empire," chapter 6 in *The Canal Builders: Making America's Empire at the Panama Canal* (New York: Penguin Press, 2010).

105. Address of President Roosevelt to the employees of the Isthmian Canal Commission at Colón, Panama, November 17, 1906, in *Special Message of the President of the United States Concerning the Panama Canal, Communicated to the Two Houses of Congress on Dec. 17, 1906* (Washington, DC: Government Printing Office, 1906).

106. Greene, *Canal Builders*, 230–232.

107. Miss J. Macklin Beattie, "The Woman's Movement," *Canal Record* 1, no. 6, October 9, 1907, 6; "Women's Clubs in Canal Zone; Miss Boswell Returns from a Tour of Observa-

tion and Organization. Started a Federation. Four Departments in Operation Cover the Home, Education, Philanthropy, and Literature and Music," *New York Times*, October 24, 1907, 11.

108. Abbott, *Panama and the Canal*, 323.

109. Senior, *Dying to Better Themselves*, 232.

110. Ibid.

111. V. Newton, *Silver Men*, 149.

112. "A Canal Zone Family," *Canal Record* 2, no. 22, January 27, 1909 (Ancon, Canal Zone), 170.

113. "Cristobal—Folks Rivers Silver Quarters," Folder 11-E-6/A-I: Silver Quarters; Rental Rates and Regulations—Ancón-Balboa District, Record Group 185: Records of the Panama Canal, 1848–1999, Entry 30: General Correspondence Files, 1904–1914 (NARA ID: 7866849), National Archives and Records Administration, College Park, MD (NARA).

114. Letter from Silver employees to Captain R. M. Wood, Chief Quartermaster, Culebra, December 2, 1913, Folder 11-E-5A: Rented Silver Quarters—Applications, Assignments, Complaints, RG 185, Entry 30, NARA.

115. Lancelot Lewis, *The West Indian in Panama: Black Labor in Panama, 1850–1914* (Washington, DC: University Press of America, 1980), 50.

116. Clipping from *Canal Record* of February 4, 1914, "Rent of Silver Married Quarters," Folder 11-E-6 (I): Silver Quarters; Rental Rates and Regulations—General, RG 185, Entry 30, NARA.

117. Letter from Herman Caulfield, District Physician, to Director of Hospitals, June 2, 1906, Folder 2-E-6 (I): Miscellaneous information re laborers and labor situation; efficiency; health and living conditions; probably reductions in force, etc.—General, RG 185, Entry 30, NARA.

118. Marixa Lasso, *Erased: The Untold Story of the Panama Canal* (Cambridge, MA: Harvard University Press, 2019), 131.

119. V. Newton, *Silver Men*, 151.

120. Harry A. Franck, *Zone Policeman 88: A Close Range Study of the Panama Canal and Its Workers* (New York: Century, 1913), 40.

121. M. Lasso, *Erased*, 74.

122. Letter from Augusta Dunlop to Joseph Le Prince, July 9, 1908, Docket 7: In re: claim of Dunlop, Augusta, Records of the Joint Land Commission, Box 2, RG 185, NARA.

123. Letter from Herbert Canfield to Joseph Le Prince, July 9, 1908, Docket 7, NARA.

124. See, for example, letter from Augusta Dunlop to Joseph Le Prince, July 14, 1908, Docket 7, NARA.

125. Statement of Espey, Statement of George Walcott and David Harris, July 16, 1908, Docket 7, NARA.

126. Letter from T. B. Miskimon to George Goethals, July 18, 1908, Docket 7, NARA.

127. Letter from George Goethals to Augusta Dunlop, July 20, 1908, Docket 7, NARA.

128. Entry of Alfred E. Dottin, Isthmian Historical Society Competition, DLOC, accessed December 6, 2020, https://dloc.com/AA00016037/00080.

Chapter 2

1. Christine Chivallon and David Howard, "Colonial Violence and Civilizing Utopias in the French and British Empires: The Morant Bay Rebellion (1865) and the Insurrection of the South (1870)," *Slavery and Abolition* 38 (2017): 534–558; Christopher M. Church, *Paradise Destroyed: Catastrophe and Citizenship in the French Caribbean* (Lincoln: University of Nebraska Press, 2017); Jacqueline Couti, "Lumina Sophie, Nineteenth Century Martinique," in *As If She Were Free: A Collective Biography of Women and Emancipation in the Americas*, ed. Erica Ball, Tatiana Seijas, and Terri L. Snyder, 373–392 (New York: Cambridge University Press, 2020); Jill Richards, *The Fury Archives: Female Citizenship, Human Rights, and the International Avant-Gardes* (New York: Columbia University Press, 2020).

2. Tyler Stovall, *Transnational France: The Modern History of a Universal Nation* (Boulder, CO: Westview Press, 2015).

3. U.S. Senate, "Papers concerning women from Martinique," in *Investigation of Panama Canal Matters: Hearings Before the United States Senate on Interoceanic Canals*, vol. 1-4, 931–981, 59th Congress, 2nd Session (Washington, DC: Government Printing Office, 1907), 932.

4. Record of Gerald, Clemence, Department of Defense, U.S. Army Garrison Panama, Directorate of Logistics, Transportation Division, Mortuary Affairs Section, "Index to the Gorgas Hospital Mortuary Death Records, 1906–1991," Record Group 185, National Archives and Records Administration, College Park, MD, https://aad.archives.gov/aad/series-description.jsp?s=1134&cat=all&bc=sd.

5. Ann Laura Stoler, *Along the Archival Grain: Epistemic Anxieties and Colonial Common Sense* (Princeton, NJ: Princeton University Press, 2010).

6. Marisa Fuentes's methodology was deeply influential to this reading; *Dispossessed Lives: Enslaved Women, Violence, and the Archive* (Philadelphia: University of Pennsylvania Press, 2016), 52.

7. Stoler, *Along the Archival Grain.*

8. James Lull and Stephen Hinerman, *Media Scandals: Morality and Desire in the Popular Culture Marketplace* (New York: Columbia University Press, 1997), 3. They defined a media scandal as that which "occurs when private acts that disgrace or offend the idealized, dominant morality of a social community are made public and narrativized by the media."

9. Examination of Mr. J. W. Settoon, "Addendum to Exhibit D, Being Evidence Coming to Hand January 10, 1906," *Annual Report of the Isthmian Canal Commission for the Year Ending December 1, 1905*, Senate, 59th Congress, 1st Session, Document No. 127 (Washington, DC: Government Printing Office, 1906), 57.

10. Statement of John F. Stevens, Chief Engineer of the Isthmian Canal Commission, January 16, 1906, *Investigation of Panama Canal Matters*, 57.

11. The sources display some discrepancies on the number of women who arrived. In his article, Bigelow cites "several hundreds," while William Howard Taft refers to them as "a boat load" in a January 8, 1906, letter to President Roosevelt. In early correspondence, Governor Charles Magoon and Commission Chairman Theodore Shonts repeatedly use the number "150," but I ultimately follow an "official" count made after the investigation that listed 295 women (Letter of George R. Shanton to Charles Magoon, November 21, 1905); all the above

are included in U.S. Senate, *Message from the President of the United States (Transmitting Certain Papers to Accompany His Message of January 8, 1906)*, 59th Congress, 1st Session, Document No. 127, Part 2 (Washington, DC: Government Printing Office, 1906).

12. Julie Greene, *The Canal Builders: Making America's Empire at the Panama Canal* (New York: Penguin Press, 2009, 7.

13. Letter from Governor Charles Magoon to Chief Engineer John Stevens, November 14, 1905, "Exhibit D: Translation of Cablegram Received from Panama," in *Message from the President*, 42.

14. Ibid.

15. Letter from Governor Charles Magoon to Secretary of War, November 16, 1905, in *Message from the President*, 41.

16. Letter from Governor Charles Magoon to Chief Engineer John Stevens, November 14, 1905, in *Message from the President*, 42.

17. Special Correspondent of the *Herald*, "A Scandal on the Isthmus of Panama," *New York Herald*, November 25, 1905, Folder: Press clippings on Panama, Box 39, Poultney Bigelow Papers, 1855–1954, Manuscript and Archives Division, New York Public Library (hereafter cited as PB Papers, NYPL).

18. Ibid.

19. Poultney Bigelow, "Untitled" (Notes from 1906 trip to Panama), Folder: PB's Miscellaneous notes on Panama and Documents on Panama, Box 39, PB Papers, NYPL.

20. "Club Canal Workmen to Force Them to Land, Shipload from Martinique Prefer Death to Panama's terrors," *New York Times*, October 2, 1905. For more on this event, see Marianne Quijano, "'The Virus of Irreligion': Afro-Caribbean Religions, U.S. Medicine, and Imperial Anxieties in Panama's Canal Zone, 1904–1914" (Master's thesis, University of Florida, 2021).

21. Among others: "Club Canal Workmen to Force Them to Land; Shipload from Martinique Prefer Death to Panama's Terrors," *New York Times*, October 2, 1905; "Workmen Refuse to Leave Ship," *San Francisco Call* 98, no. 124, October 2, 1905.

22. Special Correspondent of the *Herald*, "A Scandal on the Isthmus of Panama."

23. Ibid.

24. "The Race Problem: Speech of Hon. Benjamin R. Tillman of South Carolina in the Senate of the United States," February 23–24, 1903, Library of Congress, accessed December 7, 2021, https://lccn.loc.gov/91898597.

25. Report from Chief of Police George Shanton to Governor Magoon, November 21, 1905, in *Message from the President*, 45.

26. Poultney Bigelow, "Our Mismanagement at Panama," *Independent*, January 4, 1906, PB Papers, NYPL. Also available in U.S. Senate, *Message from the President*, 79–91.

27. "Exhibit A: Memorandum of comments of the chief engineer of the Isthmian Canal Commission, on article written by Poultney Bigelow, M.A., as published in *The Independent* of January 4, 1906, entitled 'Our Mismanagement at Panama,'" in *Message from the President*, 22.

28. Ibid., 23.

29. John Bigelow, *The Panama Canal Report of the Hon. John Bigelow Delegated by the Chamber of Commerce of New York to Assist at the Inspection of the Panama Canal in Febru-*

ary, 1886 (New York: Press of the Chamber of Commerce, 1886), accessed December 7, 2020, http://www.archive.org/details/panamacanalrepo00bigegoog.

30. "Taft Scorns Bigelow and Panama Charges; Says Writer Investigated the Canal Less Than 28 Hours. Stevens Gives Lie Direct; Men Mentioned as Authorities for Charges Said to Be Grieved Because Disappointed," *New York Times*, January 11, 1906; "Panama; Poultney Bigelow Reaffirms His Criticisms of the Canal Work," *New York Times*, January 12, 1906.

31. "Conditions on the Isthmus: Magoon Says They Are Good, Physically and Morally," *Ocala (FL) Evening Star* 11, no. 200, January 30, 1906; "Taft 'Roasts' Bigelow," *Barre (VT) Daily Times*, January 12, 1906; "Condition a Shame," *Roswell (NM) Daily Record* 3, no. 268, January 12, 1906.

32. "Taft 'Roasts' Bigelow," *Barre (VT) Daily Times*, January 12, 1906; "Poultney Bigelow Writes from Panama: Says Conditions Are Disgraceful, Author Tells Revolting Story of Saturnalia of Graft and Crime on Isthmus—Taft and Shonts are Flayed," *Los Angeles Herald* 33, no. 95, January 4, 1906.

33. "Poultney Bigelow Reaffirms His Criticism of the Canal Work," *New York Times*, January 12, 1906.

34. "Bigelow a Panama Victim," *The Sun* (New York, NY), February 22, 1906.

35. "Poultney Bigelow Writes from Panama: Says Conditions Are Disgraceful, Author Tells Revolting Story of Saturnalia of Graft and Crime on Isthmus—Taft and Shonts are Flayed," *Los Angeles Herald* 33, no. 95, January 4, 1906.

36. "Magoon Here, Replies to Poultney Bigelow," *New York Times*, January 29, 1906.

37. Postscript in letter from Secretary of War to the President, January 10, 1906, "Addendum to Exhibit D," in *Message from the President*, 53.

38. Ibid.

39. Joan Wallach Scott, "L'ouvrière! Mot impie, sordide . . .": Women Workers in the Discourse of French Political Economy, 1840–1860," in *Gender and the Politics of History*, ed. Joan Wallach Scott, 139–164 (New York: Columbia University Press, 1999), 143.

40. "Memorandum of Inquiry made by Chairman Shonts and Chief Engineer Stevens into the Alleged Importation of Martinique Women into the Canal Zone for Immoral Purposes, the Same Being the Statement of Mr. S. W. Settoon, Recruiting Agent of the Commission, who was in direct charge of labor recruiting from Martinique, and such Memorandum being based on the stenographic notes made at the time of the Inquiry," January 9, 1906, in *Message from the President*, 58.

41. "Examination of Mr. J. W. Settoon," in *Message from the President*, 56.

42. Ibid.

43. Letter from George R. Shanton to Charles Magoon, November 21, 1905, in *Message from the President*, 45.

44. Stoler, *Along the Archival Grain*.

45. Ibid., 1.

46. U.S. Senate, "Papers concerning women from Martinique," in *Investigation of Panama Canal Matters*, 932.

47. Ibid., 932.

48. Letter from Governor Magoon to Chief of Police George Shanton, November 16, 1905, "Exhibit D," in *Message from the President*, 43.

49. U.S. Senate, "Papers concerning women from Martinique," 944.

50. Ibid., 960–961. Emphasis mine.

51. Ibid., 951.

52. Ibid., 945.

53. Ibid., 932.

54. Ibid., 975.

55. Ibid., 979.

56. Feroline on 943 and Sovos on 941, U.S. Senate, "Papers concerning women from Martinique."

57. Ibid., 951.

58. Ibid., 949.

59. Ibid., 941.

60. Ibid., 959.

61. Letter from George R. Shanton to Charles Magoon, November 21, 1905, in *Message from the President*, 45; emphasis mine.

62. This shows up in several cases involving "injuria" or "provocación" in various neighborhoods throughout Panama City among the Alcaldías y Corregidurías Files in the Panamanian National Archives. See more on this in Chapter 6.

63. U.S. Senate, "Papers concerning women from Martinique," 941.

64. Ibid., 932.

65. Matthew Parker, *Panama Fever: The Epic Story of the Building of the Panama Canal* (New York: Anchor Books, 2009), 379.

66. Harry A. Franck, *Zone Policeman 88: A Close-Range Study of the Panama Canal and Its Workers* (New York: Century, 1913), 205.

67. George Washington Goethals, *Government of the Canal Zone* (Princeton, NJ: Princeton University Press, 1915), 8.

68. Letter from Governor Magoon to Chairman Shonts, November 16, 1906, in *Message from the President*, 41.

69. Greene, *Canal Builders*, 288.

70. On enclaves, see Catherine LeGrand, "Living in Macondo: Economy and Culture in a United Fruit Company Banana Enclave in Colombia," in *Close Encounters of Empire: Writing the Cultural History of U.S.–Latin America Relations*, ed. Gilbert Joseph, Catherine LeGrand, and Ricardo Salvatore, 333–368 (Durham, NC: Duke University Press, 1998); and Lara Putnam, *The Company They Kept: Migrants and the Politics of Gender in Caribbean Costa Rica, 1870–1960* (Chapel Hill: University of North Carolina Press, 2002), 12.

71. Putnam, *Company They Kept*, 87, where she says the system in Limón was "never effectively repressive and was often entirely unworkable."

72. See, as one example, the *Annual Report of the Governor of the Panama Canal, 1918* (Washington, DC: Government Printing Office, 1918), 309–311, for a later attempt to control prostitution in the terminal cities. Other reports from the era supply similar examples.

73. For more on this subject, see Jeffrey W. Parker's excellent dissertation, "Empire's Angst: The Politics of Race, Migration, and Sex Work in Panama, 1903–1945" (PhD diss., University of Texas at Austin, 2013), particularly chapter 2.

74. Parker, "Empire's Angst," 81.

75. Joan Flores-Villalobos, "Freak Letters: Tracing Gender, Race, and Diaspora in the Panama Canal Archive," *Small Axe* 23, no. 2 (July 2019): 34–56.

Chapter 3

1. The ordinance is printed in Folder 62-B-248, Part 1: Cohabitation and immoral conduct of white employees with native and colored women, RG 185, Entry 30, National Archives and Records Administration, College Park, MD (NARA).

2. For more on this vision, see Alexander Missal, *Seaway to the Future: American Social Visions and the Construction of the Panama Canal* (Madison: University of Wisconsin Press, 2008); and Ricardo Salvatore, "Imperial Mechanics: South America's Hemispheric Integration in the Machine Age," *American Quarterly* 58, no. 3 (2006): 662–691. For a broader view, see Emily Rosenberg, *Spreading the American Dream: American Economic and Cultural Expansion, 1890–1945* (New York: Hill and Wang, 2011).

3. Letter from Judge Thomas E. Brown Jr. to M. H. Thatcher, September 18, 1912, Folder 62-B-8: Misc. Police Investigation and reports for which there is no subject file or classification under Arrest or Crimes, RG 185, Entry 30, NARA.

4. On the suburbanization of the Zone, see Stephen Frenkel, "Geographical Representations of the 'Other': The Landscape of the Panama Canal Zone," *Journal of Historical Geography* 28, no. 3 (2002): 85–99.

5. For more on anti-Black racism and the penal system of the Canal Zone (though not in relation to women), see Benjamin D. Weber, "The Strange Career of the Convict Clause: US Prison Imperialism in the Panamá Canal Zone," *International Labor and Working-Class History* 96 (Fall 2019): 79–102.

6. Lara Putnam, *The Company They Kept: Migrants and the Politics of Gender in Caribbean Costa Rica, 1870–1960* (Chapel Hill: University of North Carolina Press, 2002), 78.

7. Thomas Miller Klubock, *Contested Communities: Class, Gender, and Politics in Chile's El Teniente Copper Mine, 1904–1951* (Durham, NC: Duke University Press, 1998).

8. Eileen Findlay, *Imposing Decency: The Politics of Sexuality and Race in Puerto Rico, 1870–1920* (Durham, NC: Duke University Press, 2000).

9. Willis John Abbott, *Panama and the Canal in Picture and Prose* (New York: Syndicate, 1913), 335.

10. Letter from "A Wife" to Governor Goethals, November 30, 1915, Folder 28-B-3 (II): Anonymous letters for which there is no subject file, RG 185, Entry 30, NARA.

11. Rose Van Hardeveld, *Make the Dirt Fly!* (Hollywood, CA: Pan Press, 1956), 120.

12. U.S. Senate, "Papers concerning women from Martinique," in *Investigation of Panama Canal Matters: Hearings Before the United States Senate on Interoceanic Canals*, vol. 1-4, 931–981, 59th Congress, 2nd Session (Washington, DC: Government Printing Office, 1907), 941.

13. Julie Greene, *The Canal Builders: Making America's Empire at the Panama Canal* (New York: Penguin Press, 2010), 291.

14. Mattie Udora Richardson, "No More Secrets, No More Lies: African American History and Compulsory Heterosexuality," *Journal of Women's History* 15, no. 3 (Autumn 2003): 63–76.

15. Isthmian Canal Commission, *Annual Report of the Isthmian Canal Commission for the Fiscal Year Ending June 30, 1909* (Washington, DC: Government Printing Office, 1909).

16. Letter from John O'Collins (Assistant to the ICC Secretary) to W. H. May (Secretary to the ICC Chairman), October 22, 1908, Folder 28-A-31 (I): Religious Organizations, Policy Towards, Privileges Allowed, Etc., RG 185, Entry 30, NARA.

17. *Colón Starlet*, April 30, 1908, in Olive Senior, *Dying to Better Themselves: West Indians and the Building of the Panama Canal* (Kingston: University of the West Indies Press, 2014), 250.

18. Isthmian Canal Commission, *Annual Report of the Isthmian Canal Commission for the Fiscal Year Ended June 30, 1908* (Washington, DC: Government Printing Office, 1908), 270.

19. Isthmian Canal Commission, *Annual Report of the Isthmian Canal Commission for the Fiscal Year Ended June 30, 1911* (Washington, DC: Government Printing Office, 1911), 499.

20. With a much smaller smattering of arrests of women for other crimes such as "Fighting" and "Petit Larceny."

21. See n. 1 for the title of Folder 62-B-248, RG 185, Entry 30, NARA.

22. Letter from Anita Seaman to Col. George Goethals, May 2, 1913, Folder 62-B-248: Cohabitation, RG 185, Entry 30, NARA.

23. H. G. Belknap, Memorandum to Division of Police and Prisons, June 10, 1913, Folder 62-B-248: Cohabitation, RG 185, Entry 30, NARA.

24. Belknap, Memo to Division of Police, June 10, 1913.

25. Ibid.

26. Letter from Assistant Chief of Division Belknap to Captain Barber, June 23, 1913, Folder 62-B-248: Cohabitation, RG 185, Entry 30, NARA.

27. Series of correspondence from Folder 46-D-1, Part 1, RG 185, NARA, in Matthew Scalena, "Illicit Nation: State, Empire, and Illegality on the Isthmus of Panama" (PhD diss., Stony Brook University, 2013), 80n55.

28. Letter from Sergeant William Rutherford to Chief of Division, August 10, 1913, Folder PCC-81-Z-1/0: Freak Letters (Obscene), RG 185, Entry 30, NARA.

29. Martha Hodes, *White Women, Black Men: Illicit Sex in the Nineteenth-Century South* (New Haven, CT: Yale University Press, 1997).

30. Letter from B. W. Caldwell to Governor of the Canal Zone, June 22, 1906, Folder 62-B-248: Cohabitation, RG 185, Entry 30, NARA. All spelling in original.

31. There were rape cases in other Judicial Circuits where similar patterns stood—the prevalence of West Indian men and a low level of convictions.

32. Letter from Judge Thomas E. Brown Jr. to M. H. Thatcher, September 18, 1912, Folder 62-B-8, RG 185, Entry 30, NARA.

33. Saidiya Hartman, *Scenes of Subjection: Terror, Slavery, and Self-Making in Nineteenth-Century America* (Oxford: Oxford University Press, 1997), particularly chapter 3, "Seduction and the Ruses of Power."

34. Isthmian Canal Commission, "Title XII, Chapter 1: Rape, Abduction, Carnal Abuse of Children, and Seduction," in *Laws of the Canal Zone, Isthmus of Panama* (Washington, DC: Government Printing Office, 1906), 112.

35. Canal Zone v. William Wait (CZ 2nd Cir., 1905), Case 27, Record Group 21: Records of District Courts of the United States, Canal Zone Second Judicial Circuit Criminal Court, Criminal Case Files, 1904–1914, National Archives and Records Administration, Washington, DC (NARA).

36. Statement of Keturah Lewis, October 21, 1905, Canal Zone v. William Wait (CZ 2nd Cir., 1905), RG 21, NARA.

37. Statement of William Wait, October 23, 1905, Canal Zone v. William Wait (CZ 2nd Cir., 1905), RG 21, NARA.

38. George Goethals, Memo from Executive Office, Canal Zone v. William Wait (CZ 2nd Cir., 1905), RG 21, NARA.

39. Putnam, *Company They Kept*, 86.

40. Albert Edwards, *Panama: The Canal, the Country, the People* (New York: Macmillan, 1913), 503.

41. Sue Pearl Core, *Maid in Panama* (Dobbs Ferry, NY: Clermont Press, 1938), 72.

42. Core, *Maid in Panama*, 73.

43. Ibid., 43.

44. Elizabeth Kittredge Parker, *Panama Canal Bride: A Story of Construction Days* (New York: Exposition Press, 1955), 27.

45. Tracy Robinson, *Fifty Years at Panama, 1861–1911*, 2nd ed. (New York: Trow Press, 1907), 242.

46. Karen Fog Olwig, "Cultural Complexity After Freedom: Nevis and Beyond," in *Small Islands, Large Questions: Society, Culture, and Resistance in the Post-Emancipation Caribbean*, ed. Karen Fog Olwig, 100–120 (London: Frank Cass, 1995).

47. Julie Greene used these same divorce cases to briefly discuss West Indian women's experiences in *The Canal Builders*. My work here is also influenced by a larger trend in Latin American historiography that uses legal records to reconsider women's agency: Sueann Caulfield, Sarah Chambers, and Lara Putnam, eds., *Honor, Status, and Law in Modern Latin America* (Durham, NC: Duke University Press, 2005); Sueann Caulfield, *In Defense of Honor: Sexual Morality, Modernity, and Nation and Early Twentieth-Century Brazil* (Durham, NC: Duke University Press, 2000); Sarah Chambers, *From Subjects to Citizens: Honor, Gender, and Politics in Arequipa, Peru, 1780–1854* (University Park: Penn State University Press, 1999); Putnam, *Company They Kept*; and Stephanie Smith, *Gender and the Mexican Revolution: Yucatán Women and the Realities of Patriarchy* (Chapel Hill: University of North Carolina Press, 2009).

48. Core, "The Tie That Binds," in *Maid in Panama*, 18.

49. Letter from John O'Collins (Assistant to the ICC Secretary) to W. H. May (Secretary to the ICC Chairman), October 22, 1908, Folder 28-A-31 (I): Religious Organizations, Policy Towards, Privileges Allowed, Etc., RG 185, Entry 30, NARA.

50. Letter from O'Collins to May, October 22, 1908, RG 185.

51. Ibid.

52. Senior, *Dying to Better Themselves*, 244.

53. *Who's Who in Jamaica: A Biennial Biographical Record Containing Careers of Principal Public Men and Women of Jamaica* (Kingston: S. A. Hill, 1969), 193. Senior discusses the Harry family in *Dying to Better Themselves*, 242, 325.

54. Michael Donoghue, *Borderland on the Isthmus: Race, Culture, and the Struggle for the Canal Zone* (Durham, NC: Duke University Press, 2014), 115–116.

55. Ibid., 268.

56. Eric Walrond, *Tropic Death* (1926; New York: W. W. Norton, 2013).

57. George Westerman, "Historical Notes on West Indians on the Isthmus of Panama," *Phylon* 22, no. 4 (1961): 343.

58. See Ley 17 in *Gaceta Oficial de la República de Panamá*, no. 1332, January 23, 1911.

59. Letter from Theodore Roosevelt to Secretary of War, May 9, 1904, General Orders, no. 97, War Department.

60. *The Code of Civil Procedure of the Canal Zone* (Washington, DC: Government Printing Office, 1907), 274.

61. Wayne D. Bray, *The Common Law Zone in Panama: A Case Study in Reception* (San Juan, Puerto Rico: Inter-American University Press, 1977).

62. Greene, *Canal Builders*, 254.

63. Ibid., 263.

64. Ibid.

65. Annie Sparks v. Helon Sparks (CZ 1st Cir., 1912), Case 133, Record Group 21: Records of District Courts of the United States, Canal Zone First Judicial Circuit Court (1912), Civil Case Files, 1905–1914, National Archives and Records Administration, Washington, DC.

66. Eugenia Peters v. Arthur Peters (CZ 1st Cir., 1913), Case 163, RG 21, NARA.

67. For a short biographical sketch of Bruno, see Edward L. Cox, "Panama Migration and Change in Grenada and St. Vincent" (paper presented at the Annual Conference of the Caribbean Studies Association, Panama City, Panama, May 24–29, 1999), Digital Library of the Caribbean, accessed September 10, 2019, https://ufdc.ufl.edu/CA00400201/00001.

68. U.S. House of Representatives, *The Panama Canal: Hearings Before the Committee on Interstate and Foreign Commerce*, 62nd Congress, 2nd Session, April 4, 1912 (Washington, DC: Government Printing Office, 1912), 20.

69. Fog Olwig, "Cultural Complexity After Freedom."

70. Michael L. Conniff, *Black Labor on a White Canal: Panama, 1904–1981* (Pittsburgh, PA: University of Pittsburgh Press, 1985), 31–32.

71. U.S. House of Representatives, *The Panama Canal: Hearings Before the Committee on Interstate and Foreign Commerce*, 62nd Congress, 2nd Session, 20.

72. Richard Lewis v. Felicia Lewis (CZ 3rd Cir., 1905), Case 15, Record Group 21: Records of District Courts of the United States, Canal Zone Third Judicial Circuit Criminal Court, Criminal Case Files, 1904–1914, NARA.

73. Courtney Black v. Mary Black (CZ 1st Cir., 1912), Case 124, RG 21, NARA.

74. Affidavit of Courtney Black, Courtney Black v. Mary Black (CZ 1st Cir., 1912), Case 124, RG 21, NARA.

75. Ibid.

76. Decree—A mensa et Thoro, January 6, 1913, Courtney Black v. Mary Black (CZ 1st Cir., 1912), Case 124, RG 21, NARA.

77. Certainly, the situations are not equivalent when talking about slaves who were legally caught between personhood and property, with the utmost goal of erasing white culpability and violence. Yet Hartman's work helps us see Black femininity as a locus where encroachments of power have historically been formed and enacted. Saidiya Hartman, *Scenes of Subjection*.

78. Frederick Cooper, "Conflict and Connection: Rethinking Colonial African History," *American Historical Review* 99, no. 5 (December 1994), 1516–1545.

Chapter 4

1. For a discussion of this dynamic in the British imperial context, see Anne McClintock, *Imperial Leather: Race, Gender, and Sexuality in the Colonial Contest* (New York: Routledge, 1995) and Lucy Delap, *Knowing Their Place: Domestic Service in Twentieth-Century Britain* (Oxford: Oxford University Press, 2011).

2. Micki McElya, *Clinging to Mammy: The Faithful Slave in Twentieth-Century America* (Cambridge, MA: Harvard University Press, 2007); Deborah Gray White, *Ar'n't I a Woman? Female Slaves in the Plantation South* (New York: W. W. Norton, 1985); Grace Elizabeth Hale, *Making Whiteness: The Culture of Segregation in the South, 1890–1940* (New York: Vintage Books, 1999); Kimberly Wallace-Sanders, *Mammy: A Century of Race, Gender, and Southern Memory* (Ann Arbor: University of Michigan Press, 2008).

3. Vincente L. Rafael, *White Love and Other Events in Filipino History* (Durham, NC: Duke University Press, 2014); Renato Rosaldo, "Imperialist Nostalgia," in "Memory and Counter-Memory," special issue, *Representations* 26 (Spring 1989): 107–122.

4. Tara McPherson, *Reconstructing Dixie: Race, Gender, and Nostalgia in the Imagined South* (Durham, NC: Duke University Press, 2003), 52.

5. For more on working women and their labor struggles throughout Latin America, see Ann Farnsworth-Alvear, *Dulcinea in the Factory: Myths, Morals, Men, and Women in Colombia's Industrial Experiment* (Durham, NC: Duke University Press, 2000); John D. French and Daniel James, eds., *The Gendered Worlds of Latin American Women Workers: From Household and Factory to the Union Hall and Ballot Box* (Durham, NC: Duke University Press, 1997); Susie S. Porter, *Working Women in Mexico City: Public Discourses and Material Conditions, 1879–1931* (Tucson: University of Arizona Press, 2003); Heidi Tinsman, *Partners in Conflict: The Politics of Gender, Sexuality, and Labor in the Chilean Agrarian Reform, 1950–1973* (Durham, NC: Duke University Press, 2002); Elizabeth Quay Hutchison, *Labors Appropriate to Their Sex: Gender, Labor, and Politics in Urban Chile, 1900–1930* (Durham, NC: Duke University Press, 2001); and Barbara Weinstein, "They Don't Even Look Like Women Workers": Femininity and Class in Twentieth-Century Latin America," *International Labor and Working-Class History* 69 (Spring 2006): 161–176. On the inattention to women's domestic labor in the region, see Marie Eileen Francois, "The Products of Consumption: Housework in Latin American Political Economies and Cultures," *History Compass* 6, no. 1 (2008):

207–242; and Jocelyn Olcott, "Introduction: Researching and Rethinking the Labors of Love," *Hispanic American Historical Review* 91, no. 1 (2011): 1–27.

6. Stephanie Camp, *Closer to Freedom: Enslaved Women and Everyday Resistance in the Plantation South* (Chapel Hill: University of North Carolina Press, 2004).

7. Ronald Harpelle has written about this specific topic in the context of the white company enclaves of the United Fruit Company in Central America, which shared many characteristics with the Canal Zone. White residents of these enclaves traveled back and forth to the Zone, which served as a regional hub. Ronald Harpelle, "White Zones: American Enclave Communities of Central America," in *Black and Blackness in Central America: Between Race and Place*, ed. Lowell Gudmundson and Justin Wolfe, 307–333 (Durham, NC: Duke University Press, 2010). For similar dynamics in other contexts, see also Thavolia Glymph, *Out of the House of Bondage: The Transformation of the Plantation Household* (Cambridge: Cambridge University Press, 2008); Amy Kaplan, "Manifest Domesticity," *American Literature* 70, no. 3 (September 1998): 581–606; Rosemary Marangoly George, "Homes in the Empire, Empire in the Home," *Cultural Critique*, no. 26 (Winter 1993–94): 95–127; Vicente Rafael, "Colonial Domesticity: White Women and United States Rule in the Philippines," *American Literature* 67, no. 4 (December 1995): 639–666; Ann Laura Stoler, *Carnal Knowledge and Imperial Power: Race and the Intimate in Colonial Rule* (Berkeley: University of California Press, 2002); Laura Wexler, *Tender Violence: Domestic Visions in an Age of U.S. Imperialism* (Chapel Hill: University of North Carolina Press, 2011); and Nupur Chaudhuri and Margaret Strobel, eds., *Western Women and Imperialism: Complicity and Resistance* (Bloomington: Indiana University Press, 1992).

8. Julie Greene, *The Canal Builders: Making America's Empire at the Panama Canal* (New York: Penguin Press, 2009), 228. See also Harpelle, "White Zones."

9. See the work of Glymph, *Out of the House of Bondage*, for more on Black women's "hidden transcripts."

10. Isthmian Canal Commission, Quartermaster's Department, *Census of the Canal Zone, February 1, 1912* (Mount Hope, Canal Zone: I.C.C. Press, 1912), 52.

11. *Census of the Canal Zone*, 1912, 54.

12. Ibid., 55.

13. Ibid., 55.

14. For more information on West Indian teachers and ICC employees, see Eyra Marcela Reyes Rivas, *El trabajo de las mujeres en la historia de la construcción del canal de Panamá, 1881–1914* (Panama: Universidad de Panamá, Instituto de la Mujer, 2000).

15. U.S. Senate, "Papers concerning women from Martinique," in *Investigation of Panama Canal Matters: Hearings Before the United States Senate on Interoceanic Canals*, vol. 1-4, 59th Congress, 2nd Session (Washington, DC: Government Printing Office, 1907), 951.

16. Hilary Beckles, *Natural Rebels: A Social History of Enslaved Black Women in Barbados* (New Brunswick, NJ: Rutgers University Press, 1989), 72; Rashauna Johnson, *Slavery's Metropolis: Unfree Labor in New Orleans During the Age of Revolutions* (New York: Cambridge University Press, 2016); Natasha Lightfoot, *Troubling Freedom: Antigua and the Aftermath of*

British Emancipation (Durham, NC: Duke University Press, 2015); Shauna Sweeney, "Market Marronage: Fugitive Women and the Internal Marketing System in Jamaica, 1781–1834," *William and Mary Quarterly* 76, no. 2 (April 2019): 197–222.

17. Beckles, *Natural Rebels*, 75–76.

18. Jessica B. Harris, "Same Boat, Different Stops: An African Atlantic Culinary Journey," in *African Roots/American Cultures: Africa in the Creation of the Americas*, ed. Sheila S. Walker, 169–182 (Lanham, MD: Rowman and Littlefield, 2001), 177.

19. Lightfoot, chapter 4, *Troubling Freedom*.

20. Sweeney, "Market Marronage."

21. Herbert George de Lisser, *Susan Proudleigh* (London: Methuen, 1915), 57, Digital Library of the Caribbean (DLOC), accessed September 30, 2019, https://dloc.com/UF00081174/00001.

22. Olive Senior, *Dying to Better Themselves: West Indians and the Building of the Panama Canal* (Kingston: University of the West Indies Press, 2014), 242.

23. Willis John Abbot, *Panama and the Canal in Picture and Prose* (New York: Syndicate, 1913), 336.

24. Greene, *Canal Builders*, 129.

25. J. Wynne, "Housekeeping in 1906," in *Yearbook, Society of the Chagres* (Balboa Heights, Canal Zone: John O. Collins, 1914), 87, accessed December 7, 2021, http://ufdc.ufl.edu/AA00013083/00004.

26. Reyes Rivas, *El trabajo de las mujeres*, 129–130.

27. Abbot, *Panama and the Canal*, 335.

28. Ibid., 336.

29. Along with the volume edited by Mrs. Ernest von Muenchow, *The American Woman on the Panama Canal: From 1904 to 1916* (Panama: Star and Herald, 1916), which includes further excerpts from Rose Van Hardeveld's life, these are the only three memoirs published about the construction era by "regular" white American women (that is, not married to the top authorities of the Canal Commission) and continue to receive attention from expatriates and historians as representative accounts of life during construction.

30. For a similar situation, see Rafael, "Colonial Domesticity."

31. McPherson, *Reconstructing Dixie*, 1.

32. Sarah J. Moore, *Empire on Display: San Francisco's Panama-Pacific International Exposition of 1915* (Norman: University of Oklahoma Press, 2015).

33. Carla Burnett, "Unity Is Strength: Labor, Race, Garveyism, and the 1920s Panama Canal Strike," in "Interoceanic Diasporas and the Panama Canal's Centennial," special issue, *Global South* 6, no. 2 (Fall 2012): 39–64.

34. Marixa Lasso, "Race and Ethnicity in the Formation of Panamanian National Identity: Panamanian Discrimination Against Chinese and West Indians in the Thirties," *Revista Panameña de Política* 4 (July–December 2007): 61–92.

35. Michael Thomas Caroll, *Popular Modernity in America: Experience, Technology, Mythohistory* (Albany: State University of New York Press, 2000), 22.

36. Elizabeth Kittredge Parker, *Panama Canal Bride: A Story of Construction Days* (New York: Exposition Press, 1955), 33.

37. Margaret Jacobs, *White Mother to a Dark Race: Settler Colonialism, Maternalism, and the Removal of Indigenous Children in the American West and Australia, 1880–1940* (Lincoln: University of Nebraska Press, 2009); Peggy Pascoe, "Race, Gender, and the Privileges of Property: On the Significance of Miscegenation Law in the U.S. West," in *Over the Edge: Remapping the American West*, ed. Valerie J. Matsumoto and Blake Allmendinger, 215–230 (Berkeley: University of California Press, 1999).

38. Jan later received the Roosevelt Medal of Honor for serving the longest time at the construction of the Canal. They eventually moved back to the United States, and Rose died in San Antonio, Texas, in 1969 at the age of ninety-two; "Mrs. Van Hardeveld, 92, Ex-Tucsonian, Is Dead," *Tucson Daily Citizen*, June 19, 1969.

39. Rose Van Hardeveld, *Make the Dirt Fly!* (Hollywood, CA: Pan Press, 1956), 26.

40. Van Hardeveld, *Make the Dirt Fly!*, 25–26.

41. Ibid., 34.

42. Mary Louise Pratt, *Imperial Eyes: Travel Writing and Transculturation* (New York: Routledge, 2007).

43. Parker, *Panama Canal Bride*, 17.

44. Ibid., 27.

45. "Retirements in May," *Panama Canal Review* 2, no. 11 (June 6, 1952): 14. Although the Canal Commission required teachers in the Zone to stay single, Core had a long-term relationship with John "Doc" Odom, head of the quarantine station at Corozal at the time, and married him after retiring. During her tenure as teacher, Core published fifteen books on Panama, mostly children's books like *Panama's Jungle Book* (1936), *Christmas on the Isthmus* (1935), and the children's history book *Panama's Trail of Progress, or the Story of Panama and Its Canal* (1925). She gained some renown as a local historian and in 1952 offered a one-semester no-credit course at the Canal Zone Junior College's Extension Division on Panamanian history, which focused on "the history of the Isthmus from the earliest known geologic period through the present and [combined] actual history with some folklore and legends." Her work was rewarded with Panama's Order of Vasco Nuñez de Balboa, an award for civic commitment.

46. Canal Zone Brats, accessed December 7, 2021, http://www.czbrats.com.

47. Sue Pearl Core, *Maid in Panama* (Dobbs Ferry, NY: Clermont Press, 1938), 44–45.

48. Ibid., 83, xiii.

49. Camp, *Closer to Freedom*; see also Beckles, *Natural Rebels*; David Barry Gaspar and Darlene Clark Hines, eds., *More Than Chattel: Black Women and Slavery in the Americas* (Bloomington: Indiana University Press, 1996).

50. Van Hardeveld, *Make the Dirt Fly!*, 41. None of the memoirists ever refer to their maids' last names, which forced me to exclusively use the first names of Black women present in these sources.

51. Ibid.

52. Core, *Maid in Panama*, 120.

53. Ibid., 45.

54. McClintock, *Imperial Leather*; Leonore Davidoff, *Worlds Between: Historical Perspectives on Gender and Class* (New York: Routledge, 1995); Mary Douglas, *Purity and Danger: An Analysis of the Concepts of Pollution and Taboo* (New York: Routledge, 2002).

55. Douglas, *Purity and Danger*, 2–3.

56. Alice Childress, *Like One of the Family: Conversations from a Domestic's Life* (1956; Boston: Beacon Press, 2017); Patricia Hill Collins, "Like One of the Family: Race, Ethnicity, and the Paradox of US National Identity," *Ethnic and Racial Studies* 24, no. 1 (2001): 3–28; Premilla Nadasen, *Household Workers Unite: The Untold Story of African American Women Who Built a Movement* (Boston: Beacon Press, 2015), Rhacel Salazar Parreñas, "Migrant Domestic Workers as 'One of the Family,'" in *Migration and Care Labour: Theory, Policy, and Politics*, ed. Bridget Anderson and Isabel Shutes, 49–64 (London: Palgrave Macmillan, 2014).

57. McClintock, *Imperial Leather*.

58. Ibid., 45.

59. See Kaplan, "Manifest Domesticity," on the boundedness of the American home in empire.

60. Parker, *Panama Canal Bride*, 22.

61. Ibid., 19.

62. Van Hardeveld, *Make the Dirt Fly!*, 74.

63. Ibid.

64. Glymph, *Out of the House of Bondage*.

65. Lara Putnam, *The Company They Kept: Migrants and the Politics of Gender in Caribbean Costa Rica, 1870–1960* (Chapel Hill: University of North Carolina Press, 2002), 61.

66. Anyaa Anim-Addo, "Reading Postemancipation In/Security: Negotiations of Everyday Freedom," *Small Axe* 22, no. 3 (November 2018): 105–114.

67. Rose Van Hardeveld, "From 1906 to 1916," in *The American Woman on the Panama Canal: From 1904 to 1916*, ed. Mrs. Ernest von Muenchow, 10–18 (Panama: Star and Herald, 1916), 14.

68. Van Hardeveld, *Make the Dirt Fly!*, 39.

69. Noel Maurer and Carlos Yu, *The Big Ditch: How America Took, Built, Ran, and Ultimately Gave Away the Panama Canal* (Princeton, NJ: Princeton University Press, 2010), 192.

70. Van Hardeveld, *Make the Dirt Fly!*, 40.

71. Ibid., 90.

72. Greene, *Canal Builders*, 150.

73. Ibid., 148.

74. Entry of Amos Clarke, Isthmian Historical Society Competition for the Best True Stories of life and work on the Isthmus of Panama during the construction of the Panama Canal (Panama: Isthmian Historical Society, 1963), accessed December 6, 2020, Digital Library of the Caribbean, http://ufdc.ufl.edu/AA00016037/00001.

75. Index to the Gorgas Hospital Mortuary Death Records, 1906–1991, Record Group 185, National Archives and Records Administration, College Park, MD (NARA).

76. Van Hardeveld, *Make the Dirt Fly!*, 41.

77. "Fruit Trees," Docket 7: In re claim of Dunlop, Augusta, Records of the Joint Land Commission, Docket Files, Box 2, RG 185, NARA.

78. Core, "Philosophy of Life," in *Maid in Panama*, 1–5.

79. Ibid., 1.

80. Ibid., 5.

81. Van Hardeveld, *Make the Dirt Fly!*, 55.

82. Core, "The Dividing Line," in *Maid in Panama*, 33.

83. U.S. House of Representatives, *The Panama Canal: Hearings Before the Committee on Interstate and Foreign Commerce*, 62nd Congress, 2nd Session, April 4, 1912 (Washington, DC: Government Printing Office, 1912), 88.

84. John Owen Collins, *The Panama Guide* (Mount Hope, CZ: ICC Press, Quartermaster's Department, 1912), 24.

85. Abbot, *Panama and the Canal*, 152. Abbot's book collects previously syndicated journalistic photographs along with some watercolors about the Canal.

86. Van Hardeveld, *Make the Dirt Fly!*, 35.

87. U.S. House of Representatives, *The Panama Canal: Hearings Before the Committee on Interstate and Foreign Commerce*, 62nd Congress, 2nd Session, April 4, 1912, 88.

88. Wynne, "Housekeeping in 1906," 100.

89. Core, *Maid in Panama*, 181.

90. Van Hardeveld, "From 1906 to 1916," 15.

91. John F. Wallace, "Summary of Work on Panama Canal—July 1, 1904–June 30, 1905," in *Investigation of Panama Canal Matters, Hearings Before the Committee on Interoceanic Canals of the United States* (Washington, DC: Government Printing Office, 1907), 1:620.

92. Wallace, "Summary," 620.

93. *Robert Newman v. Jane Hall* (CZ 2nd Cir. 1907), Case 93, Record Group 21: Records of District Courts of the United States, Canal Zone Second Judicial Circuit Civil Court (Empire, Gorgona, Ancon), Civil Case Files, 1904–1914, National Archives and Records Administration, Washington, DC (NARA).

94. *Rufus Melhado v. Jane Hall* (CZ 2nd Cir. 1906), Case 62, RG 21, NARA.

95. Paulette Kerr, "Victims or Strategists? Female Lodging-House Keepers in Jamaica," in *Engendering History: Caribbean Women in Historical Perspective*, ed. Verene Shepherd and Bridget Brereton, 197–212 (New York: Palgrave Macmillan, 1995).

96. *Jane Hall v. China Byasta* (CZ 2nd Cir. 1907), Case 89, RG 21, NARA.

Chapter 5

1. Entry of Alfred E. Dottin, Isthmian Historical Society Competition for the Best True Stories of life and work on the Isthmus of Panama during the construction of the Panama Canal (Panama: Isthmian Historical Society, 1963), Digital Library of the Caribbean, accessed December 9, 2020, http://ufdc.ufl.edu/AA00016037/00001.

2. U.S. Congress, Senate, Panama Canal Treaties, *Report of the Committee on Foreign Relations, United States Senate, with Supplemental and Minority Views*, 95th Congress, 2nd Session (Washington, DC: Government Printing Office, 1978), 54.

3. Ibid.

4. Taken from yearly annual reports of the Isthmian Canal Commission, which start counting these deaths in fiscal year 1906–7. See Table 1 in this chapter.

5. This does not include noncontracted labor, which Bonham Richardson estimates at least doubled that number. Bonham Richardson, *Panama Money in Barbados, 1900–1920* (Knoxville: University of Tennessee Press, 1985), 125.

6. Lisa Levenstein, *A Movement Without Marches: African-American Women and the Politics of Poverty in Postwar Philadelphia* (Chapel Hill: University of North Carolina Press, 2009); Jocelyn Olcott, "Introduction: Researching and Rethinking the Labors of Love," *Hispanic American Historical Review* 91, no. 1 (2011): 1–27.

7. Vincent Brown, *Reaper's Garden: Death and Power in the World of Atlantic Slavery* (Cambridge, MA: Harvard University Press, 2008).

8. This chapter is also heavily influenced by the work of Daina Ramey Berry in understanding both the commodification of enslaved Black people and enslaved people's awareness of their own monetary value, *The Price for Their Pound of Flesh: The Value of the Enslaved, from Womb to Grave, in the Building of a Nation* (Boston: Beacon Press, 2017).

9. Claude McKay, *Complete Poems*, ed. William J. Maxwell (Urbana: University of Illinois Press, 2004), 9–12; originally published in the *Kingston Daily Gleaner*, January 27, 1912.

10. *Barbados Advocate*, November 14, 17, 1905, in Richardson, *Panama Money*, 115.

11. For more on disease and environmental history of the Canal, see Ashley Carse, *Beyond the Big Ditch: Politics, Ecology, and Infrastructure at the Panama Canal* (Cambridge, MA: MIT Press, 2014); and Paul Sutter, "The First Mountain to Be Removed: Yellow Fever Control and the Construction of the Panama Canal," in Ashley Carse et al., "Panama Canal Forum: From the Conquest of Nature to the Construction of New Ecologies," *Environmental History* 21 (2016): 206–287; and Paul Sutter, "Nature's Agents or Agents of Empire? Entomological Workers and Environmental Change During the Construction of the Panama Canal," *Isis* 98 (December 2007): 724–754.

12. Richardson, *Panama Money*, 116.

13. "The Panama Canal Commission's Barbados Recruiting Arrangements," *Weekly Illustrated Paper* (Bridgetown, Barbados), August 21, 1909, in Richardson, *Panama Money*, 117.

14. Albert Edwards (pseudonym for Arthur Bullard), "With a Cargo of Black Ivory," *Harper's Weekly*, July 2, 1910, 10–12. Also reprinted in Arthur Bullard, *Panama: The Canal, the Country, and the People* (New York: Macmillan, 1914), 31.

15. Richardson, *Panama Money*, 132.

16. Olive Senior, *Dying to Better Themselves: West Indians and the Building of the Panama Canal* (Kingston: University of the West Indies Press, 2014), 103.

17. Congressional Record—Senate, Proceedings of April 17, 1902, "Practical Experience," *Congressional Record: Containing the Proceedings and Debates of the Fifty-Seventh Congress, First Session* (Washington, DC: Government Printing Office, 1902), 35:4293.

18. Entry of Constantine Parkinson, Isthmian Historical Society Competition for the Best True Stories of life and work on the Isthmus of Panama during the construction of the

Panama Canal (Panama: Isthmian Historical Society, 1963), Digital Library of the Caribbean, accessed December 9, 2020, http://ufdc.ufl.edu/AA00016037/00001.

19. Entry of Amos Parks, Isthmian Historical Society Competition for the Best True Stories of life and work on the Isthmus of Panama during the construction of the Panama Canal (Panama: Isthmian Historical Society, 1963), Digital Library of the Caribbean, accessed December 9, 2020, http://ufdc.ufl.edu/AA00016037/00001.

20. Letter from Acting Chief Sanitary Officer to Col. George Goethals, January 15, 1909, Folder 2-L-080000: [Untitled], Record Group 185: Records of the Panama Canal, Entry 30: General Correspondence, 1905–1914, National Archives and Records Administration, College Park, MD (NARA).

21. Canal Zone Police Sergeant No. 15 Charles Kreuger, Report of Death, October 20, 1907, Folder 2-L-040000: [Untitled], RG 185, Entry 30, NARA.

22. Coroner's Report, October 12, 1908, Folder 2-L-080000: [Untitled], RG 185, Entry 30, NARA.

23. Coroner's Verdict, November 30, 1906, Folder 2-L-040000: [Untitled], RG 185, Entry 30, NARA.

24. Letter from A. T. Luther to James MacFarlane, Superintendent of Dredging, January 12, 1914, Folder 2-L-100000: [Untitled], RG 185, Entry 30, NARA.

25. Letter from Charles Palacio to J. P. Fyffe, Chief of Police, March 11, 1911, Folder 2-L-100000: [Untitled], RG 185, Entry 30, NARA.

26. Letter from Zone Police Lieutenant #3 to Chief of Division, Ancon, January 29, 1914, Folder 2-L-100000: [Untitled], RG 185, Entry 30, NARA.

27. Letter from Gilbert Thomas Carter to Claude Mallet, April 27, 1908, FO 288/109: From Miscellaneous, 1908, January 1–June 30, folio 158, Records of the Foreign Office, Consulate: Panama, National Archives, Kew, Richmond, UK (hereafter cited as FO: Panama, Kew).

28. Peter Stearns, *Revolutions in Sorrow: The American Experience of Death in Global Perspective* (New York: Routledge, 2007).

29. Act No. 9: Sanitary Rules and Regulations: An Act to provide sanitary rules and regulations for the Canal Zone, Isthmus of Panama, and for the enforcement thereof, Section 26: "Certificate of Death, Burial Permits, Etc.," in *Laws of the Canal Zone, Isthmus of Panama* (Washington, DC: Government Printing Office, 1906), 74.

30. M. C. Stayer, *Report of the Health Department of the Panama Canal for the Calendar Year 1943* (Mount Hope, CZ: Panama Canal Press, 1943), 76.

31. See, for one example, Letter from Zone Police Lieutenant #3, Empire Central Station to Chief of Division, Ancon, January 29, 1914, where the Lieutenant notes that West Indians in the area, "not caring to undergo the delay and expense incident to conveying the body to Empire for burial, placed it where it was found as the most convenient way of disposing of it," Folder 2-L-100000: [Untitled], RG 185, Entry 30, NARA.

32. Rose Van Hardeveld, *Make the Dirt Fly!* (Hollywood, CA: Pan Press, 1956), 49.

33. Ibid., 50.

34. Ibid., 50.

35. Note the similarity in an observer's description of a funeral among enslaved people in Jamaica in 1740: "then the Body is put in the Ground, all the while they are covering it with Earth, the Attendants scream out in a terrible manner, which is not the Effect of Grief but of Joy, they beat on their wooden Drums, and the Women with their Rattles make a hideous Noise." Charles Leslie, *A New History of Jamaica: From the Earliest Accounts to the Taking of Porto Bello by Vice-Admiral Vernon* (1740; Cambridge: Cambridge University Press, 2015), 309.

36. Senior, *Dying to Better Themselves*, 165.

37. Maarit Forde, "Governing Death in Trinidad and Tobago," in *Passages and Afterworlds: Anthropological Perspectives on Death in the Caribbean*, ed. Maarit Forde and Yanique Hume, 176–198 (Durham, NC: Duke University Press, 2018), 17. See also Diana Paton, *The Cultural Politics of Obeah: Religion, Colonialism and Modernity in the Caribbean World* (Cambridge: Cambridge University Press, 2015); Diana Paton and Maarit Forde, eds., *Obeah and Other Powers: The Politics of Caribbean Religion and Healing* (Durham, NC: Duke University Press, 2012); Reinaldo Román, *Governing Spirits: Religion, Miracles, and Spectacles in Cuba and Puerto Rico, 1898–1956* (Chapel Hill: University of North Carolina Press, 2007); and Alexander Rocklin, *The Regulation of Religion and the Making of Hinduism in Colonial Trinidad* (Chapel Hill: University of North Carolina Press, 2019). Thank you to Alexander Rocklin for these references.

38. Forde, "Governing Death in Trinidad and Tobago."

39. Yanique Hume, "Death and the Construction of Social Space: Land, Kinship, and Identity in the Jamaican Mortuary Cycle," in Forde and Hume, *Passages and Afterworlds*, 111.

40. Hume, "Death and the Construction of Social Space."

41. Forde, "Governing Death in Trinidad and Tobago," 17. For more on the policing of West Indian immigrant religious practices in this period, see Lara Putnam, "Rites of Power and Rumors of Race: The Circulations of Supernatural Knowledge in the Greater Caribbean, 1890–1940," in Patton and Forde, *Obeah and Other Powers*, 243–267.

42. Letter from Corporal #10 to Chief of Police, January 11, 1914, Folder 2-L-100000: [Untitled], RG 185, Entry 30, NARA.

43. Verdict of Coroner's Jury in the Case of an: UNIDENTIFIED–black–male–adult found January 10, 1914, January 20, 1914, Folder 2-L-100000: [Untitled], RG 185, Entry 30, NARA.

44. Letter from Corporal #10 to Chief of Police, January 11, 1914, Folder 2-L-100000: [Untitled], RG 185, Entry 30, NARA.

45. Leonard P. Fletcher, "The Decline of Friendly Societies in Barbados," *Caribbean Studies* 15, no. 4 (January 1976): 73–85.

46. Howard Johnson, "Friendly Societies in the Bahamas 1834–1910," *Slavery and Abolition: A Journal of Slave and Post-Slave Studies* 12, no. 3 (December 1991): 183–199; Tyesha Maddox, "More Than Auxiliary: Caribbean Women and Social Organizations in the Interwar Period," *Caribbean Review of Gender Studies* 12 (2018): 67–94. Thank you to Tyesha Maddox for these references.

47. Letter from Acting Colonial Secretary of Barbados to Her Majesty's Consul in Panama Claude Mallet, October 2, 1906, FO 288/101: From Miscellaneous, 1906, July 20–December 31, folio 110, FO: Panama, Kew.

48. Letter from Secretary of Lodge to Her Majesty's Consul in Panama Claude Mallet, January 30, 1912, FO 288/143: From Miscellaneous, 1912, folio 89, FO: Panama, Kew.

49. Sue Pearl Core, "Social Security," in *Maid in Panama* (Dobbs Ferry, NY: Clermont Press, 1938), 85–87.

50. Robin Elizabeth Zenger, "West Indians in Panama: Diversity and Activism, 1910s–1940," (PhD diss., University of Arizona, 2015), 74, accessed December 9, 2021, https://repository.arizona.edu/handle/10150/581411. The bylaws of this lodge were registered in 1918, four years after the Canal's completion, which means they might not be directly representative of how funerals were held in the early years of construction. However, many lodges drew on long-standing traditions from the islands for their funeral practices and thus could have maintained certain similarities throughout construction.

51. Zenger, "West Indians in Panama."

52. Richardson, *Panama Money*, 146.

53. Ibid., 118.

54. Letter from S. W. Knaggs to Claude Mallet, September 12, 1907, folio 138; Letter from Chief of Police of Ancon Station to Thomas Broadwood, British Vice-Consul in Panama, October 7, 1907, folios 186–187, FO 288/104: From Miscellaneous, 1907, July 1–December 31, FO: Panama, Kew.

55. Letter from Maud Louise Weeks to Colonial Secretary of Barbados, September 7, 1906, FO 288/101, folio 88, FO: Panama, Kew.

56. I refer to the participants by their first names because John, Frederick, and Margaret all have the last name Smith. Letter from John A. Smith to Margaret Smith, September 12, 1906, FO 288/101, folios 221–222, FO: Panama, Kew.

57. Copy of Report of Death, FO 288/100: From Miscellaneous, 1906, January 1–July 19, folio 88, FO: Panama, Kew.

58. Letter from H. D. Reed, Executive Secretary, to Mrs. Frances Mahon, December 2, 1905, FO 288/100, folio 111, FO: Panama, Kew.

59. Letter from Frances Mahon to the Governor of Barbados, February 23, 1906, FO 288/100, folio 110, FO: Panama, Kew.

60. Letter from Basil Blackburn to Claude Mallet, July 21, 1908, FO 288/110: From Miscellaneous, 1908, July 1–December 31, folio 21, FO: Panama, Kew.

61. Senior, *Dying to Better Themselves*, 242.

62. Letter from Mary Gibson to Government Secretary, Georgetown, British Guiana, September 18, 1908, FO 288/110, folios 168–169, FO: Panama, Kew.

63. List of Contract Labourers, *Trent*, September 20, 1905, in "United States, Panama Canal Zone, Employment Records and Sailing Lists" database, *FamilySearch*, accessed January 30, 2020, https://familysearch.org/ark:/61903/1:1:QVSH-4BKX: images 27–31, from Sailing Lists of Contract Laborers, 1905–1910, Box 2, RG 185, National Personnel Records Center, St. Louis, Missouri.

64. Letter from Wilbert Senhouse to Mary Ann Gibbs, December 12, 1905, FO 288/100, folios 103–104, FO: Panama, Kew.

65. Letter from Mary Ann Gibbs to S. W. Knaggs, March 12, 1906, FO 288/100, folio 102, FO: Panama, Kew.

66. Letter from Mary Gibson (written by J. G. Applewhaite, Lacytown, Guyana) to Government Secretary, Georgetown, Guyana, June 16, 1908, FO 288/110, folios 172–173, FO: Panama, Kew.

67. Letter from S. W. Knaggs to Claude Mallet, March 15, 1906, FO 288/100, folio 101, FO: Panama, Kew.

68. Barbados Savings Bank Ledgers, 1907, Barbados National Archives, Cave Hill, Barbados.

69. Letter from Wilbert Senhouse to Mary Ann Gibbs, December 12, 1905, FO 288/100, folio 103, FO: Panama, Kew.

70. U.S. Congress, House of Representatives, H.R. 21844, Chap. 236: *An Act Granting to certain employees of the United States right to receive from it compensation for injuries sustained in the course of their employment*, Public Law 176, *Statutes at Large* 35, 60th Congress, 1st Session (1908): 556–558.

71. De Alva Stanwood Alexander, U.S. Congress, House of Representatives, *Report to Accompany H.R. 21844*, H. Report no.1669, 60th Congress, 1st Session (1908), 1.

72. U.S. Bureau of Labor Statistics, *Report of Operations Under the Act of May 30, 1908* (Washington DC: Government Printing Office, 1914), 8.

73. Theda Skocpol, *Protecting Soldiers and Mothers: The Political Origins of Social Policy in the United States* (Cambridge, MA: Harvard University Press, 1992).

74. Donald Shaffer, "I Do Not Suppose That Uncle Sam Looks at the Skin": African Americans and the Civil War Pension System, 1865–1934," *Civil War History* 46, no. 2 (June 2000): 133.

75. Brandi Clay Brimmer, *Claiming Union Widowhood: Race, Respectability, and Poverty in the Post-Emancipation South* (Durham, NC: Duke University Press, 2020); Allison Dorsey, "'I Brought Them out of My Bounty-money': USCT Veterans and the Struggle for Land" (conference paper presented at the Association for the Study of the Worldwide African Diaspora (ASWAD) 10th Biennial Conference, Williamsburg, Virginia, November 5–9, 2019); Larry M. Logue and Peter Blanck, "Benefit of the Doubt: African-American Civil War Veterans and Pensions," *Journal of Interdisciplinary History* 38, no. 3 (Winter 2008): 377–399; Shaffer, "I Do not Suppose That Uncle Sam Looks at the Skin."

76. U.S. Bureau of Labor Statistics, *Report of Operations*, 15.

77. In 1908 amendment H.R. 22340 modified the law as it referred to the Isthmian Canal Commission, adding that the ICC would have final say over granting compensation, despite the dispensations of the initial bill that placed it under a federal umbrella. The application of the compensation bill for ICC employees thus remained entirely at the discretion of the commission.

78. U.S. Congress, House of Representatives, H.R. 21844, Chap. 236: *An Act Granting to certain employees of the United States right to receive from it compensation for injuries sustained in the course of their employment*, Public Law 176, *Statutes at Large* 35, 60th Congress, 1st Session (1908), 557.

79. Alexander, *Report to Accompany H.R. 21844*, H. Report no. 1669, 60th Congress, 1st Session, (1908), 1.

80. Ibid., 29.

81. Letter from Acting Governor of Jamaica Philip Clark Cork to Claude Mallet, August 6, 1909, FO 288/117: From Miscellaneous, 1909, June 22–October 1, folio 139, FO: Panama, Kew.

82. U.S. Bureau of Labor Statistics, *Report of Operations*, 30.

83. Ibid., 39.

84. Ibid.

85. Letter from Millicent Marshall to Lord Basil Blackwood, July 4, 1908, FO 288/110, folios 22–23, FO: Panama, Kew.

86. Letter from Clara Jones to Sir Gilbert Carter, no date, ca. July 1909, FO 288/117, folio 120, FO: Panama, Kew.

87. Letter from Elma Washington to Sir Sydney Olivier, FO 288/134: From Miscellaneous, 1911, July 19–December 31, folio 501, FO: Panama, Kew.

88. Some claims would simply not go forward to the consideration stage.

89. Letter from Claims Officer Frank Ward to British Charge d'Affaires in Panama H. O. Chalkley, November 23, 1909, FO 288/118: From Miscellaneous, 1909, October 2–December 31, folio 173, FO: Panama, Kew.

90. Letter from Claim Officer J. H. Helmer to British Vice-Consul in Panama, December 5, 1911, FO 288/134, folio 468, FO: Panama, Kew.

91. U.S. Bureau of Labor Statistics, Table: "Average Cost of Compensation for Fatal Injuries," *Report of Operations*, 43. A note on the exchange rate: There was no official "exchange rate" as we know it now between American dollars and British pounds during this period, though both countries followed the gold standard. The pound, bound to the gold standard, was perhaps the most important global currency in the late nineteenth century as almost two-thirds of total world trade was transacted in this currency, though by the early twentieth century, New York rivaled London as a financial center. The U.S. adopted the gold standard in 1900. The gold standard was at its "zenith" in the period of the Panama construction, propped up in part by the growth of multilateral trade. In 1904, at the beginning of construction, 100 pounds sterling (£) was quoted at an exchange of 486.92 U.S. dollars. In 1914 it equaled $487.07, meaning that the minimum compensation payment in U.S. dollars ($) neared £100. For a detailed explanation of these exchange rates, see Markus A. Denzel, *Handbook of World Exchange Rates, 1590–1914* (Farnham, England: Ashgate, 2010).

Chapter 6

1. Complaint of Rebecca Williams, May 22, 1917, Folder 39: Memoriales y diligencias policivas, 26 de Mayo de 1917, Box 65: Calidonia, 1911–1919, Series: Alcaldías y Corregidurías, Administración del Estado, Archivo Nacional de Panamá (ANP), Panama City, Panama (hereafter cited as ANP).

2. Mimi Sheller, *Citizenship from Below: Erotic Agency and Caribbean Freedom* (Durham, NC: Duke University Press, 2012); Lauren Berlant, *The Queen of America Goes to Washington City: Essays on Sex and Citizenship* (Durham, NC: Duke University Press, 1997).

3. Sheller, *Citizenship from Below*, 10.

4. Carolyn Cooper, *Noises in the Blood: Orality, Gender, and the "Vulgar" Body of Jamaican Popular Culture* (Durham, NC: Duke University Press, 1995); Lara Putnam, "Sex and Standing in the Streets of Port Limón, Costa Rica, 1890–1910," in *Honor, Status, and Law in Modern Latin America*, ed. Sueann Caulfield, Sarah Chambers, Lara Putnam, 155–175 (Durham, NC: Duke University Press, 2005). On jamettes, see Rosamond S. King, "New Citizens, New Sexualities: Nineteenth-Century Jamettes," in *Sex and the Citizen: Interrogating the Caribbean*, ed. Faith L. Smith, 214–223 (Charlottesville: University of Virginia Press, 2011); Allison O. Ramsay, "Jametes, mas and bacchanal: A Culture of Resistance in Trinidad and Tobago," in *The Routledge Companion to Black Women's Cultural Histories*, 213–222 (New York: Routledge, 2021); Rhoda Reddock, *Women, Labor, and Politics in Trinidad and Tobago: A History* (Kingston: Ian Randle, 1994); David Trotman, "Women and Crime in Late Nineteenth-Century Trinidad," *Caribbean Quarterly* 30, nos. 3–4 (1984): 60–72.

5. Putnam, "Sex and Standing," 159.

6. Putnam, "Sex and Standing," 164, 171.

7. Caulfield, Chambers, and Putnam, *Honor, Status, and Law*.

8. A long historiography on honor in Latin America from the colonial period to the twentieth century informs my work here, including but not limited to Sueann Caulfield, *In Defense of Honor: Sexual Morality, Modernity, and Nation in Early Twentieth-Century Brazil* (Durham, NC: Duke University Press, 2000); Caulfield, Chambers, and Putnam, *Honor, Status, and Law*; Sarah Chambers, *From Subjects to Citizens: Honor, Gender, and Politics in Arequipa, Peru, 1780–1854* (University Park: Pennsylvania State University Press, 1999); Arlene Díaz, *Female Citizens, Patriarchs, and the Law in Venezuela, 1786–1904* (Lincoln: University of Nebraska Press, 2004); Lyman Johnson and Sonya Lipsett-Rivera, eds., *The Faces of Honor: Sex, Shame, and Violence in Colonial Latin America* (Albuquerque: University of New Mexico Press, 1998); Evelyne Laurent-Perrault, "Black Honor, Intellectual Marronage, and the Law in Venezuela, 1760–1809" (PhD diss., New York University, UMI Dissertations, 2015); Pablo Picato, *The Tyranny of Opinion: Honor in the Construction of the Mexican Public Sphere* (Durham, NC: Duke University Press, 2010); Lara Putnam, *The Company They Kept: Migrants and the Politics of Gender in Caribbean Costa Rica* (Chapel Hill: University of North Carolina Press, 2002); and Ann Twinam, "Honor, Sexuality, and Illegitimacy in Colonial Spanish America," in *Sexuality and Marriage in Colonial Latin America*, ed. Asunción Lavrin, 118–155 (Lincoln: University of Nebraska Press, 1992).

9. On U.S. and Panamanian "rival visions of honor," see "The Riots of Cocoa Grove," chapter 8 in Julie Greene, *The Canal Builders: Making America's Empire at the Panama Canal*, 303–333 (New York: Penguin Press, 2009).

10. Peter Wilson, *Crab-Antics: The Social Anthropology of English-Speaking Negro Societies of the Caribbean* (New Haven, CT: Yale University Press, 1973).

11. Jean Besson, "Reputation and Respectability Reconsidered: A New Perspective on Afro-Caribbean Peasant Women," in *Women and Change in the Caribbean: A Pan-Caribbean Perspective*, ed. Jane Momsen, 15–37 (Kingston: Ian Randle, 1993); Karen Fog Olwig, "The Struggle for Respectability: Methodism and Afro-Caribbean Culture on

19th Century Nevis," *Nieuwe West-Indische Gids / New West Indian Guide* 64, no. 3/4 (1990): 93–114.

12. Cecilia Green, "Between Respectability and Self-Respect: Framing Afro-Caribbean Women's Labour History," *Social and Economic Studies* 55, no. 3 (September 2006): 1–31; Shalini Puri, "Beyond Resistance: Notes Toward a New Caribbean Cultural Studies," *Small Axe* 7, no. 2 (September 2003): 23–28.

13. Green, "Between Respectability and Self-Respect."

14. República de Panamá, Gaceta Oficial, Serie 1, No. 4 (December 3, 1903), "Decreto número 10 de 1903 sobre organización judicial," Justia Panamá, accessed April 4, 2022, https://panama.justia.com/federales/decretos-legislativos/19-de-1903-dec-3-1903/gdoc/.

15. Carlos H. Cuestas G., "La justicia panameña durante la república: 1903–2003," in *Nueva Historia General de Panamá*, vol. 3, t. 1, ed. Alfredo Castillero Calvo, 111–146 (Panamá: Editorial Novo Art, Biblioteca 500, 2019).

16. Libro III: Delito contra los particulares y sus penas, Título 1: Delitos contra las personas, Capítulo 7: Riñas y peleas, Código Penal Colombiano 1890 (Bogota: Librería Colombia, C. Roldán y Tamayo, 1890), 58, accessed December 9, 2021, http://www.archive.org/details/codigo_penal_colombiano_1890.

17. Ibid., Título 2: Delitos contra la honra, fama y tranquilidad de los particulares, Capítulo 2: Injurias, art, 755, 64.

18. Ibid., Libro III, Título 1, Capítulo 4: Aborto, art, 642, 56. Cassia Roth shows that, in Rio de Janeiro around the same time, legal doctrines on abortion and infanticide were rarely used to actually persecute or punish women for these crimes. Rather, poor Brazilian women faced exclusion through other routes, bolstered by legal and medical expertise that positioned them as unfit for citizenship and only able to contribute to the nation through motherhood. I have no evidence of whether women were actually persecuted for the same crimes in Panama. Nevertheless, legal codes on honor, whether applied or not, contributed to broader elite and popular discourses that condemned certain women for dishonorable behavior and excluded them from the body politic. Cassia Roth, *A Miscarriage of Justice: Women's Reproductive Lives and the Law in Early Twentieth Century Brazil* (Palo Alto, CA: Stanford University Press, 2020).

19. Aura E. Guerra de Villalaz, "Historia de la Codificación Penal Durante la época Republicana," Órgano Judicial de la República de Panamá, Centenario 1903–2003, Suplemento Conmemorativo No 13, Panamá, 2003, http://www.organojudicial.gob.pa/cendoj/wp-content/blogs.dir/cendoj/13-historiadelacodificacionpena.pdf.

20. Título XI, República de Panamá, Codigo Penal (Barcelona: Talleres de Artes Gráficas de Henrich, 1917), Procuraduría de la Administración, accessed April 4, 2022, http://gacetas.procuraduria-admon.gob.pa/codigo_penal_1916.pdf.

21. Ibid., Capítulo 2: Injurias, art, 465, 99.

22. Ibid.

23. Ibid., Título IX: Delitos contra las personas, Capítulo 5: Infanticidio, Capítulo 6: Aborto, 89–90.

24. For the administrative organization of local politics and geographic limits of each province, district, and corregiduría, see Art. 65 of the Administrative Code, República de

Panamá, Codigo Administrativo (Barcelona: Talleres de Artes Gráficas de Henrich, 1917), Procuraduría de la Administración, accessed April 4, 2022, http://gacetas.procuraduria -admon.gob.pa/codigo_administrativo.pdf.

25. See "Capítulo Séptimo: Alcaldías, Corregimientos, Regidurías y Barrios" of the Codigo Administrativo, Ibid., 160–162.

26. Ibid. Libro I: Asuntos Fundamentales, Título 3: Nacionalidad y ciudadanía, extranjería y naturalización, Capítulo Séptimo: Extranjería, art, 163, 65.

27. Marixa Lasso, *Erased: The Untold Story of the Panama Canal* (Cambridge, MA: Harvard University Press, 2019), 168.

28. Lasso, *Erased*, 167.

29. The process of naturalization was not ostensibly difficult, requiring only that foreigners declare their intent after ten or more years in residence, but in reality, it privileged those who owned businesses or real estate, had a special skill, or had the money to bribe officials. After 1914, Goethals refused to recognize Panamanian citizens naturalized after 1914, so as not to confer Gold Roll status on West Indians (if they did manage to become citizens of Panama). Few West Indians lived as Panamanian citizens at the end of construction. All West Indian children born in Panama did enjoy Panamanian citizenship, until a constitutional amendment in 1928 thrust children of prohibited immigrants (including West Indians) into limbo. West Indians born on the Canal Zone were not conferred U.S. citizenship. Michael L. Conniff, *Black Labor on a White Canal: Panama, 1904–1981* (Pittsburgh, PA: University of Pittsburgh Press, 1985), 66.

30. All are still heavily populated by West Indian–descended Panamanians.

31. Ana Luisa Sanchez Laws, *Panamanian Museums and Historical Memory* (New York: Berghahn Books, 2011), 88.

32. Advertisement, *Daily Star and Herald* (Panama City, Panama), February 8, 1914, 11.

33. "In the matter of the claim of Alberto B. de Obarrio," *Panama Canal Record* 13, no. 1, August 20, 1919, 31 (Balboa Heights, CZ)

34. For more on land claims in the Canal Zone and the Joint Land Commission, see the work of Allison Powers Useche, *Settlement Colonialism: Life and Property in the United States Empire* (Oxford University Press, forthcoming).

35. Winifred James, *The Mulberry Tree* (London: Chapman and Hall, 1913), 232.

36. Complaint of Maud Aitken, July 9, 1921, Folder: Asunto, Calumnia e Injuria Contra: Winifred Buckner Demandante: Catherine Scott, Box 69: Calidonia, 1921, Alcaldías, ANP.

37. Henry de Lisser, *Jamaicans in Colón and the Canal Zone* (Kingston: Gleaner, 1906), 5, quoted in Velma Newton, *The Silver Men: West Indian Migration to Panama, 1850–1914*, rev. ed. (1985; Kingston: Ian Randle, 2004), 151.

38. Samuel A. Gutiérrez, *Arquitectura Panameña: Descripción e historia* (Panamá: Editorial Litográfica, 1966): "una arquitectura un tanto popular y espontánea, y, a la vez, rigurosamente comercial," 386; "El criterio que guiaba a los propietarios y constructores, era el de obtener el máximo de cuarto individuales para los obreros e inquilinos de ocasión . . . sin ninguna consideración por la vida humana," 336.

39. Olive Senior, *Dying to Better Themselves: West Indians and the Building of the Panama Canal* (Kingston: University of the West Indies Press, 2014), 260.

40. Decree No. 48 of 1912, Folder 37-H-10: Venereal Diseases on the Isthmus; Policy and Procedure for Control; Cooperation between U.S. and Panama officials, etc., Record Group 185: Records of the Panama Canal, Entry 30: General Correspondence, 1904–1914, National Archives and Records Administration, College Park, MD.

41. Letter from Walter Stephens to Acting Governor Chester Harding, July 9, 1916, Folder 64-Y-4 (II): Segregation of Prostitutes, Red Light District Limits, Etc. from August 1, 1915 to May 31, 1933, RG 185, Entry 30, NARA.

42. Letter from J. P. Fyffe to H. H Rousseau, June 6, 1911, Folder 64-Y-4 (I), RG 185, Entry 30, NARA.

43. Letter from Federico Boyd to H. H. Rousseau, June 17, 1911, Folder 64-Y-4 (I), RG 185, Entry 30, NARA.

44. Jeffrey W. Parker, "Empire's Angst: The Politics of Race, Migration, and Sex Work in Panama, 1903–1945" (PhD diss., University of Texas at Austin, 2013), 110.

45. "September 1916, Plan of Cocoa Grove or Restricted District—Panama City," Folder 64-Y-4 (II), RG 185, Entry 30, NARA.

46. Untitled property list, Folder 64-Y-4 (II), RG 185, Entry 30, NARA.

47. Parker, "Empire's Angst," 75.

48. Letter from Vincent Lindsay, Jonas T. M. Wilson, St. Aubyn Yearwood, William B. Niles (Pastor and Members of the Baptist Church), and Luther F. Lewis (Pastor, Committee, and Members of Christian Mission Church) to M. H. Thatcher, August 23, 1911, Folder 64-Y-4 (I), RG 185, Entry 30, NARA.

49. Declaration of Thomas Price, January 12, 1914, Docket 3: Maltratamiento de Obra, Thomas Price, Ercilia Clair, Box 52: Calidonia, 1914, Alcaldías, ANP.

50. Declaration of Ercilia Clair, January 12, 1914, Docket 3, Box 52, Alcaldías, ANP.

51. Mary Louise Pratt, "Arts of the Contact Zone," *Profession* (1991): 33–40.

52. For more information on Cocoa Grove and the 1912 riots, see Greene, "Riots of Cocoa Grove."

53. Greene, *Canal Builders*, 313.

54. Harry A. Franck, *Zone Policeman 88: A Close Range Study of the Canal and Its Workers* (New York: Century, 1913), 206.

55. Letter to the Editor from "A Sympathizer," "Panama's Modern (?) Police Methods," *Daily Star and Herald* (Panama City, Panama), December 10, 1914.

56. Cecilia A. Green, "'The Abandoned Lower Class of Females': Class, Gender, and Penal Discipline in Barbados, 1875–1929," *Comparative Studies in Society and History* 53 (January 2011): 172.

57. Ibid.

58. King, "New Citizens, New Sexualities"; Reddock, *Women, Labor, and Politics in Trinidad and Tobago*; Trotman, "Women and Crime in Late Nineteenth-Century Trinidad." Though very few Haitians traveled to Panama during this period, Anne Eller identifies a similar dynamic in urban Haitian market women's political participation during the nineteenth century. Anne Eller, "Skirts Rolled Up: The Gendered Terrain of Politics in Nineteenth-Century Port-au-Prince," *Small Axe* 25, no. 1 (March 2021): 61–83.

59. Trotman, "Women and Crime in Late Nineteenth-Century Trinidad," 71.

60. The missing cases appear random, so I assume the remaining cases to be representative of the courts as a whole.

61. Docket 63: Ultrajes, Querella de Irene Geddes contra Delfina Todman, July 6, 1914, Box 52, Alcaldías, ANP.

62. Docket 113: Injurias, Ambrosina Prescott, Claris Bennett, August 26, 1914, Box 52, Alcaldías, ANP.

63. Complaint of Claris Bennett, August 24, 1914, Docket 113: Injurias, Ambrosina Prescott, Claris Bennett, Box 52, Alcaldías, ANP.

64. Ibid.

65. Witness Statement of Rosa Williams, Docket 113: Injurias, Ambrosina Prescott, Claris Bennett, Box 52, Alcaldías, ANP.

66. Putnam, *Company They Kept*, 148.

67. Interrogation of Ambrosina Prescott, Docket 113: Injurias, Ambrosina Prescott, Claris Bennett, Box 52, Alcaldías, ANP.

68. Docket 116: Querella de Sarah Bryan contra Luisa Spencer por Insultos, December 4, 1914, Box 52, Alcaldías, ANP.

69. Docket 63: Ultrajes, Querella de Irene Geddes contra Delfina Todman, July 6, 1914, Box 52, Alcaldías, ANP.

70. Docket 117: Querella de Salomón Hylton, November 13, 1914, Box 52, Alcaldías, ANP.

71. Docket 10: Ultrajes, Querella de Isaac Cooper contra James Gittens, February 2, 1914, Alcaldías, ANP.

72. Complaint of Julia Evans, August 26, 1914, Docket 79: Querella de Julia Evans contra Charles y Rosa Patterson por provocaciones y escándalos, Box 52, Alcaldías, ANP.

73. Denuncia de Bertha Alleyne, April 14, 1914, Docket 47: Injurios y ultrajes, Beatríz Taylor, Bertha Alleyne, barbadenses de oficios domésticos, Box 52, Alcaldías, ANP.

74. Ibid.

75. Jennifer Morgan, *Laboring Women: Reproduction and Gender in New World Slavery* (Philadelphia: University of Pennsylvania Press, 2004); Katherine Paugh, *The Politics of Reproduction: Race, Medicine, and Fertility in the Age of Abolition* (Oxford: Oxford University Press, 2017); Sasha Turner, *Contested Bodies: Pregnancy, Childbearing, and Slavery in Jamaica* (Philadelphia: University of Pennsylvania Press, 2017); Suman Seth, *Difference and Disease: Medicine, Race, and the Eighteenth-Century British Empire* (Cambridge: Cambridge University Press, 2018).

76. Juanita de Barros, *Reproducing the British Caribbean: Sex, Gender, and Population Politics After Slavery* (Chapel Hill: University of North Carolina Press, 2014).

77. Ibid., see chapter 4.

78. Docket 1: Hurto, Contra: Nemesio Noyola Demandante: Adina Harper, October 17, 1914, Box 52, Alcaldías, ANP.

79. Father of Ewart and Lani Guinier.

80. Docket 13: Sumarias contra Jose D. Perez por ultrajes, 25 de febrero, Demandante: Pedro de Icaza, February 25, 1914, Box 52, Alcaldías, ANP.

81. Witness statement of Annie Brown, Docket 47: Injurios y ultrajes, Beatríz Taylor, Bertha Alleyne, barbadenses de oficios domésticos, April 14, 1914, Box 52, ANP.

82. Court declaration, July 4, 1914, Docket 66: Fuerza y violencia, Barballis (Barboly) Pallis, Maria Miguel, Box 52, Alcaldías, ANP.

83. Docket 109: Querella de J. Green contra Veroni Bernard, October 2, 1914, Box 52, Alcaldías, ANP.

84. Docket 89: Provocaciones, Denuncia de Atilio Pecorini contra Maria Ponticelli, January 24, 1914, Box 52, Alcaldías, ANP.

85. Docket 92: Denuncia de Rebecca Jordan contra Adolphus Spencer por Herida, August 3, 1914, Box 52, Alcaldías, ANP.

Chapter 7

1. The past two decades have seen increased scholarly attention to Black internationalism: Keisha Blain, *Set the World on Fire: Black Nationalist Women and the Global Struggle for Freedom* (Philadelphia: University of Pennsylvania Press, 2018); James Cantres, *Blackening Britain: Caribbean Radicalism from Windrush to Decolonization* (Lanham, MD: Rowan and Littlefield, 2020); Brent Hayes Edwards, *The Practice of Diaspora: Literature, Translation, and the Rise of Black Internationalism* (Cambridge, MA: Harvard University Press, 2003); Winston James, *Holding Aloft the Banner of Ethiopia: Caribbean Radicalism in Early Twentieth Century America* (New York: Verso, 1998); Minkah Makalani, *In the Cause of Freedom: Radical Black Internationalism from Harlem to London, 1917–1939* (Chapel Hill: University of North Carolina Press, 2011); Louis J. Parascandola, ed., *Look for Me All Around You: Anglophone Caribbean Immigrants in the Harlem Renaissance* (Detroit, MI: Wayne State University Press, 2005); Lara Putnam, *Radical Moves: Caribbean Migrants and the Politics of Race in the Jazz Age* (Chapel Hill: University of North Carolina Press, 2013); Michelle Ann Stephens, *Black Empire: The Masculine Global Imaginary of Caribbean Intellectuals in the United States, 1914–1962* (Durham, NC: Duke University Press, 2005); among others.

2. Blain, *Set the World on Fire*; Carole Boyce Davies, *Left of Karl Marx: The Political Life of Black Communist Claudia Jones* (Durham, NC: Duke University Press, 2008); Ula Yvette Taylor, *The Veiled Garvey: The Life and Times of Amy Jacques Garvey* (Chapel Hill: University of North Carolina Press, 2002); Irma Watkins-Owens, "Early Twentieth-Century Caribbean Women: Migration and Social Networks in New York City," in *Islands in the City: West Indian Migration to New York*, ed. Nancy Foner, 25–51 (Berkeley: University of California Press, 2001).

3. Winston James, "Explaining Afro-Caribbean Social Mobility in the United States: Beyond the Sowell Thesis," *Comparative Studies in Society and History* 44, no. 2 (April 2002): 218–262.

4. The phrase "triple oppression" is credited to Louise Thompson and Claudia Jones, two Black Communist women. Davies, *Left of Karl Marx*; Erik McDuffie, *Sojourning for Freedom: Black Women, American Communism, and the Making of Black Left Feminism* (Durham, NC: Duke University Press, 2011).

5. Erika Lee, *At America's Gates: Chinese Immigration During the Exclusion Era, 1882–1943* (Chapel Hill: University of North Carolina Press, 2003); Mae Ngai, *Impossible Subjects:*

Illegal Aliens and the Making of Modern America (Princeton, NJ: Princeton University Press, 2004).

6. Ngai, *Impossible Subjects*.

7. Kelly Lytle Hernandez, *Migra! A History of the U.S. Border Patrol* (Berkeley: University of California Press, 2010).

8. Lara Putnam, "The Ties Allowed to Bind: Kinship Legalities and Migration Restriction in the Interwar Americas," in "Strikes and Social Conflicts: Towards a Global History," ed. Kate Brown, Marjoleine Kars, and Marcel van der Linden, special issue, *International Labor and Working-Class History* 83 (Spring 2013): 201.

9. Ibid., 192.

10. Ibid., 206.

11. Putnam, *Radical Moves*; George Reid Andrews, *Afro-Latin America, 1800–2000* (Oxford: Oxford University Press, 2004).

12. Nancy Appelbaum, Anne Macpherson, and Karin Alejandra Rosenblatt, eds., *Race and Nation in Modern Latin America* (Chapel Hill: University of North Carolina Press, 2003); Alejandro de la Fuente, *A National For All: Race, Inequality, and Politics in Twentieth-Century Cuba* (Chapel Hill: University of North Carolina Press, 2001); Carla Guerrón-Montero, "Racial Democracy and Nationalism in Panama," *Ethnology* 45 (Summer 2006): 209–228; Jeffrey L. Gould, *To Die in This Way: Nicaraguan Indians and the Myth of Mestizaje, 1880–1965* (Durham, NC: Duke University Press, 1998); Emilia Viotti da Costa, "The Myth of Racial Democracy: A Legacy of Empire," in *The Brazilian Empire: Myths and Histories*, 234–246 (1985; Chapel Hill: University of North Carolina Press, 2000); Barbara Weinstein, *The Color of Modernity: São Paulo and the Making of Race and Nation in Brazil* (Durham, NC: Duke University Press, 2015); Winthrop Wright, *Café con Leche: Race, Class, and National Image in Venezuela* (Austin: University of Texas Press, 1990).

13. Aline Helg, *Our Rightful Share: The Afro-Cuban Struggle for Equality, 1886–1912* (Chapel Hill: University of North Carolina Press, 1995); Reid Andrews, *Afro-Latin America*, chapter 4.

14. Sadith Esther Paz, "The Status of West Indian Immigrants in Panama from 1850–1941" (master's thesis, University of Massachusetts Amherst, 1977).

15. Law 79 on July 25, 1941, chapter 2, title 7, in Paz, "Status of West Indian Immigrants," 71.

16. "Como se quiere que sea Costa Rica: blanca o negra?," *Reportorio Americano*, San José, September 13, 1930, in Reid-Andrews, *Afro-Latin America*, 235n70.

17. The phrase "xenophobic nationalism" comes from Lara Putnam, *Radical Moves*.

18. Conniff locates the rise of a West Indian subculture in Panama in this period, Michael L. Conniff, *Black Labor on a White Canal: Panama, 1904–1981* (Pittsburgh, PA: University of Pittsburgh Press, 1985).

19. The net outflow was only four thousand people because many West Indians kept arriving in Panama during those years, Conniff, *Black Labor on a White Canal*, 49.

20. *Censo demográfico de la Provincia de Panamá* (Panama: Imprenta Nacional, 1920), 94.

21. Putnam estimates that including the locally born second generation would bring the number of West Indians in Panama to sixty thousand by 1930. Lara Putnam, "Borderlands

and Border-Crossers: Migrants and Boundaries in the Greater Caribbean, 1840–1940," *Small Axe* 18, no. 1 (March 2014): 12–14.

22. Título II: Nacionalidad y Ciudadanía, Articulo 6, Constitución de la República de Panamá, 1904, Biblioteca Parlamentaria Dr. Justo Arosemena, accessed December 8, 2021, https://asamblea-dspace.metabiblioteca.com/bitstream/001/8/3/constitucion%20de%20 1904%20edicion%20oficial.pdf.

23. Marzia Milazzo, "White Supremacy, White Knowledge, and Anti–West Indian Discourse in Panama," in "The Interoceanic Diasporas and the Panama Canal's Centennial," special issue, *Global South* 6, no. 2 (Fall 2012): 65–86.

24. Ley 13 de 1926, Gaceta Oficial, 28 de octubre de 1926, Panamá, accessed December 8, 2021, https://docs.panama.justia.com/federales/leyes/13-de-1926-oct-28-1926.pdf.

25. Acto Legislativo de 1928 (de 19 de octubre), por el cual se subroga el articulo 6 de la Constitución Nacional, Gaceta Oficial, 20 de octubre de 1928, Panamá Año 25, Numero 5388, accessed December 8, 2021, https://docs.panama.justia.com/federales/actos-legislativos /acto-legislativo-6-de-1928-oct-20-1928.pdf.

26. Conniff, *Black Labor on a White Canal*, 49.

27. Ibid., 70.

28. Putnam, *Radical Moves*, chapter 4.

29. Katherine Zien, *Sovereign Acts: Performing Race, Space, and Belonging in Panama and the Canal Zone* (New Brunswick, NJ: Rutgers University Press, 2017), 79–80.

30. Barbara Bair, "True Women, Real Men: Gender, Ideology, and Social Roles in the Garvey Movement," in *Gendered Domains: Rethinking Public and Private in Women's History*, ed. Dorothy O. Helly and Susan M. Retherby, 154–166 (Ithaca, NY: Cornell University Press, 1992); Jorge L. Giovannetti-Torres, "The Elusive Organization of 'Identity': Race, Religion, and Empire Among Caribbean Migrants in Cuba," *Small Axe* 10, no. 1 (March 2006), 1–27; Jorge L. Giovannetti-Torres, *Black British Migrants in Cuba: Race, Labor, and Empire in the Twentieth-Century Caribbean, 1898–1948* (Cambridge: Cambridge University Press, 2018); Frank Guridy, *Forging Diaspora: Afro-Cubans and African-Americans in a World of Empire and Jim Crow* (Chapel Hill: University of North Carolina Press, 2010); Asia Leeds, "Toward the 'Higher Type of Womanhood': The Gendered Contours of Garveyism and the Making of Redemptive Geographies in Costa Rica, 1922–1941," *Palimpsest: A Journal on Women, Gender, and the Black International* 2, no. 1 (2013): 1–27; Jeffrey Parker, "Sex at a Crossroads: The Gender Politics of Racial Uplift and Afro-Caribbean Activism in Panama, 1918–32," *Women, Gender, and Families of Color* 4, no 2 (Fall 2016): 196–221; Irma Watkins-Owens, *Blood Relations: Caribbean Immigrants and the Harlem Community, 1900–1930* (Bloomington: Indiana University Press, 1996).

31. Carla Burnett, "'Unity Is Strength': Labor, Race, Garveyism, and the 1920 Panama Canal Strike," in "Interoceanic Diasporas and the Panama Canal's Centennial," special issue, *Global South* 6, no. 2 (Fall 2012): 39–64; Jeffrey Parker, chapter 2, "Sacrificed on the Altar of Vice": Afro-Caribbean Activism and Sexuality in Panama, 1914–1930," in "Empire's Angst:

The Politics of Race, Migration, and Sex Work in Panama, 1903–1945" (PhD diss., University of Texas at Austin, 2013), 82–144.

32. Conniff, *Black Labor on a White Canal*, 54.

33. "All in Favor Say 'Aye!,'" *Workman*, July 5, 1919, Digital Library of the Caribbean (DLOC), accessed December 8, 2021, https://original-ufdc.uflib.ufl.edu/AA00027053/00142.

34. "Our Local Strikes," *Workman*, May 10, 1919, DLOC, accessed December 8, 2021, https://original-ufdc.uflib.ufl.edu/AA00027053/00135.

35. "Who Will Help the Negro?," *Workman*, December 6, 1919, DLOC, accessed December 8, 2021, https://original-ufdc.uflib.ufl.edu/AA00027053/00165.

36. "Our Women," *Workman*, September 20, 1919, DLOC, accessed December 8, 2021, https://ufdc.ufl.edu/AA00027053/00154.

37. Blain, *Set the World on Fire*; Edwards, *Practice of Diaspora*; Leeds, "Toward the 'Higher Type of Womanhood'"; Courtney Desiree Morris, "Becoming Creole, Becoming Black: Migration, Diasporic Self-Making, and the Many Lives of Madame Maymie Leona Turpeau de Mena," *Women, Gender, and Families of Color* 4, no. 2 (Fall 2016): 171–195.

38. Kaysha Corinealdi, "A Section for Women: Journalism and Gendered Promises of Anti-Colonial Progress in Interwar Panama," in "Gender and Anti-Colonialism in the Interwar Caribbean," ed. Reena L. Goldthree and Natanya Duncan, special issue, *Caribbean Review of Gender Studies* 12 (December 2018): 91–120.

39. Parker, "Sex at a Crossroads."

40. Kaysha Corinealdi, "Local Internationalists: Activist Women in 1940s Panama" (presentation at the 134th Annual Meeting of the American Historical Association, New York City, January 3–6, 2020).

41. Lara Putnam, "Citizenship from the Margins: Vernacular Theories of Rights and the State from the Interwar Caribbean," *Journal of British Studies* 53, no. 1 (2014): 162–191.

42. Paule Marshall, *Triangular Road: A Memoir* (New York: Basic Civitas Books, 2009), 61.

43. Marshall, *Triangular Road*, 66.

44. Watkins-Owens, *Blood Relations*, 19.

45. Bonham Richardson, *Panama Money in Barbados, 1900–1920* (Knoxville: University of Tennessee Press, 1985) notes, but does not explore, the substantial participation of women in these financial practices.

46. See table in Richardson, *Panama Money*, 157.

47. Letter from Charles Magoon to Leon Pepperman, Chief of Administration, September 3, 1906, Records of the Foreign Office, Consulate: Panama, FO 288/103: "From Miscellaneous, 1907, January 1–June 30," National Archives, Kew, Richmond, UK.

48. *Barbados Agricultural Reporter*, November 18, 1911, in Bonham Richardson, "The Impact of Panama Money in Barbados in the Early Twentieth Century," *Nieuwe West-Indische Gids / New West Indian Guide* 59, no. 1/2 (1985): 13.

49. Richardson, *Panama Money*, 167.

50. Ibid., 192.

51. Ibid., 168.

52. Woodville Marshall, "Routes to Chattel Village: Bequest and Family Villages in Post-Slavery Barbados," *Journal of Caribbean History* 48, nos. 1 and 2 (2014): 86–107.

53. Ibid., 89.

54. Ibid., 94.

55. James, *Holding Aloft the Banner of Ethiopia*, 45.

56. Ibid.

57. Sharon Milagro Marshall, *Tell My Mother I Gone to Cuba: Stories of Early Twentieth-Century Migration from Barbados* (Kingston: University of the West Indies Press, 2016), Chapter 11: "Earl Alonzo 'Panama' Greaves," Kindle.

58. Minutes of the Council and Assembly, 1911–1912, Document 162: *Report on the Census of Barbados, 1911*, 6, quoted in Aviston Decourcei Downes, "Barbados, 1880–1914: A Socio-Cultural History" (PhD diss., University of York, 1994), 69.

59. Eleanor Marie Lawrence Brown, "The Blacks Who 'Got Their Forty Acres': A Theory of Black West Indian Migrant Asset Acquisition," *New York University Law Review* 89, no. 1 (April 2014): 46n61.

60. Lawrence Brown, "The Blacks Who 'Got Their Forty Acres'"; Richard Frucht, "A Caribbean Social Type: Neither 'Peasant' nor 'Proletarian,'" *Social and Economic Studies* 16, no. 3 (September 1967): 295–300.

61. Paule Marshall, "Black Immigrant Women in *Brown Girl, Brownstones*," in Delores Mortimer and Roy Bryce-Laporte, eds. *Female Immigrants to the United States: Caribbean, Latin American, and African Experiences* (Washington, DC: Research Institute on Immigration and Ethnic Studies, Smithsonian Institution, 1981), 7.

62. Ed Edwin, ed., *The Reminiscences of Kenneth B. Clark* (Alexandria, VA: Alexander Street Press for the Oral History Research Office, Columbia University, 1989), 12.

63. Ibid., 13.

64. Walter Laidlaw, ed., *Population of the City of New York, 1890–1930* (New York: Cities Census Committee, 1932).

65. Putnam, "Borderlands and Border-Crossers," 11.

66. Watkins-Owens, *Blood Relations*, 2; Putnam, *Radical Moves*.

67. Watkins-Owens, "Early Twentieth-Century Caribbean Women," 26.

68. Lara Putnam, "Kenneth Bancroft Clark," in *Dictionary of Caribbean and Afro–Latin American Biography*, ed. Henry Louis Gates Jr. and Franklin W. Knight (New York: Oxford University Press, 2016), accessed March 25, 2022, https://www-oxfordreference-com.proxy.library.nyu.edu/view/10.1093/acref/9780199935796.001.0001/acref-9780199935796-e-502.

69. Watkins-Owens, *Blood Relations*, 50.

70. Janette Gayle, "'Invaders': Black Ladies of the ILGWU and the Emergence of the Early Civil Rights Movement in New York City," *Gotham: A Blog for Scholars of New York City*, Gotham Center for New York City History, October 19, 2016, accessed July 1, 2020, https://www.gothamcenter.org/blog/invaders-black-ladies-of-the-ilgwu-and-the-emergence-of-the-early-civil-rights-movement-in-new-york-city.

71. Ibid.

72. Watkins-Owens, *Blood Relations*, 45.

73. Jacqueline Jones, *Labor of Love, Labor of Sorrow: Black Women, Work, and the Family, from Slavery to the Present* (1985; New York: Basic Books, 2010); Carole Marks, "The Bone and Sinew of the Race: Black Women, Domestic Service and Labor Migration," *Marriage and Family Review* 19 (1993): 149–173.

74. Ella Baker and Marvel Cooke, "The Bronx Slave Market," *Crisis* 42 (November 1935): 330–331; Paula Giddings, *When and Where I Enter: The Impact of Black Women on Race and Sex in America* (New York: William Morrow, 1984), 204.

75. Elizabeth Clark-Lewis, *Living In, Living Out: African-American Domestics in Washington, D.C., 1910–1940* (Washington, DC: Smithsonian Books, 1994).

76. Watkins-Owens, "Early Twentieth-Century Caribbean Women."

77. LaShawn Harris, *Sex Workers, Psychics, and Numbers Runners: Black Women in New York City's Underground Economy* (Champaign: University of Illinois Press, 2016).

78. G. W. Roberts, Table 5: Sources and Values of Emigrant's Transfers to Barbados by Money Order, in "Emigration from the Island of Barbados," *Social and Economic Studies* 4, no. 3 (September 1955): 286.

79. *Reminiscences of Kenneth B. Clark*, 31.

80. Watkins-Owens, *Blood Relations*, 50.

81. Yevette Richards, *Maida Springer: Pan-Africanist and International Labor Leader* (Pittsburgh, PA: University of Pittsburgh Press, 2000).

82. Transcript of Oral History Interview with Maida Springer Kemp, 6, Black Women Oral History Project Interviews, 1976–1981, Harvard Radcliffe Institute, Schlesinger Library, accessed December 8, 2021, https://iiif.lib.harvard.edu/manifests/view/drs:45172388$1i.

83. Blain, *Set the World on Fire*.

84. James, *Holding Aloft the Banner of Ethiopia*, 1.

85. Blain, *Set the World on Fire*; Davies, *Left of Karl Marx*.

86. Marshall, *Tell My Mother I Gone to Cuba*, Chapter 10: Maradell Atwell Greene.

87. Isthmian Canal Commission, *Annual Report of the Isthmian Canal Commission and the Panama Canal for the Year Ending June 30, 1914* (Washington, DC: Government Printing Office, 1914), 516.

88. Marshall, *Tell My Mother I Gone to Cuba*, Chapter 6: Relief and Repatriation.

89. Glenn Chambers, *Race, Nation, and West Indian Immigration to Honduras, 1890–1940* (Baton Rouge: Louisiana State University Press, 2010); Aviva Chomsky, *West Indian Workers and the United Fruit Company in Costa Rica, 1870–1940* (Baton Rouge: Louisiana State University Press, 1996); Lara Putnam, *The Company They Kept: Migrants and the Politics of Gender in Caribbean Costa Rica* (Chapel Hill: University of North Carolina Press, 2002).

90. Elizabeth McLean Petras, *Jamaican Labor Migration: White Capital and Black Labor, 1850–1930* (1988; New York: Routledge, 2018), chapter 9.

91. Giovannetti-Torres, *Black British Migrants in Cuba*, 50.

92. César J. Ayala, *American Sugar Kingdom: The Plantation Economy of the Spanish Caribbean, 1898–1934* (Chapel Hill: University of North Carolina Press, 1999), 92.

93. Ayala, Table 7.8: U.S. Corporate Mills Built in Cuba during World War I, in *American Sugar Kingdom*, 218.

94. Jorge L. Giovannetti-Torres, "Historia visual y etnohistoria en Cuba: Inmigración antillana e identidad en 'Los hijos de Baraguá,'" *Caribbean Studies* 30, no. 2 (July–December 2002): 216–252; Robert Whitney and Graciela Chailloux Laffita, *Subjects or Citizens: British Caribbean Workers in Cuba, 1900–1960* (Gainesville: University Press of Florida, 2013).

95. Giovannetti-Torres, *Black British Migrants in Cuba*, 65.

96. "Appendix III: Moral Environment of Immigrant Girls in Cuba," in Margery Corbett Ashby to the Secretary, Colonial Office, June 24, 1921, FO 369/1597, Records of the Foreign Office, National Archives, Kew, Richmond, UK, from Giovannetti-Torres, *Black British Migrants*, 67n81.

97. Tiffany A. Sippial, *Prostitution, Modernity, and the Making of the Cuban Republic, 1840–1920* (Chapel Hill: University of North Carolina Press, 2013), 163.

98. Sippial, *Prostitution, Modernity, and the Making of the Cuban Republic*, 175–176.

99. Matthew Casey, *Empire's Guestworkers: Haitian Migrants in Cuba During the Age of U.S. Occupation* (Cambridge: Cambridge University Press, 2017), 130–131.

100. Giovannetti-Torres, *Black British Migrants in Cuba*, 68.

101. Marshall, *Tell My Mother I Gone to Cuba*, Chapter 10.

102. Ibid., Chapter 9: Celia Leonora Campbell Jones.

103. Ibid., Chapter 13: Delcina Esperanza Marshall.

104. Whitney and Chailloux Laffita, *Subjects or Citizens*, 51.

105. Marshall, *Tell My Mother I Gone to Cuba*, Chapter 10.

106. Ibid., Chapter 13.

107. Giovannetti-Torres, "Elusive Organization of 'Identity,'" 19.

108. Ibid.

109. Letter from William Stoute to Marcus Garvey, July 8, 1919, in *The Marcus Garvey and UNIA Papers*, vol. 11, *The Caribbean Diaspora, 1910–1920*, ed. Robert A. Hill (Durham, NC: Duke University Press, 2011), 229.

110. Conniff, *Black Labor on a White Canal*, 54–61.

111. Giovannetti-Torres, "Elusive Organization of 'Identity'"; Giovannetti-Torres, *Black British Migrants in Cuba*; Frank Guridy, "'Enemies of the White Race': The *Machadista* State and the UNIA in Cuba," in "Garveyism and the Universal Negro Association in the Hispanic Caribbean," special issue, *Caribbean Studies* 31, no. 1 (January–June 2003): 107–137; Guridy, *Forging Diaspora*; Marc McLeod, "'Sin dejar de ser cubanos': Cuban Blacks and the Challenges of Garveyism in Cuba," in "Garveyism and the Universal Negro Association in the Hispanic Caribbean," special issue, *Caribbean Studies* 31, no. 1 (January–June 2003): 75–105.

112. Andrea Queeley, *Rescuing Our Roots: The African Anglo-Caribbean Diaspora in Contemporary Cuba* (Gainesville: University Press of Florida, 2015), 60.

113. Queeley, *Rescuing Our Roots*, 50–51.

114. Ibid., 51.

115. Marshall, *Tell My Mother I Gone to Cuba*, Chapter 13.

116. Queeley, *Rescuing Our Roots*, 53.

117. Ibid., 39.

118. Ibid., 38.

119. *My Footsteps in Baragua,* directed by Gloria Rolando (Mundo Latino, 1996), DVD. Thank you to Devyn Spence Benson for helping me acquire a copy of this film!

Conclusion

1. George Priestley and Alberto Barrow, "The Black Movement in Panama: A Historical and Political Interpretation, 1994–2004," *Souls* 10 (2008): 227–255. Along with SAMAAP's work, see the activism of the Red de Mujeres Afropanameñas, the Red de Mujeres Afrodescendientes Profesionales y Empresariales, and the Corozal-Gatun-Mt. Hope Cemetery Preservation Foundation/Pan-Caribbean Sankofa, groups founded and led by West Indian women.

2. Maya Doig-Acuña, "As Brooklyn Continues Changing: A Reflection on Crown Heights' Panamanian Community," *Remezcla*, October 22, 2018, https://remezcla.com/features/culture /as-brooklyn-continues-changing-a-reflection-on-crown-heights-panamanian-community/; Jenise Miller, "We Are Our Own Multitude: Los Angeles' Black Panamanian Community," *Boom California*, October 24, 2019, https://boomcalifornia.org/2019/10/24/we-are-our-own -multitude-los-angeles-black-panamanian-community/.

3. Maya Doig-Acuña, "The Most Caribbean of Stories," *Southern Cultures* 26 (Winter 2020): 12–23.

4. Henry Burnett, ICC Chief of Labor and Quarters, quoted in "A Scandal on the Isthmus of Panama," *New York Herald*, November 25, 1905.

5. Letter from Herman Caulfield to Director of Hospitals, June 2, 1906, Folder 2-E-6 (I): Miscellaneous information re laborers and labor situation; efficiency; health and living conditions; probably reductions in force, etc., RG 185, Entry 30, NARA.

6. Silvia Federici, *Caliban and the Witch: Women, the Body, and Primitive Accumulation* (New York: Autonomedia, 2004).

7. Shauna J. Sweeney, "Black Women in Slavery and Freedom: Gendering the History of Racial Capitalism," *American Quarterly* 72, no. 1 (2020): 277–289.

INDEX

ACKNOWLEDGMENTS

My family's recent history has been defined by immigration. My cousins, aunts, uncles, and family friends now live scattered across Costa Rica, Panama, Peru, Mexico, Chile, Kentucky, Texas, England, Spain, and many yet remain in Venezuela. Every single one of them has made this book possible, though my primos José Alirio Almarza, José Rafael Almarza, and Amaya Urbieta, who housed me and kept me company during research stays in Panama, deserve special attention. Most importantly, I would like to thank my mom and dad, Angela and Yhonny Flores, who sacrificed their home, language, jobs, and family to move to the United States to create better opportunities for me. They have unfailingly expressed their love and support for my decisions, even if they do not often understand them. My home will always be where they are.

My earliest mentors, J. Celso Castro Alves, Rhonda Cobham-Sander, Jeffrey Ferguson, Dale Hudson, and Margaret Hunt, helped me believe I could become a scholar.

My advisers, Michael Gomez, Barbara Weinstein, Ada Ferrer, and Sinclair Thomson, each brought a particular gift to completing this book. Thanks to those who have mentored and aided in this process, especially Theodora Dragostinova, Alice Echols, Jorge Giovannetti-Torres, Julie Greene, Koritha Mitchell, Nathan Perl-Rosenthal, Lara Putnam, George Sanchez, Stephanie Smith, and David Steigerwald, alongside many others.

My team of friends and collaborators who read, contributed to, and improved this work includes Westenley Alcenat, Alice Baumgartner, Emilie Connolly, Jennifer Eaglin, Jeannette Estruth, Philip Gleissner, Connor Guy, Anasa Hicks, Clayton Howard, Dominique Jean-Louis, Ebony Jones, Tyesha Maddox, Katherine Marino, Celeste Menchaca, Alaina Morgan, Wendy Muñiz,

A. J. Murphy, Rachel Nolan, Ketaki Pant, Joseph Parrott, Briana Royster, Amy Sheeran, Ashanti Shih, Ahmad Shokr, Sara Sligar, Seguin Strohmeier, Emma Teitelman, Aro Velmet, and Amy Zanoni.

Thank you to all the friends, staff, and wonderful colleagues at New York University, The Ohio State University, and the University of Southern California, too innumerable to name. Special thanks to the students in my Fall 2021 graduate seminar on Intimacy and Empire, the last readers of the manuscript before it went to press. Thanks as well to the 2017–2018 fellows of the NYU Center for the Humanities and participants of the Tepoztlán Institute for the Transnational History of the Americas, the Association of Caribbean Historians, the Business History Conference, the American Historical Association, the Association for the Study of the African Diaspora in the World, the History of Women and Gender Program at NYU, the African Diaspora Graduate History Workshop at NYU, the Racial Capitalism Reading Group, and my dedicated 2020–2021 "pandemic" writing group.

Doing research in the National Archives of Panama was not always an easy task but archivists Hercilia Torres and Lic. Jorge Luis Nuñez made the process as easy as possible. Annie Ramos and Michael Granadillo of the United Nations Development Program (UNDP) office in Panama provided crucial access to the archives on my last visit. In Barbados, Frederick Alleyne from the University of the West Indies–Cave Hill provided invaluable research assistance for Chapter 5. I would not have made it through London without the support of Zainab Abbas, who housed me in her beautiful Fulham home. Thank you as well to the archivists and librarians of the George A. Smathers Libraries at the University of Florida and the Digital Library of the Caribbean, who have made invaluable contributions to the preservation of historical material about the Panama Canal construction.

This book exists due to the support and masterful editing of Bob Lockhart and the rest of the team at Penn Press. Thanks as well to Keisha Blain and Stephen Pitti, the series editors of Politics and Culture in Modern America who first read the proposal, and the two anonymous reviewers who encouraged this work and pushed me to refine my argument. I would further like to thank the Ford Foundation, the Mellon Foundation, the American Historical Association, the Society for Historians of American Foreign Relations, and the American Association of University Women for making this work financially possible. Material in Chapter 4 previously appeared in the following publication and is reprinted with permission: Joan Flores-Villalobos, "Gender, Race, and Migrant Labor in the 'Domestic Frontier' of the Panama Canal Zone," *International Labor and Working-Class History* 99 (2021): 96–121. Scattered material throughout the introduction and Chapter 3 previously appeared in the following publication and is also reprinted with permission: Joan Flores-Villalobos, "'Freak Letters': Tracing Gender, Race, and Diaspora in the Panama Canal Archive," *Small Axe* 23, no 2 (July 2019): 34–56.

A book comes out of so many moments that cannot be captured in a list of acknowledgments—inspiration over coffee or drinks with friends, the anonymous readers' comments on a journal article that never saw the light, the frantic 1 A.M. texts on the group chat, the unexpected Twitter replies. Dinners, beach time, and hugs with Sam Keller gave me many happy, peaceful moments through this difficult process. I definitely forgot some people, which makes them no less important to this book's trajectory. This work is a testament to my friends' and family's patience and confidence in me. All of those interactions are in here and I am grateful for each of them.